In a Southern Garden

*Twelve Months of Plants
and Observations*

CAROL BISHOP HIPPS

A **HORTICULTURE** BOOK
Macmillan • USA

To my parents, Betty Ann and Jesse Earl Bishop, and in memory of my grandmother, Allie Venia Bishop.

MACMILLAN
A Prentice Hall Macmillan Company
15 Columbus Circle
New York, NY 10023

MACMILLAN is a registered trademark of Macmillan, Inc.

Library of Congress Cataloging-in-Publication Data

Hipps, Carol Bishop.
    Horticulture : in a southern garden : twelve months of plants &
observations / Carol Bishop Hipps.
      p.   cm.
    Includes index.
    ISBN 0-671-87151-X
    1. Gardening—Southern States.   2. Landscape gardening—Southern
States.   3. Plants, Ornamental—Southern States.   I. Title.
SB453.3.S63H56   1995   94-23465
712'.6'0976—dc20   CIP

Designed by Levavi & Levavi

Manufactured in the United States of America

10 9 8 7 6 5 4 3 2 1

Acknowledgments

Knowingly or not, a multitude of individuals have contributed to the creation of this book. I am most deeply indebted to my lightning-fingered husband, Jesse, whose pity at my manual ineptitude led him to type my manuscript from a draft which was in places illegible even to me. "Bear in mind," he points out, "your readers will really be reading my typing, not your writing."

I would like to thank the editors at *Horticulture* magazine — Thomas C. Cooper, Teri Dunn, Rosalie Davis, Thomas Fischer, Deborah Starr, and Roger Swain — whose encouraging response to my efforts over the years has saved me from switching to a career in pizza delivery. Thanks, too, are due Rebecca Atwater at Prentice Hall (now Macmillan General Reference), who, along with Thomas Cooper, awarded me this lovely opportunity and then patiently and persistently saw to it that I eventually produced an actual book.

I am greatly indebted to the Huntsville Wildflower Society and to the volunteers and staff of the Huntsville-Madison County Botanical Garden, whose companionship I have relished and from whom I have learned so much, especially Harvey Cotton, Mary Ann Ely, Arthel Frith, Val Fulmer, Mike Gibson, Catherine Hall, Max Harmon, Charles Higgins, Terry Lee, Willodene Mathews, Louise McDowell, Mary Lou McNabb, Inge Paul, Al Privette, Margaret Vann, Wade Wharton, and Gordon White.

I owe many thanks to my mother- and father-in-law, Lois and Dwight Hipps, for their knowledge and support. Special thanks are also due Sally Elliott, David Byers, the late Beatrice Hall, and my generous and long-suffering next-door neighbor, Patricia Roth. Thanks, too, to Drs. Caula C. Beyl, Cathy Sabota, Vallabdas Sapra, and Mahasin G. Tadros of Alabama A&M University.

Many authors, both living and long gone, have contributed to this work and inspired shameless imitation on my part, among them Gertrude Jekyll, Celia Thaxter, James Underwood Crockett, Thalassa Cruso, Elizabeth Lawrence, Henry Mitchell, Christopher Lloyd, and Michael A. Dirr, without whose magnificent *Manual of Woody Landscape Plants* I obviously could not get through the day.

And I am grateful beyond words for the elegant contributions of my fellow photographers and good friends, Elsabe Holst-Webster, Daniel Little, Robert McNabb, and, most of all — for supreme sacrifice in the line of duty — Pat Gardner.

Contents ❧

Introduction

I never actually *read* how-to and encyclopedic garden books; I consult them for specifics. Even with lush illustrations, they fail to hold my attention for long. But just as reading biographies is a relatively painless way to learn history, reading about the personal experiences of other gardeners is—for me, at least—a comparatively effortless (and amusing) way to learn about plants and gardening and to keep my enthusiasm charged. Strange, perhaps, that one should find the trial and error that leads to fact more absorbing than the fact itself, but there you go.

Since gardening is for most of us a lonesome pursuit, sometimes what we need from a gardening book is not so much cold, hard fact as inspiration and confirmation that we are not alone in our struggles and shortcomings. It does my heart good to read that the gardeners I most admire in the world on occasion allow impatience, stubbornness, ignorance, or sheer laziness to lead to embarrassing loss. I have tried, then, in writing this book, to produce the kind of book that I myself exult in as a reader—a book that, as much as anything, is a celebration of the adventure of gardening. Thus, it is full of rueful confessions, utterly unjustified prejudice, lame humor, and, I hope, even useful information, much of it gleaned from sources far more knowledgeable than me.

For the most part, I have written about genera with which I have some experience—or at least passing acquaintance—so there are glaring omissions. Peonies, for instance. Where the heck are the peonies? Have I sulkily ignored them because I've grown only one peony in my life, and it had the audacity to die, when everybody knows peonies live for centuries? Or have I left them out because there simply isn't room for everything? I'm not sure.

My husband has objected that I've made our home sound more like an estate than like the modest brick-rancher-on-a-third-of-an-acre that it is. That's his problem. Gardening is three-fourth's imagination, after all. When we insert a spindly, bare root stick into the ground, we already see the billowing shade tree we've envisioned for that spot. And we can be as blind to our garden's imperfections as we are to those of the people we love. This is not a fault—it's a blessing. It lets us go on pretending, carrying a childlike enjoyment of gardening as a form of play into old age.

This, of course, is a *southern* garden book. Have you ever noticed that, when a northern gardener writes a book, it's a *gardening* book; when a southerner pens or pecks a gardening book, it's a *southern* garden book? But then perhaps our erratic climate qualifies us for separate treatment from the rest of the planet.

The Gulf states, in particular, are something of a war zone between the warm, wet fronts that push up from the Gulf of Mexico and the waves of arctic chill that sweep down from the north. While summers are hot, sticky, and usually drought plagued, (last July the mercury here in Huntsville topped 90°F every single day of the month, hitting a record 104°F at mid-month), winter weather is far from consistent. Last February a record low of 14°F was followed two days later by a bark-splitting record high of 73°F, and we typically lack an insulating snow cover to mitigate the impact of such rapid reversals. On this January evening as I write, the predicted low temperature is 5°F, and there's nary a snowflake in sight.

Southern gardening publications often feature maps dividing the southeastern states into the Upper, Middle, Lower, Coastal, and Tropical South—designations that don't conform at all to the zonal boundaries of the USDA plant hardiness map. For my purposes, I've considered the Upper South as Zone 6, the Middle Zone 7, the Lower Zone 8, and the Coastal Zone 9. I've rudely snubbed the Florida peninsula, a vast, steaming sandspit overrun with mysterious, exotic flora and prehistoric fauna of mythological proportions and powers, like that thought by scientific visionaries of centuries past to populate the planet Venus.

The South is blessed with a long growing season (usually six or seven months from last to first frost in our back yard), and winter is liberally punctuated with mild spells, making gardening, if desired, a year-round sport. I'm tempted to say I wouldn't want to garden anywhere else, but then I haven't tried anyplace else. Perhaps I'd like Tahiti even better. Or maybe it's just like South Florida.

January

January in our part of the South is cruel, luring the common white garden iris into bud with the false promise of spring borne on the Gulf's moist breath, then rushing in with a frigid ferocity to blight the pearllike petals before they've begun to unfurl. For a day or two the bare branches clatter when moved together by the wind, and the ground crunches beneath our step. Then the harsh wind stalls, the clouds gather, and the hint of spring edges back.

Already hepatica and winter honeysuckle are blooming in the woods. Even though the handsomely dappled, leathery leaves of our native *Hepatica acutiloba* and *H. americana* are hidden beneath the tan layer of freshly sifted leaves, this tough little woodland perennial herb has pushed its fuzzy shepherd's crook bloomstalks up to toad's eye level, where they respond to the sunshine by unfurling saucers of white or lavender sepals topped by dazzling white anthers.

With winter honeysuckle (*Lonicera fragrantissima*) you catch the delicious lemony scent of its inconspicuous, cream-colored flowers long before your eye locates the source. This Chinese native is one of several imported honeysuckles that now ramp through southern fields and forests.

Though at the turn of the year winter honeysuckle's remaining leaves may take on a welcome yellow to counter the surrounding grayness, it is not a particularly showy shrub, even in full bloom, for the small flowers, borne in pairs along the arching stems, look rather dingy from a distance. In leaf it is almost invisibly unremarkable but for the berries, which rapidly metamorphose from green to red to purple-black in spring before being consumed and distributed by the birds.

I've seen winter honeysuckle used as a formal, sheared hedge, but as such it is downright ugly in winter — a see-through wall of sawed-off sticks. I grow this graceful, invasive shrub simply for the divine fragrance of its flowers which, when brought indoors, tinge the air with the promise of spring.

Nearby in Huntsville's Old Town historic district, winter jasmine (*Jasminum nudiflorum*) is in full bloom now, cascading over old stone walls in a thick spray of wandlike, deep green stems pierced by luminous, inch-wide yellow stars.

This stiffly sprawling shrub is easily propagated and makes a fine groundcover for a slope, rooting anew where stem tips touch the ground.

One can truly *see* a garden in winter, when its supporting framework of wood, stone, and evergreens is most evident, and one may most readily study its design and contemplate changes. Whether our home is the house we were born in or one of an endless series of rental properties, there are likely to be elements of its exterior environment which grate on our sensibilities or fail to satisfy our needs, elements which one aches to change. A sunny, mild midwinter day is custom-made for a critical stroll around the grounds with pen and pad in hand and our sweater pockets stuffed with Kleenex.

Do our fences, decks, drives, walks, hedges, trees, and shrub beds present a cohesive, visually appealing whole? Are there eyesores that can be screened or removed? Can groceries be hauled in and the trash hauled out without undue effort? Are there drainage problems — erosion or standing water — that need attention? Is there adequate lighting? Do hobby and entertainment areas lack needed privacy? Are pets and young children safely restrained? Well?

Now let's go back inside and have a sip of coffee while we check the view from the windows. Is it so inviting that we can hardly take our eyes away, or does it make us cringe? Have our collector's instincts run amok, leaving us with an assortment of radically mismatched shrubs, chaotically dotted about the yard, giving our agitated eyes no logical resting point? Ah, dear, such a garden lacks repose. Even horticultural Noahs, incurably afflicted with a compulsion to have one (and in the case of dioecious shrubs, two) of everything, can present their collections harmoniously, grouping all but the showiest specimens into beds and carefully blending color, form, and texture so that both similarities and differences are exploited to advantage.

Evergreens for Structure

Whether sparkling in the sun or contrasting with the rare snowfall, evergreen shrubs and trees impart lively relief from winter's dreariness, and, along with well-placed, attractive walls, fences, paved areas, and other "hardscape" features, provide a defining framework for the garden. An evergreen hedge or screen is an especially strong feature, denoting boundaries, assuring privacy, and serving as a backdrop for showier companions in their spells of glory.

PHOTINIA

Perhaps the most done-to-death broadleaf evergreen for hedging in the South in recent years has been the Fraser photinia (*Photinia* ×*fraseri*). A cross between *P. glabra* and *P. serrulata*, it reportedly originated in a Birmingham nursery around the middle of the century. New growth sports a ruby glow. One of the most unusual hedges I've ever seen featured reddish, squared-off photinias alternating down the line with shorter, flat-topped golden forsythias in the style of a castle wall. Give a retired man an electric hedge clipper, and the possibilities are endless.

Left unshorn, a photinia develops an understated grandeur, growing into a rosy-hued small tree, with a roundly columnar, bushy habit reminiscent of *Magnolia grandiflora* and with lacelike clusters of creamy flowers the size of salad plates in spring.

Unfortunately, above USDA Zone 8 photinia occasionally freezes to the ground in winter — not a desireable trait in a hedge, though we put up with it occasionally in our crapemyrtles and pyracanthas.

ELAEAGNUS

In Zones 7 through 9 thorny elaeagnus (*Elaeagnus pungens*) makes a great, ungainly thicket of a hedge or screen, needing frequent pruning unless it's given plenty of room to start with (at least ten by ten feet). The backs of the unevenly cut, crinkled leaves appear to have been sprayed silver and then dusted with cinnamon. This pallor may lack the dramatic definition of darker-leaved evergreens, perhaps, but in autumn the sweetness of the myriads of dainty, bell-like blossoms is intoxicating, and the bush squirms with honeybees topping off their winter grocery cache. Later, birds find the elongated, dangling fruits equally alluring.

OSMANTHUS

Osmanthus is another acutely fragrant evergreen shrub common to southern gardens. I regret I've little experience with members of this genus. It wasn't until I took a landscape materials course at Alabama A&M University that I was formally introduced to the false holly (*Osmanthus heterophyllus*) and learned to distinguish it from the true holly by the fact that the spiny leaves of the osmanthus oppose one another, while those of a holly are arranged alternately on the stem.

The curlyleaf tea olive (*O. heterophyllus* 'Rotundifolius') is a slow-growing dwarf, one of only a few osmanthus hardy into the upper South, that is, Zone 6. There are variegated and purple-leaved varieties of *O. heterophyllus*.

The most familiar member of the genus is the fragrant tea olive (*O. fragrans*), a kinder, gentler shrub with broad, sleek, medium-green leaves that narrow to a fine point at the tips and small, intensely sweet white flowers in fall or winter. The Fortune tea olive (*O. ×fortunei*), like most osmanthus, grows too large for a foundation plant, and though not what I could call low maintenance, is handsome for screening or hedging, particularly by a driveway or patio where the flower's scent can be savored.

GARDENIA

In the deepest South the dizzying scent of Cape jasmine (*Gardenia jasminoides*) is as much a part of summer evenings as the drone of mosquitoes. But from Birmingham northward, gardenias are apt to freeze to the ground in winter, and, given that they flower on old wood, remain flowerless the following summer. My mother-in-law in Anniston for years kept a gardenia among her foundation shrubs, but the cutting she started for me died young here in Huntsville. Some years she had flowers, others she didn't. But, when that gardenia was good, it was *very* good, with polished, rippling, dark green leaves and fist-sized, creamy, rumpled flowers. Wayside Gardens recommends the "improved" *G. jasminoides* 'August Beauty' for Zones 7 through 9, but I would certainly give it a warm, sheltered site in Zone 7. One might also want to try *G. jasminoides* 'Radicans', a low, spreading version with smaller leaves and two-inch flowers.

CAMELLIA

Once upon a time the state flower of Alabama was the goldenrod (*Solidago*), a sensible choice because one or more species of the genus is endemic to every part of the state. But this rough and ready wildflower, indifferent to its celebrity, allowed itself to be outpoliticked by the temperamental camellia, a Far Eastern exotic, which performs as advertised only in the southern half of the state, its fragile, autumn-to-spring blossoms often freezing in bud here in the northern counties. The flowers and buds on all of the literally thousands of camellia cultivars are susceptible to frost damage to varying degrees. Allowing morning sun to strike a frost-encrusted bud is said to heighten the risk of damage. My neighbors drape their camellias with old blankets on cold nights to protect the tender flower buds from frost (an aesthetically acceptable practice when one considers that the original reason for putting shrubbery around a house may have been to provide a handy, airy surface upon which to dry laundry).

Garden camellias are derived principally from three species and their hybrids: *Camellia japonica* and *C. sasanqua*, both from Japan and the immediate vicinity, and *C. reticulata*, from China. The large, showy flowers may be single, semidouble, or double, or may be classified as anemone, peony, or rose form, while their colors range from white through pink to red and magenta. The shrubs themselves have glossy, leathery leaves and assume a lumpily rounded or columnar habit. They are deemed tolerant of all manner of cruelty; they can be sheared into formal hedges, espaliered against walls, trundled around in tubs, and whacked off top and bottom and stuffed into bonsai containers. But they are most commonly seen as specimens and as oversized foundation plants, hardly noticeable until they burst into bloom at the most incongruous times of the year. I've seen camellias transform winter-weary Birmingham streets into an after-Christmas fairyland of pink and red and white.

Although they are especially attractive used as informal hedges, camellias are best sheltered from harsh, drying winds. Prolonged periods of sub-freezing temperatures, combined with drought, can kill back even very old plants . A wall or evergreen windbreak combined with a thick organic mulch protects the plants from dehydration and cold. Good drainage is also critical, because water-logged soil leads to root rot (caused by the fungus *Phytophthora cinnamomi*, which also affects rhododendrons).

As with ferns, azaleas, and other lovers of moist, bright shade, care must be taken not to plant camellias more deeply than they grew originally.

Their soil can be kept acid, if need be, with an occasional application of sulfur, aluminum sulfate, or an acidic azalea-camellia fertilizer (best applied in late spring). Municipal water is often buffered with a calcium compound to retard pipe corrosion and may raise soil pH over time. Withholding water in late summer allows new growth to harden off, but camellias should be watered well just before the first winter freeze.

Stem dieback is caused by the fungus *Glomerella cingulata* (sounds like one of Cinderella's ugly stepsisters). Prune out dead or discolored wood on sight to thwart the spread of this fungus.

Scale and, occasionally, red spider can be troublesome on camellias.

As if frost-blackening weren't threat enough, buds and flowers must contend with petal blight, *Sclerotinia camelliae*. Controlling this blight requires removing affected fallen flowers from beneath the shrub and, perhaps, spraying the ground with a fungicide. Open blossoms shatter when struck by heavy rain, and bud drop may occur when any little thing (culture, siting, or weather) displeases the fussy camellia.

The much-loved formal double 'Alba Plena' has been listed in catalogs since at least 1827. Japonicas given high marks for cold resistance include the early-flowering semidouble red 'Christmas Beauty' and the late-blooming 'Blood of China'. 'Pink Perfection', a formal double, has an extra-long season of bloom, and the white rose form double 'Purity' kicks in as 'Alba Plena' calls it quits. My mother-in-law and I are especially fond of the peppermint-striped semidouble peony blooms of her 'Governor Mouton'.

In recent years exceptionally winter-hardy hybrid camellias have emerged from work done by William L. Ackerman and others at the U.S. National Arboretum, where crosses were made involving a cold-resistant specimen of *C. oleifera* from northern China. The cultivars all have wintry names: 'Snow Flurry', 'Winter's Charm', 'Winter's Rose', and 'Winter's Waterlily' are a few.

The authentic tea plant, *C. sinensis*, is well-suited to informal situations, with its dark, lustrous foliage, a loose habit, and small, scented, creamy fall flowers with golden centers. This species is a bit less hardy than the japonicas and sasanquas.

EUONYMUS

There is a confusing variety of *Euonymus* species and cultivars in use as "evergreen" landscape material, but most that I've seen get ragged, and some, if the winter is harsh, wind up as naked as the frankly deciduous sorts. At our old house on Ewing Street, we had a great, dark, billowing euonymus which I now suspect to have been *Euonymus kiautschovicus* (I don't pronounce 'em; I just spell 'em), for it was a fence-climbing spreader that went leafless in rough winters but sheltered the sparrows in mild ones. The birds made quick work of the innumerable small scarlet fruits and promptly seeded them all over the yard. The seedlings, if not soon weeded out, spread into stubbornly rooted mats that had to be grubbed out with a mattock.

The shrub made a handsome, contrasting background for my gaudy old red *Hibiscus coccineus*, but I could hardly stand to be around that shrub in summer when it bloomed, for its perfume struck me as more of a stench. What bitter honey the bees must have made from its nectar! I was surprised, therefore, when admiring the exquisite new landscape at one of our local hospitals, to see a cozy sitting area surrounded by a sea of variegated euonymus. Ah, well, the blooming period probably won't last more than a few weeks.

Euonymus is not the least bit fussy as to culture; it will take whatever lot is meted out to it and make do. Scale, mattock-wielding gardeners, and, to a lesser extent, mildew are its only enemies.

CHERRY LAUREL

I've come to have great admiration for the cherry laurels. Such functional, dependable, handsome, weatherproof (most winters) workhorse plants they are. Their habit — casually outspread, yet dense — gives them enormous versatility; they are compatible with any architectural style. The lower-growing types, like *Prunus laurocerasus* 'Otto Luyken', 'Schipkaensis', or

'Zabeliana', are superb in foundation plantings, retaining a lusty, dark green vigor year-round and needing little pruning to keep them presentable.

The taller sorts, such as *P. laurocerasus* 'Magnoliafolia' (say that three times real fast), are excellent as windbreaks, screens, or hedges, and, with judicious pruning, as small specimen trees. The native *P. caroliniana*, however, is probably the least desirable for most yards, vaulting to thirty or forty feet if unclipped and bribing the birds to seed its offspring into every bed and border.

All cherry laurels release a characteristic cherry aroma when bruised. At least some are considered toxic to livestock and, supposedly, are not sought-after by deer.

Cherry laurels prosper in any well-drained, moisture-retentive soil. They do less well in a drought, taking on a dejected look during long dry spells. The upward-pointing, fingerlike racemes of too-sweet white flowers appear in profusion in either sun or shade. Even if they become so riddled by insects and the shothole fungus to which they are susceptible that they look as if they've been used for target practice by a kid with a BB gun, cherry laurels somehow manage to give an impression of orderliness and exuberant health.

PRIVET

I'm not sure how the craze for the common privet hedge ever got started, but I understand it's been going on for centuries. Certainly no other plant makes the transition from a cutting to a sizeable shrub more rapidly or inexpensively than privet (*Ligustrum*), and no plant tolerates a more diverse set of conditions or recovers more rapidly from inept, dull-bladed butchery.

There are enough privets and their hybrids to be confusing, especially since some advertised as "evergreen" are actually deciduous in the North, while the "deciduous" privets hold their leaves over winter in the Deep South.

Unfortunately, both Chinese privet (*Ligustrum sinense*) and European privet (*L. vulgare*), the species most often seen as hedging, are semievergreen at best and present a shabby appearance in all but the mildest winters. Both privets have jubilantly escaped into the wild.

Japanese, or wax, privet (*L. japonicum*) is a better choice for a hedge, being denser, darker, and reliably evergreen. Its thick, deep green lustrous leaves give it something of the still serenity of a tropical houseplant. Variety 'Fraseri' shows yellow on its new growth, while the leaves of 'Jack Frost' are edged in white.

Two yellow-leaved privets, golden vicary privet (*L. ×vicaryi*) and *L. sinense* 'Variegatum', make eye-catching specimens when set against a darkly billowing yew or hemlock.

Curlyleaf ligustrum (*L. japonicum* 'Rotundifolium') is a slow-growing, rigidly upright shrub suitable for containers. *L. lucidum* is a taller, more open species, which makes a graceful informal screen along the rear of a property.

Privet blooms in May or June with panicles of creamy flowers that fill the air with a scent many people find objectionable. I once worked in a day care center where the only spot of shade on the playground lay beneath a tough old tree of European privet under which teachers and children alike huddled like Texas cattle beneath a billboard. I don't recall our taking exception to the fragrance of the flowers, but we did mind the overloaded honeybees falling down our necks. In autumn, however, we took delight (from a safe distance) as the scruffy little tree flashed with cedar waxwings gorging on the grapelike clusters of purple drupes.

BOXWOOD

Being dense and slow-growing, boxwood, primarily selections of *Buxus sempervirens* and *B. microphylla*, has for centuries been a top-rated choice for topiary and formal hedging and edging. It is thus both the most useful and the most boring of shrubs, under the best of circumstances just sitting there, seemingly unchanged day after day, year after year. Only the bees are apt to spot its tightly clutched clusters of tiny, fragrant flowers in spring.

One occasionally sees a very old house embedded to the second story in a pillow of *B. sempervirens*. Box is best kept at the desired size once it finally gets there, for recovery from major surgery takes time. Unfortunately, the prevailing style is to shear it into balls. Treated like this and lined across the front of a house the plants look like a strand of pearls. For heaven's sake, if you must do this, leave the two plants at either end larger than the rest to give the effect of matching earrings. There is an even more atrocious fad of carving boxwood into cylinders, which gives a house a gap-toothed, jack-o'-lantern look. I much prefer to see box allowed to flow together so that it becomes impossible to tell where one plant stops and the next begins.

Buxus sempervirens var. *suffruticosa*, a dwarf boxwood, is the variety traditionally used as edging in formal designs. Some gardeners also use the exceedingly dwarf *B. microphylla* 'Kingsville' for the same purpose. I have a specimen given me years ago by Mike Gibson, who's now in charge of the greenhouse at our botanical garden here in Huntsville. It has been moved twice but never trimmed and is no more than ten inches tall, with minute, closely spaced leaves. At the Ewing Street house it squatted beneath a Japanese maple, where it served as a dark background for the petite, lavender blossoms of a dainty spurred violet (*Viola rostrata*). When we moved to our present place I resituated it beneath another Japanese maple, but it is in danger of being consumed by a lusty *Heuchera* 'Palace Purple'.

It is best not to shear boxwood in late summer or fall, as this promotes tender new growth which will be singed by winter's cold, drying winds. A good mulch will protect the shallow roots (and thus the leaves) from winter desiccation. 'Wintergreen', a cultivar of *B. microphylla* var. *koreana*, is said to resist winter damage even into Zone 5.

Boxwood is often confused with certain small-leaved evergreen hollies which are used in similar ways. Dwarf yaupon holly (*Ilex vomitoria* 'Nana'), a southern native, is dense and compact, with a low, spreading habit. It tolerates almost any soil, from hard, dry subsoil, to butterscotch pudding, in either sun or shade. It takes salt spray, too. This holly is probably the closest thing to a maintenance-free shrub. There's nothing exciting about it — not even a berry, since 'Nana' is a male clone. But the trio of dwarf yaupons out front have grown so slowly and evenly — almost imperceptibly — that in three years I've not once had to prune them.

Japanese holly (*I. crenata*) is very similar but the leaf margin is a bit less scalloped (that is, the leaf of *I. crenata* is actually *less* crenate than that of *I. vomitoria*), and the berries, when present, are black rather than the yaupon's red or yellow, and the yaupon is more likely to have purplish stem tips. The cultivars 'Repandens', 'Kingsville' (not to be confused with the boxwood by that name), and 'Helleri' can be used as edgers like box. 'Black Beauty' and 'Border Gem' are dark green, compact cultivars known for extreme hardiness — to Zone 5. 'Carefree' has a slightly uneven, more relaxed look suitable to less formal settings. 'Tiny Tim' is a low shrub with branches stretching stiffly upward and outward — angular, yet somehow casual.

To distinguish dwarf yaupon and Japanese holly from boxwood, remember that box leaves sit directly opposite one another on the stem, while those of holly are arranged alternately. And box leaves have smooth margins; a holly's are scalloped.

Most hollies are in heaven if given moist, humusy, well-drained acid soil in either sun or part shade. They can be amazingly compliant, however, when their preference is ignored. Thus I am gratified that the row of "professionally installed" Burford hollies the previous owner stretched between our attached garage and the front door thrive so lustily given that they are rather heavily shaded and that beneath the neat groundcover of black plastic topped with pine bark, their shallow roots are gripped in a sour, heavy subsoil. These are probably *I. cornuta* 'Burfordii Nana', the comparatively dwarf version of *I. cornuta* 'Burfordii', though, judging by the hefty leaves, I'm not so sure. I keep them about thigh-high with a February heading-back with the hand pruners. The convex leaves have a single spine on the tip and are deep green with a high polish, giving a streak of real vibrancy to the winter landscape and serving as a contrasting backdrop to fiery *Salvia splendens* in summer. 'Burfordii Nana' sets fruit only sparingly, but the full-sized (to fifteen feet or more) original *I. cornuta* 'Burfordii' is obscenely weighted with orange berries in fall and winter. Burford holly sets fruit parthenocarpically, that is, without the presence of a male pollinator.

Ilex cornuta 'Carissa' is superior to 'Burfordii Nana' in that it is such a densely packed, slow-growing dwarf that it never needs pruning — a very well-behaved little green mound.

Now if you like your hollies bristling with killer spines, then horned Chinese holly is your ticket. Years ago I purchased an *I. cornuta* 'Rotunda', the dwarf Chinese holly, to place at the corner of a flower bed at the intersection of the driveway and the front walk where the kids tended to take a bit of a shortcut across the bed. The holly's multispined, saddle-shaped leaves drew instant respect, and all trespassing ceased. 'Rotunda' eventually reaches three feet or so in height, so I had to give it an annual haircut to preserve its diminutiveness — a daunting task given its fearsome weaponry. I recall that when I bought this shrub (at a florist's shop, of all places) it was unlabeled, so I took a leaf to a local nursery where I asked the lady in charge if she could identify it. "I can't tell what a shrub is by looking at a single leaf," she sniffed. She was not amused when I assured her they all looked just about like this one.

One of the handsomest hollies for southern gardens, with heavily ribbed, dark blue-green leaves that crackle with luster, is *Ilex* 'Nellie R. Stevens', a cross between *I. aquifolium* and *I. cornuta*. Left unpruned, Nellie grows into a thick, dark, comfortably lumpy small tree. She needs a male *I. cornuta* as a pollinator. (Well, heck, who doesn't?)

Unfortunately our native American holly (*I. opaca*) is considered inferior to the English holly (*I. aquifolium*) in every respect except sheer size. (They both become sizeable trees if you care to wait.) Taken on the whole, *I. opaca* cultivars tend to be paler of leaf — rather yellowish and dull — buggy, and more prone to disease. Nevertheless, there is a host of cultivars advertised as superior to the type. 'Rotunda', for instance, is claimed to have virtually spineless, dark green glossy leaves and an excellent fruit set. 'Croonenburg' is densely columnar, dark green, and to some degree self-fertile. 'Wayside's Christmas Tree' has a natural Christmas-tree shape, of course, and is liberally decorated with clusters of red berries. 'Goldie' and 'Canary' are yellow-fruiting forms.

English holly is more tightly packed and typically has very dark, lustrous, prickly leaves and glistening red berries. There are many fancy cultivars including 'Hastata', a dwarf male with small spiny leaves; 'Aurea Mediopicta', a variety whose yellow-centered leaves are margined in green; and even 'Argenteo-marginata Pendula', a silver-variegated weeper. Some cultivars are available in both male and female versions. Both American and English hollies are rated hardy to Zone 6; American holly is the better suited for Zone 9.

Dahoon holly, *I. cassine*, is a bit skimpy as hollies go, but puts on a brilliant show from late summer all the way into spring as its red, orange, or yellow berries, produced in profusion, flash among the slender, rather yellowish leaves. It is especially effective as a vivid, airy accent against a stage of dark brown wood.

A native of southern swamps, dahoon is a good choice for poorly drained ground. Though it prefers sand over clay, it will accept most garden conditions. Its hardiness is iffy above the southern half of Zone 7.

At its best, Foster hybrid holly (*I.* ×*attenuata* 'Fosteri', a selection of a cross between *I. cassine* and *I. opaca*), is a great asset to a landscape. Left to its own devices, Foster holly quickly builds into a loosely cylindrical, medium-green tree with short, narrow leaves, lavish clusters of scarlet berries, and lower branches that rest on the ground. It makes a showy hedge or specimen; it is most often seen, however, sheared into fanciful forms — bullet and toad-stool shapes are always popular — and used as a foundation shrub, especially at the corners of houses. But its frisky rate of growth makes its maintenance in a foundation planting burdensome.

We've a much-overgrown Foster holly slap against the front of our house. It visually bisects the house and blocks the view and light from the living-room window. I've thought of limbing it from the top of the window down-ward and of cutting the whole thing off to make it lower than the window, and I've considered doing away with it entirely. But a solitary robin calls it home every winter, taking his meals on the limb, as it were, and he insists that we leave it just the way it is.

I see an awful lot of sick Foster hollies about town. Commercial land-scapers like to trap them between concrete barriers where, once the mulch of pine bark has floated away, the poor roots burn in the sun and the meager ration of soil is soon depleted of nutrients. Such parking-lot hollies are apt also to be eaten alive by spider mites. A bit of iron sulfate and nitrogen, a generous mulch, and weekly water do wonders for a holly of this sort.

At a glance the large, flat, leatherlike, medium green leaves of the lusterleaf holly (*I. latifolia*) might be taken for those of a sweet bay magnolia or, per-haps, a fringe tree. But a single touch will reveal the error, for the leaf margins are as finely and sharply serrated as the blade of a handsaw. It is surprising that this stalwart shrub is so seldom seen, for it is handsome year-round and its required care is no different from that of any other holly. Lusterleaf holly is especially flamboyant in fall and winter, with its dense clusters of scarlet berries.

One last evergreen holly that I feel deserves more attention is *I. pedunculosa*, the longstalk holly. Among the hardiest and least finicky hol-lies, this dioecious native of China and Japan endures winters to Zone 5, tolerates heavy soil, and takes drying winds and summer heat better than most other hollies, though it much prefers moist soil. While hollies are often installed to give a garden a rigid, controlled look — and *I. pedunculosa* will accept espaliering — it displays a friendly, relaxed habit that should be en-couraged. The narrow, pea green leaves are spineless, and the sparkling red berries dangle like cherries from long pedicels. A variegated version exists.

BARBERRY

If you want to erect a barrier around your castle or pumpkin patch that shows you mean business, you would do well to consider the barberries (*Berberis*). *Berberis julianae*, for instance, the wintergreen barberry, is a handsome, toler-ant, impenetrably branched hedge or background shrub with whorls of narrow, spiny-edged, deep green leaves and convincing triple-pronged thorns. It takes pruning well, if one dares get so close, and is hardy to Zone 5, or thereabouts, but extremely cold weather will bronze or even kill the leaves. We are having a mild winter at the moment, and the local *B. julianae*, while a bit shopworn, is predominantly green and rather attractively flecked with scarlet.

Mentor barberry (*B. ×mentorensis*) is another rough customer. Optimistically described as semievergreen, this purple-tinged cross between *B. julianae* and the Japanese *B. thunbergii* is heat- and drought-resistant and forms a deceptively frothy-looking hedge when viewed from afar. It is so thickly branched that even in winter, near leafless, it commands considerable presence in the landscape.

The Mentor barberry's other parent, *B. thunbergii*, the Japanese barberry, is among the most popular of landscape plants, particularly dwarf cultivars of the variety *atropurpurea*, which sport deciduous, teardrop-shaped leaves of reddish purple and are hung in autumn with elongated, beadlike, enameled red berries. This is often coupled with the yellow *B. thunbergii* 'Aurea' in front of gas stations, where they glitter with gum wrappers all winter.

Barberry flowers are small and appear to have been carved into six sections with admirably neat precision. Though somewhat concealed by the foliage, they are borne in profusion, erupting from globose buds mounted on stalks, lollipop-style. Eventually the yellow to red blossoms give way to fruits of virtually any color, depending on the species.

Berberis candidula, paleleaf barberry, and *B. verruculosa*, warty barberry, are fairly low-growing evergreen species with a spreading habit ideal for massing on banks, where an absence of maintenance would be welcome. Both have rich, lustrous green foliage which turns burgundy in winter and bears pristine yellow blossoms in late spring.

YUCCA

The yucca is a wicked plant. Just the thing to mass beneath a wayward teenage daughter's bedroom window. One might regard this evergreen succulent with its menacing, daggerlike leaves as out of character for a southern garden except perhaps along the coast, yet at least six species of this striking member of the agave family are native to the Southeast.

Adam's needle (*Yucca filamentosa*) presents a squat starburst of very narrow, rather spatulate, medium-green, pointed leaves whose margins are festooned with long, frizzly threads. A squatter, this yucca is an excellent plant to mass before the taller (to six feet or more) Spanish dagger or Roman candle (*Y. gloriosa*), or the majestic (to ten feet or more) Spanish bayonet (*Y. aloifolia*). As stunning as the leaves are, the real fireworks begin in late spring and early summer when *Y. filamentosa* and *Y. aloifolia* send up towering stalks bearing enormous panicles of white or off-white, evening-scented bell-like blossoms. *Yucca gloriosa* reserves its display of pink-tinged bells for mid- to late summer. I've seen *Y. gloriosa* used as a hedge around a small front yard, but really, this is about as inviting as a yard full of pit bulls. The taller sorts are best reserved as specimens or perhaps accents in a mixed planting. However you use them, yuccas should be placed well off the beaten path, certainly away from children's play areas. They never need pruning, but even to remove spent foliage one would be wise to don goggles.

Yucca does well in either sun or part-shade and is accommodating as to soil so long as it is very well-drained. Long rainy spells promote fungal diseases.

Yucca filamentosa, the hardiest of the lot, can survive in Zone 6. *Yucca gloriosa* is a common fixture in Zones 7 through 9, while *Y. aloifolia* should be reserved for Zones 8 and 9 unless given winter protection.

LEUCOTHOE

Not all broadleaf evergreen shrubs are cut out to be bold barriers and definers of boundaries. Leucothoe, a shade-loving member of the heath family, is one such gentle shrub that seems happiest in a supporting role: massed along a streambank or as filler beneath a taller, bare-stemmed companion. If given an abundantly mulched, unfailingly moist, acid, friable soil, leucothoe creeps around and makes a thicket of itself.

Known variously as drooping leucothoe, dog hobble, or fetterbush, *Leucothoe axillaris* and *L. fontanesiana*, both southeastern natives, reach two to six feet in height. The sleek leaves, arranged alternately along the gracefully arching stems in a fernlike fashion, begin life strongly colored — red, pink, cream, or rust, depending on the cultivar — then settle down to a deep green. In winter they go swarthy purple. In spring small, urn-shaped white flowers dangle in racemes from the leaf axils.

The red stems of *L. fontanesiana* 'Girard's Rainbow' sport new growth freckled in shades of pink and yellow. *Leucothoe fontanesiana* 'Scarletta', at two feet, is compact and topped with garnet-red foliage — a complementary facer for leggy nandina, mahonia, mountain laurel, or native azalea.

Blissfully resistant to the leaf spot fungi which often disfigure the other species, Florida leucothoe (*L. populifolia*, also listed as *Agarista populifolia*), at twelve feet, serves a naturalized setting as an airy screen, much like bamboo. Pruning out older canes stimulates bushier growth if desired.

AUCUBA

Another winter-worthy evergreen shrub for massing in shade is *Aucuba japonica*. With bold, toothy leaves spurting from the upper reaches of stiff, green, canelike branches, aucuba bears a rigid, humorless aspect. Maybe it's worried about its health, for aucuba must be sited carefully. It will burn black in full sun, and will freeze to the ground — even in Zone 8 — during severe winters without protection. Recovery from either trauma is slow unless the patient is tenderly plied with water and fertilizer.

Aucuba is one of the few shrubs that will splash real color into even densely shaded corners, thus the favored cultivars have always been those like 'Crotonifolia', whose leaves are spattered with yellow or white. Nevertheless, aucubas going by the designations 'Angustifolia', 'Salicifolia', or 'Longifolia' have long, gracefully tapering leaves deserving of greater appreciation. Aucubas, like hollies, are dioecious, and only the females bear the plump scarlet berries which can be fashioned into snazzy Christmas decorations.

Aucubas prefer heavy, rich, wet soil. Stem cuttings root in water, but, once in the ground, they're annoyingly slow-growing unless babied. Spider mites and scale can spell trouble in summer.

MAGNOLIA

The queen of southern evergreens is no doubt the stately southern magnolia, or bull bay (*Magnolia grandiflora*). With its darkly looming, lawn-swallowing presence it is far too overwhelming for many gardens, and yet it has so much to offer where it can be comfortably fitted in. Of course, it is an awe-inspiring specimen in May and June, when deliciously fragrant ivory blossoms of pre-historic proportions contrast with the highly glossed, cucumber-green leaves. But here in winter it serves as a near pitch-dark backdrop for pampas grass plumes lit by the low-slung sun. The rigid, boatlike leaves with their rusty velvet backs are practically indestructible and, ground up, are becoming a popular decorative mulch.

Though southern magnolia takes pruning well (I've even seen it espaliered onto the side of a tall building), I much prefer to see it left alone, its broad branches sweeping the ground, providing a secret playhouse for the neighborhood children. But a note of caution here: Magnolias and other bulky vegetation are hazardous when planted streetside. I once nearly struck a small boy who pedaled his tricycle from behind a large, dense magnolia into the street in front of my car.

Southern magnolia may sucker or develop multiple trunks. When the lower limbs are removed to make it a routine shade tree, the resulting puddle of shade is so dense and so dry that it takes real determination to get anything but ants to thrive in it.

Good *M. grandiflora* cultivars include 'Samuel Sommer', a fast-growing selection with huge flowers; 'Goliath' another large-flowered type with a long season of bloom; 'Praecox Fastigiata', which has a narrow profile for smaller sites; 'Charles Dickens' with large flowers and conspicuous red fruit; and the densely branched 'Bracken's Brown Beauty' and 'Edith Bogue' for hardiness above Zone 7.

If your yard is small and you choose to have a lawn rather than a southern magnolia, you might give the sweet bay magnolia (*M. virginiana*) a try, though it, too, can become something of a behemoth in the southern portions of its range. Normally, however, it is treated as a deciduous-to-evergreen shrub for a sheltered spot where the lemony fragrance of its blossoms, which, though scaled down, are much like those of *M. grandiflora*, can be savored.

Magnolias need damp soil in either sun or partial shade. My parents' *M. grandiflora* is blissfully content directly over their septic tank. The conelike fruits of both magnolias are red-seeded and showy.

A N I S E   T R E E

A magnolia relative I've repeatedly admired on visits to the wildflower garden at Birmingham's botanical garden is the Florida anise tree (*Illicium floridanum*). With smooth, somewhat whorled anise-scented leaves resembling those of *Magnolia virginiana*, this casually upright evergreen shrub presents a look that is both loose and neat and has, when grown in perpetually moist soil, something of a year-round tropical lushness. The spidery, maroon flowers are interesting and unusual, but not outstandingly showy. The Florida anise tree would likely be a disappointment north of Zone 7, as would the similarly tender white-flowering Japanese anise tree (*I. anisatum*).

A   T R I O   O F   C E D A R S

There are other broadleaf evergreens — rhododendron and leatherleaf viburnum (*Viburnum rhytidophyllum*) are two — which, while fitting the definition of an evergreen, nonetheless, droop so forlornly during winter that one can only conclude they silently wish for dormancy. There is a host of conifers, however, which make a vigorous statement in the landscape all winter.

If one were to seek something of the grace of a weeping willow in a pyramidal evergreen, one's choice would undoubtedly be the deodar cedar (*Cedrus deodara*). Though books optimistically rate it hardy to Zones 7 and even 6, this softly pendulant conifer is killed to the ground during the occasional severe winter. I am not aware of a single mature specimen here in Huntsville, but I vividly recall from my Carolina Piedmont childhood how an enormous, matched pair of shimmering deodars on either side of the front walk could dominate a front yard.

It is criminal to remove the pendulous lower branches, so this elegant tree should be situated where this won't become necessary over time. The silvery blue cultivar 'Kashmir' and the bluish 'Shalimar' are as hardy as any. 'Pendula' is particularly weepy.

While we may lack deodar cedar, Huntsville definitely has fine, mature specimens of its cousins, Atlas cedar (*C. atlantica*) and cedar of Lebanon

(*C. libani*). The courthouse square, in fact, is graced with a venerable Atlas cedar whose rugged woodpecker-drilled trunk is overspread by a broad, seemingly windswept canopy of gnarled branches grasping short, steel-blue needles.

A mighty-limbed, century-old cedar of Lebanon lends similar grizzled distinction to the front yard of an old home on Eustis Avenue. But for its dark green needles it is very like the Atlas.

All of these true cedars start out shaped like Christmas trees and develop character — and a wide-reaching canopy — with age. All need full sun and well-drained soil, preferably on the dry side, so they do especially well on hillsides.

One might be reluctant to plant a tree which will not likely reach maturity in one's lifetime. How selfish! There is no finer memorial or gesture of faith in future generations.

JUNIPER

The eastern red cedar, which most likely springs to mind at the mention of "cedar" is actually a juniper — *Juniperus virginiana*. It is so plentiful in the eastern United States, dotting fields and roadsides for miles on end, that we tend to assign it status as a junk tree and thus may fail to consider either its value as a source of food and shelter for wildlife or its landscape potential. The huge variation in individuals always fascinates me when I travel. One will go along for miles seeing only fat-around-the-middle junipers, then a few thinner specimens start to appear among the chunky ones. Soon one is seeing more and more narrow trees and fewer and fewer wide ones, until eventually, every juniper in sight is decidedly columnar. Sometimes the predominant form will be weepy.

We've a large, frankly scruffy *J. virginiana* outside our bedroom window that favors us by blocking the early morning sun and shading the cooling system compressor, which also serves as my potting table. This cedar shares a nasty case of cedar apple rust with the backyard apple tree and so, in spring is festooned with fungal fruiting bodies that look like shriveled apricots from hell. I assume it is a male, since I don't believe it bears the berrylike blue cones so popular with wildlife, but it cradles a squirrel's nest near the very top and the bird feeder slung beneath the branch nearest the back porch is frequented by cardinals, titmice, and chickadees.

Eastern red cedar's stringy, splintery bark, vertically streaked with red and white, grows bleached with age. A very old specimen of this slow-growing, adaptable species projects great character though not on the scale of the true cedars. Like other trees whose branches grow vertically, junipers are apt to be pried open — and often broken — by the weight of winter snow and ice.

Ordinary eastern red cedars range in color from yellowish to very dark green with a bluish blush as the cones mature and a muddy cast in winter. But the many cultivated varieties offer a selection of frosty blues and silvers and an assortment of useful shapes. 'Gray Owl', for example, is a spreading, three-foot shrub with feathery silver foliage and an upward-reaching habit similar to Pfitzer's juniper. The blue-gray 'Stover', on the other hand, is as statuesque and narrow as an exclamation point. One could conceivably design an entire landscape completely dependent on this genus. Admittedly, there would be little variation of texture, but there could be wonderful diversity of form, color, and size.

Let's see: One could have a pool of steely-blue creeping juniper (*J. horizontalis* 'Wiltoni' — the familiar, heat-resistant 'Blue Rug') seeping from a fluffy wave of rich, blue-green *J. conferta* 'Emerald Sea'. This, in turn, would seem to slip from the weeping, gold-tipped grasp of *J. chinensis* 'Pfitzeriana Gold Star'. The whole could be backed by a chunky, bright green wall of Hollywood juniper (*J. chinensis* 'Kaizuka'), or, perhaps, more in keeping with our watery metaphor, a cerulean tidal wave of *J. scopulorum* 'Wichita Blue'.

Junipers need full sun and will do well in almost any soil so long as it doesn't stay soggy. Winter foliage on some species is an attractive bronze or purple. Depending on variety and region, major problems include *Phomopsis* blight, cedar-apple rust, bagworm, spider mite, redcedar bark beetle, scale, wilt, juniper midge, webworm, and certain aphids.

PINE

The coniferous evergreen most prevalent in the Southeast is the pine, of which we have at least eight native species, and, of course, for our landscapes we've imported many more.

One of the most beautiful natives for Zone 7 southward is the longleaf pine (*Pinus palustris*) which, with its widely stretched branches and tufts of exquisitely long (to over a foot), bright green needles, has a fluffy, airy look and is far more graceful than the more common, though somewhat hardier, loblolly pine (*P. taeda*). Both these pines grow rapidly to produce a quick screen (while young) or shade, but become tall and, since they can clog gutters with fallen needles and are readily split when weighted with ice, are really not a good choice for planting beside a dwelling. (Why do we really need gutters anyway? Rain diverters over doorways should be sufficient.) Maintaining a lawn under pines takes a bit of raking, since they shed half their leaves every autumn, but the needles make a fragrant, attractive mulch to spread at the base of azaleas, camellias, and the like.

Pinus strobus, the Eastern white pine, is distinctive in that the needles have a bluish cast and the limbs are arranged in great horizontal whorls about the trunk. The whole tree exudes a heady, *concentrated* pine scent. With its soft, Christmas-tree outline and long, blue needles twinkling in the sunshine, a healthy white pine is wondrous to behold. It is not always a long-lived tree in hotter parts of the South, especially under drought conditions, which lessen its resistance to a wide assortment of insects and diseases. There are many funny-looking cultivars, quite a few of which fit neatly into small areas, but the original species is hard to beat for sheer beauty.

One of the hardiest, most unique, and long-lived pines is the lacebark pine (*P. bungeana*). With multiple trunks mottled with shades of green and freshly exfoliated flecks of bright yellow, the tree has about it an exotic elegance and lightness. It makes a fine specimen for an outdoor entertainment area where the bark can be observed.

Mugo pine (*Pinus mugo*) is, perhaps, the most versatile of pines, its customary small size qualifying it for many uses about the yard. The variety *mugo* (*P. mugo* var. *mugo*) may develop a substantial, leaning trunk, giving the plant a Far Eastern, windswept look that nicely complements modern architecture. Ultra-compact forms like 'Gnome' are fine for containers, foundations, and even low hedges, and they add substance to a mixed border of perennials.

Mugo pine is tolerant of alkaline soil. It does best from Zones 2 to 8. If one examines the tuffets of short needles with a hand lens, it will likely reveal astonishing numbers of scale insects.

SPRUCE

The appealing thing, to most people, about the Colorado blue spruce (*Picea pungens*) is its light blue coloring and matte finish. This is the very thing that sets off its critics, who wail that it combines poorly with almost every other plant on earth and attracts so much attention to itself that guests can't find the front door or some such foolishness. Well, you might as well say the *sky* distracts from the landscape. Personally, I think this tree slips nicely and not too obtrusively into a landscape in which the *house* is stained blue or gray and the theme is carried about the yard here and there in other plantings. I especially like this and other blues with yellows, a combination that is universally adored in flowers but raises eyebrows when applied to shrubs and trees, at least here in the traditional, conservative South.

A western mountain species, Colorado blue spruce needs full sun but is uncomfortable with hotter regions of the South and will languish below Zone 7. It is drought-resistant, but its excruciatingly slow rate of growth is prodded a bit by watering during dry spells. Several diseases and insects can be dishearteningly disfiguring.

'Foxtail' is a selection noted for heat resistance, 'Thompsonii' (Thompson's Colorado blue spruce) is one of the prettiest, with extra-large silvery leaves.

There are numerous dwarf, globular, or prostrate cultivars, some of which are handsome in containers and, at any rate, are less overpowering in the landscape. 'Glauca Globosa' is a milky blue, flattened ball reaching some three feet in diameter. 'Glauca Procumbens' is a crawler.

Several green-leaved spruces also do reasonably well in the middle and upper South provided they're watered well the first few years. The darkly brooding Norway spruce (*Picea abies*) is often seen, its ascending branches draped with ropy olive-drab branchlets resembling the ringlets in which little girls wore their hair in bygone days. The cultivar 'Argenteo-spica', with milk-white new shoots, is said to be especially stunning. Many scaled-down cultivars are available for the shrub border, some attractive, others merely bizarre. 'Little Gem' is a densely packed puff of tiny, bright green needles no larger than a house cat and almost as inviting to touch. The form 'Nidiformis', bird's nest spruce, is larger and looser, usually with a sunken middle. Wayside Gardens offers *P. abies* 'Mucronata' as a grafted standard suitable for a formal setting.

Many slow-growing dwarf cultivars of white spruce (*P. glauca*) are outstanding in the home landscape. 'Rainbow's End' reminds one of an old-fashioned Christmas tree lit with candles, for the pale yellow tips of the new growth virtually seem to shine. Both this and the long-popular 'Conica' seldom exceed ten feet.

I've not been enchanted with the Serbian spruce (*P. omorika*), though some find it hauntingly beautiful. It's interesting, yes, having a highly irregular, asymmetrical outline, even in full sun, but the dead interior needles show through the significant gaps in the drooping branch structure, giving the tree, I think, a mangy appearance. It, too, can only be expected to succeed in cooler parts of the South (Zones 6 and 7). There are a few dwarf forms.

Oriental spruce (*P. orientalis*) is perkier and fresher looking, but it, too, resents heat and drought. 'Gracilis' is a highly recommended cultivar with a compact, dense habit, reaching only fifteen to twenty feet. It is said to do well in containers. There are several yellow-leaved cultivars and a dwarf weeping form.

HEMLOCK

There is about the hemlocks a warmth that kindles affection. Perhaps it's because the olive green needles are attached to the downy stems by petioles that Canadian and Carolina hemlock (*Tsuga canadensis* and *T. caroliniana*, respectively) are as soft to the touch and as graceful as any fern.

Last year I gathered cones from beneath Alabama's state champion hemlock. Amazingly, it seemed, the cones of this giant, whose roughly furrowed, arrow-straight trunk soared out of sight into the forest canopy, were of normal size — no larger than a child's thumbprint.

Hemlocks seldom thrive below Zone 7. Soil structure is not critical, but it must be moist, well-drained, and acid. Very tolerant of shade, hemlocks, nevertheless, grow fuller and more handsome in sun, though persistent winds and high temperature may be damaging.

Fortunately for hemlock lovers who haven't room for a state champion tree, hemlocks can be pruned or sheared to any size or shape and thus make wonderful screens and hedges. Also, there are compact or dwarf cultivars suitable for a small garden. *Tsuga canadensis* 'Dawsoniana' is described as compact and slow-growing to six feet. *Tsuga caroliniana* 'Compacta' is short, rounded, and dense. The intriguing sargent's weeping hemlock (*T. canadensis* 'Pendula') should be trained upward for a few feet and then allowed to weep to its heart's content. It can reach six feet or so with a sprawl twice its height. Especially lovely beside a small pool is the very dwarf weeping *T. canadensis* 'Gracilis' ("Gracilis" just means graceful), a dainty, miniature version of *T. c.* 'Pendula'.

YEW

Yews (*Taxus* species) are said to resent heat and drought, and since no southern summer is complete without a leisurely stretch of stultifyingly humid yet rainless 95 degree Fahrenheit days (or weeks), Alabama and Georgia aren't crisscrossed with fine, English-style yew hedges. Still, with proper care, yews, including *Taxus baccata*, the yew of English hedges, do nicely in gardens in the middle and upper South (Zones 6 and 7); one species, Florida yew (*T. floridana*), is native to Florida, while the natural range of Canadian yew (*T. canadensis*) dips down to Virginia. Yews are adaptable as to soil, as long as it's well-drained — they are adamant on this point. They are among the few conifers that relish shade, though they prosper in sunny sites if well-watered and protected from drying winds.

The bushy branchlets with their pliant, petioled leaves are invitingly soft to touch. Yews are slow-growing and amenable to all sorts of pruning and shearing, so they can be well-behaved, fluffy little geometric solids or sculptural, wide-spreading small trees. Almost all parts of the plant are extremely toxic to people and other animals, an exception, I've read, being the alluring red seed-covering. Since the poisonous seed is likely to pass through Junior undigested, it is probably not necessary to run red lights on the way to the emergency room should he swallow one. I would try syrup of ipecac first, anyway.

The wealth of *Taxus* cultivars available for the home landscape are derived from English (*T. baccata*) and Japanese (*T. cuspidata*) yews and their hybrids (*T.* ×*media*, the Anglojap yews). English yews actually hail from widely separated parts of the Old World, while the ancestral homes of the Japanese yews are scattered about the Orient.

LEYLAND CYPRESS

Whenever visitors to the Birmingham Botanical Garden stroll down the blacktop path between the Southern Living Garden and the daylily garden, they invariably unconsciously reach out and let their hands brush against the twin rows of Leyland cypress on either side. The featherlike branchlets — as flat as if they'd been ironed — are irresistibly soft and inviting.

Leyland Cypress (×*Cupressocyparis leylandii*), an intergeneric cross between Monterey Cypress (*Cupressus macrocarpa*) and Nootka cypress (*Chamaecyparis nootkatensis*), a false cypress, is gaining popularity as a graceful alternative to the ubiquitous arborvitae (*Thuja*), for it screens better from the ground up, takes pruning and shearing far better, and looks right at home in either a formal or informal setting. It needs full sun but is content with almost any soil, rich or poor. Yellow-leaved conifers are usually slow-growing (I've never been able to shake the notion that they're really sick), but 'Castlewellan', a yellow form of this fast-growing hybrid, can reach one hundred feet within sixty years, so I've read. I'm not aware of any dwarf cultivars, though 'Robinson's Gold' is said to have a compact habit. Bluish forms include 'Naylor's Blue', a narrowly columnar selection, and 'Silver Dust', which has an open, spreading habit. Sadly, I've seen Leyland Cypress stripped bare by bagworms, so it might be necessary to spray from time to time. And, as with eastern red cedar, ice damage is a real possibility.

CRYPTOMERIA

It's surprising to me that cryptomeria (*Cryptomeria japonica*) is not grown more often in the South, for it thrives from Zone 9 northward to 5. We have a local specimen — I suspect it is the cultivar 'Lobbii' or perhaps, 'Compacta' — that I have often admired. It lives in a little, bark-mulched island in a sea of concrete and asphalt on one of Huntsville's busiest streets. Perhaps it is watered automatically, since the species is reported to resent drought, but surely it cooks on summer days and breathes polluted air year-round. Yet it looks green and content. I've spotted a couple of bagworm sacks on it, but it is as thick as a haystack and, with its lower limbs removed, looks like a very tidy, partially opened toadstool.

For mixed borders and foundation plantings there are three-foot cultivars like 'Globosa' with blue-green leaves which get rusty in winter, and 'Elegans Nana', whose needles go purplish in cold weather. The slender branchlets of cryptomerias, borne in sprays, resemble small versions of those of the familiar Norfolk Island pine of indoor culture.

CHINA FIR

One last evergreen conifer to mention, which I only recently discovered, is the China fir (*Cunninghamia lanceolata*), which, upon scrutiny, appears rather like an exaggerated version of its close relative, the cryptomeria, the leaves being similarly arranged but far larger and more widely spaced. On the whole it is a thin, see-through tree, interesting and tropical in appearance. It grows very tall and straight but remains narrow and sheds it lower limbs, so that it fits into snug spots where most trees won't and shows its warm, cinnamon-colored shredding bark to great effect.

China fir is more easily propagated from cuttings than most of the conifers; when cut down, it sprouts anew from the roots. Winter damage is to be expected above Zone 7. The cultivar 'Glauca' is on the bluish side.

A Winter's Dream

The holidays are finally over, and it's too soon to fret about income tax. There's nothing that *has* to be done in the yard that can't just as well be done later. January is time to sit down with the colorful stack of new catalogs and daydream. If you don't *have* a colorful stack of catalogs, God bless you. Just fill out a few of the handy coupons included in advertisements in your favorite gardening magazine and suddenly you'll be flooded with temptations. I know very well that the choicest, rarest, most interesting plants are found in the catalogs without pictures — those put out by very small specialty companies. But I am a sucker for pictures, even though I'm well aware that photos can lie even more convincingly than words. The pictures though, are an aid to fantasy, and fantasy, in the dead of winter, is the thing. Nothing is impossible when the actual expense and labor involved lie somewhere in the murky future.

I approach the catalogs as a plant enthusiast, not as a landscape designer, usually, and so I lust after particular plants that appeal to me for reasons I don't analyze. I seldom look for a particular plant to fit a certain spot in a design, at least in my own yard. I say, "Ah, there's a bottlebrush buckeye. I've longed for a bottlebrush buckeye for years. Now where will I put it?" Sometimes I have no earthly idea where the plant will go when I order it.

I operate on a slender budget, and my original list is pared down considerably over the weeks following Christmas, but, if I've consistently craved a plant for at least three years, I conclude it must be love and allow myself to buy it — if it doesn't swallow my entire spring plant budget. I try not to exceed the budget I set for myself by more than a third. Discipline, discipline.

I order a lot of seeds because acquiring a plant as a seed is usually inexpensive, though time-consuming and fraught with peril, for life is more hazardous for tiny seedlings than for "two-year field-grown stock."

Since we've only been in our current house for three years, I've not yet run out of room for major additions, and so each winter I plan either to build a new bed or to expand an existing one.

It doesn't hurt at all to dedicate a bit of time to sitting on the porch or at the window from where the bed will be viewed and doing a bit of previsualization: Imagining how you want the planting to look, considering its shape and size and the kind of materials and plants it will include. Unless you're very sure of what you want, you might explore a few landscape or garden books for inspiration and try sketching your ideas, making sure that the trees and shrubs included in your plan are going to have room to reach their potential.

If you want to take a high-tech route, there is software entering the market that, starting with a photograph or drawing of your landscape, allows you to add and subtract vegetation, walls, fences, ponds, waterfalls, and pink flamingos until you arrive at a scene that satisfies both your taste and your needs.

Soil Preparation

Once you've settled on a site and a design you must prepare your soil. Let's pretend that you're one of those rare individuals who has consulted his or her county extension agent and has submitted as instructed a sample of your soil for analysis. Now you're poised to add the recommended elements. Even if your soil contains satisfactory levels of nitrogen, phosphorus, potassium, calcium, iron, and magnesium, these and other nutrients essential to plant growth are rendered unavailable to the plant if the pH is too high (alkaline) or too low (acid). Iron compounds, for example, are soluble under acid conditions, and a pin oak grown in neutral (pH 7.0) or alkaline soil will be severely chlorotic. At the other extreme, calcium and magnesium become less available as pH drops below 6.0. pH is usually raised by adding lime and lowered by adding sulfur. Most southern soils are on the acid side, and the plants we most commonly grow are content with a pH close to 6.0 — azaleas and blueberries being the most notable exceptions. Azaleas and many other rhododendrons require a pH between 4.5 and 5.0, while blueberries need a very acid pH between 4.0 and 5.0.

But soil structure is just as important as soil chemistry. Good soil breathes. Its porosity allows plant roots and the fungi and bacteria that feed them by decomposing organic matter to take in oxygen and expel carbon dioxide. Soils with small, tightly packed particles easily become waterlogged and starved for oxygen. I've lost many plants because I was too lazy or too impatient to adequately prepare the soil. There are several ways to do this: One is to turn the soil by spading or tilling. This is hard work, and grass and weeds will quickly return, so hoeing and pulling will be necessary for a very long time — probably years. Dousing the area with an herbicide prior to tilling will save some effort here. If your soil is deep, rich loam, you might try simply scooping off the turf with a flat spade, much as you'd scrape cooked-on egg from a pan.

While either tilling or scraping facilitates new planting, the soil quickly returns to its original condition. My current favorite method of soil preparation, however, results in long-term improvement in both fertility and tilth and, while it takes a few months, saves considerable wear and tear on my weak back.

I simply cover the selected site with a *thick* layer of newspaper, top it with gypsum (about fifty pounds per thousand square feet), and cover this with a six- to ten-inch layer of grass clippings, chopped leaves, or compost.

The gypsum is recommended for loosening tight clay. For the first two years we lived here, I struggled to make a shade garden in the hard clay beneath two white dogwoods out front. I added copious quantities of grass clippings and chopped leaves, confident that in no time at all my rock-hard clay would be transformed into black, crumbly woods dirt. But nothing changed. Wet or dry my spindly impatiens gasped for breath and the perennials I set therein — ferns, hostas, and the like — grew neither large and lush as I'd envisioned nor died, but stayed essentially unchanged. Then I read William Lanier Hunt's *Southern Gardens, Southern Gardening* and followed his advice to spread agricultural gypsum over my clay. For a time thereafter, by golly, I could sink a trowel into that bed with no more effort than it takes to slice a chocolate cake, but within a few months the soil had reverted to "normal."

Though gypsum's value as a soil loosener is debated, it certainly does no harm. A hydrate of calcium sulfate, it doesn't appreciably affect soil pH, but it does add calcium and sulfur, two minerals plants need to varying degrees. It supposedly works, as best I can tell, by encouraging small soil particles to clump together, thereby making the soil more porous. Gary Murray, our county extension agent, however, tells me that just adding organic matter to the soil does exactly the same thing.

Sometimes, instead of agricultural gypsum, I amend clay soil with certain coarsely granular low-priced brands of cat litter. When we had cats, I recycled their used litter by scattering it around shrub and flower beds, taking care to keep it from direct contact with the stems and leaves lest it burn them. Over time these beds, which I also mulched regularly, also became dark, rich, and fluffy. At the time I gave the cats themselves credit for the improvement; now I suspect the litter to have been the magic ingredient. Perhaps it was crushed gypsum. (Or maybe it was uranium mine tailings — I dunno.)

Many of my ecologically unenlightened neighbors bag their yard waste and set it out on the street. I'm probably derided as something of a horticultural bag lady, but, having long ago overcome my initial embarrassment, I often stop and heave a few sacks into the rear of our station wagon (why anyone would toodle around in a mere *car* I can't imagine). I don't always compost this material properly, but sometimes dump the unopened bags against the rear wall of the house, where the contents cook in the sun and eventually grow mellow, so that they can be dug into the soil or spread directly around plants without burning them. (This is strictly a wintertime option. Treated this way in summer the bags quickly fill with disgusting maggots, and the material inside turns into a black pudding with a stench that will fell a pig farmer.)

The dust that arises from the dispersal of this rotted and/or dried plant matter is rife with mold spores and other nasty things, so if I had the sense that God gave mayonnaise, I'd wear a breathing mask for protection when I handle it.

I'm reluctant to use other people's yard waste on vegetables, particularly root crops, for I don't know what gruesome chemicals — perhaps even heavy metals — I might be introducing to my soil.

In general, the coarser the organic amendments the better. In summer I pick up a lot of grass clippings (I do not bag my own, but leave them lie in peace), which are heavy to lift and, if they've sat around in the sun, highly aromatic, so that my car, for a time, takes on the rich flavor of an unkempt stable. Grass clippings taken from a well-fed lawn are a great source of free fertilizer (and possibly herbicides, unfortunately), but will burn the daylights out of plants if they are applied while fresh. Grass, however, is fine-textured and decomposes rapidly, leaving the soil almost as hard — or as unretentive, in the case of sand — as before.

I dearly love the chopped leaves of autumn. The bags are light as air and the long-lasting contents — already dry — quite often can be applied immediately. With a little fertilizer tossed in, plants can be grown directly in mulched leaves. One of my major front beds, as a matter of fact, consists primarily of chopped leaves donated by my next-door neighbor, Pat Roth.

Ground up — that is, chipped — trees or branches are the top of the line organic mulch, bringing wonderful texture and water retention to a soil and gradually breaking down into the soft, black, deliciously fragrant humus of which gardeners dream.

Edging

Some means of separating the new bed from the surrounding lawn is helpful; otherwise the lawn quickly crawls back into the bed. Many people edge their flower beds with stones and, while others regard this as a bit primitive and unsophisticated, it can nevertheless be quite satisfactory. Of the three large borders in our backyard visible out my window, only the one lined with rocks hauled from the creek at the rear of our property has any winter presence. The other two, which I simply trench around to keep the lawn at bay, melt drearily from notice in winter, covered as they are with shredded leaf mulch.

Railroad ties and landscape timbers function well in this capacity too, of course, and are usually the materials of choice for constructing raised beds where drainage is a problem. The only disadvantage to solid boundaries for a bed is the necessity for trimming around them when the mower can't get close enough. Still I find this less aggravating than maneuvering the lawn mower neatly around the beds demarcated with wheel-gulping, blade-grabbing, shallow trenches. Filling my trenches with gravel would probably speed up the operation, but my filler materials have a propensity for getting scattered about the yard.

The most attractive, functional, and low-maintenance treatment I've seen for containing a bed is the brick mowing strip, which, being two bricks high on the inside, retains soil and mulch well, and, being about flush with the ground on the outside, accommodates mower wheels and eliminates after-mowing trimming. A mowing strip should be regarded as a permanent feature. It may be a good idea to live with a bed design for a time before adding the strip to be sure you're happy with the plan. Be sure "weep holes" are incorporated into the construction to prevent your bed from becoming a pool during rainy spells.

Where drought is of more concern than drainage, I've seen *sunken* beds used for summer vegetables and annuals.

Winter Chores

Winter is the best time to attack unwanted brush and vines, for now the mosquitoes and ticks are off duty, and you can see what your hands are doing and are less likely to accidentally bisect your favorite garter snake. Japanese honeysuckle and seedlings of euonymus, privet, wild cherry, and hackberry that threaten to engulf your shrub borders can be banished now with relative ease.

We always have a few wonderfully sunny, mild days in January and February, ideal for doing yard work. Unfortunately I'm always taking the kids to the dentist, the dog to the vet, or the car to the shop when this happens, and so I invariably end up digging new beds and attending to winter cleaning while a bone-cold wind drills out of the north and a leaden sky spits ice, and I struggle to wipe my nose with frozen fingers and manipulate my loppers without cutting off my nose.

Most trees can be safely pruned in January or early February before the buds begin to swell. This is a "sanitary" time of year, when disease organisms are less active. For the tree's part, the most stressful times to prune are just when the new leaves are coming out in spring and in fall when the leaves are falling and the tree is forming new feeder roots.

Fruit trees can be pruned in January, along with summer-blooming shrubs such as vitex, abelia, callicarpa, and crapemyrtle. Save the spring-bloomers until just after they've bloomed.

Summer pruning is preferable to winter in some cases. Michael Dirr has noted that birches, for example, are less apt to bleed excessively if pruned in summer.

Every winter I whittle a little more on the pair of white dogwoods out front. The previous owner favored a sheared, ball-like effect for these trees. But since they are situated beneath a large ash tree that has been limbed high enough to walk under comfortably, I prefer a leaner look for the dogwoods, more like the understory trees they really are. Besides, thinning them out allows more light into the little shade garden I've established beneath them. I remove all growth close to the ground and all interior branches that cross one another, all obviously dead or dying wood, and I thin the sprays of epicormic growth that have erupted around the old wounds.

Pruning often does trees more harm than good. I'm especially irked when I see a healthy, handsome tree ruined by "topping," the practice of indiscriminately lopping off every branch at a certain length. Such sawing away between limbs induces rot to spread below the wound and produces fountains of weakly attached branches, which tear away as they grow heavier. And it spoils the tree's natural winter silhouette.

If it is necessary to remove a limb, make your cut just at the edge of the branch collar — the swollen area at the base of the branch. This collar contains chemicals that wall off the injury so disease-causing organisms can't reach the trunk's conductive tissue.

I much prefer to see flowering shrubs allowed to assume their natural forms rather than sheared into cubes and spheres. Prune an *Abelia* ×*grandiflora*, for example, by cutting out some of the oldest growth from the base of the plant. Such pruning rejuvenates the plant and preserves its fountainlike profile.

Hardy annuals like larkspur, bachelor buttons, and poppies, sown now in *well-prepared* soil, should be up and doing in no time. Larkspur is a weed in some people's gardens, but I needed several tries to establish it in mine. Same with poppies. Several times I've started the seeds only to have the seedlings fall prey to damping off or some such. Determined to enjoy the big flaring bowls of oriental poppies in my garden, I finally broke down and ordered plants of *Papaver orientale* 'Brilliant'.

Bachelor's button, or cornflower (*Centaurea cyanus*), is easy to grow, and the shaggy little blue, red, and peppermint faces, borne atop slender blue-gray foliage, are the perfect counterpoint for the pretentious bearded irises, which bloom at the same time. Bachelor's buttons can be started outdoors now either in the ground or in flats. Though it is Germany's national flower, this Eurasian vagabond is hardly fancy and has generously salted itself along American railroad banks. It will do the same in your garden.

Wildflower gardeners may find, as they poke about the garden now, crouching clusters of self-sown American bellflower (*Campanula americana*) and calliopsis (*Coreopsis tinctoria*). If you have made the mistake, as I have, of allowing the annual black-eyed Susan (*Rudbeckia triloba*; actually, it often behaves as a biennial or even a perennial) into your garden, there will be myriads of fuzzy little offspring all about, even in the lawn. These should be dealt with promptly, before they begin to crowd out everything else. A few will invariably survive and, as they are irresistible in bloom — shoulder-high billows of quarter-sized, golden, dark-eyed daisies — you will invariably relent and allow them to bloom, and the next winter you will be crawling around, dabbing at your snotty nose with a wadded tissue as you carefully extricate their thousands of offspring from among your phlox and other treasures. Ever so slowly I am learning to confine their radiant largesse to the back fence, away from my "civilized" beds, and to the "wild" area under the ash by the creek, where in shade and tougher soil they flower more sparsely, as they normally do in the woods around here.

January is the absolute last chance to set bulbs of narcissus, tulip, crocus, hyacinth, and the like into the ground for spring blooms. Most bulbs left in storage this long, though, will be seriously dehydrated, and tulips, particularly, may never realize their former potential.

Established clumps of crocus and certain narcissus cultivars will be in bloom before the month is out along with a smattering of snowdrops (*Galanthus nivalis* and its relatives) and the diminutive hardy cyclamen (*Cyclamen hederifolium*) with its stunningly beautiful heart-shaped, marbled leaves. The various *Cyclamen* species take turns blooming from autumn through spring. My gardening friend Mary Lou McNabb is a great promoter of these bright little tuberous perennials, as they've naturalized with gay abandon in her woodland garden.

Unless the winter is unusually severe, January should see new foliage of biennials and perennials gathering momentum down low to the ground — creeping tufts of physostegia (false dragonhead, or obedient plant), flattened wheels of the biennial evening primrose (*Oenothera biennis*), narrow, fuzzy leaves of *Anchusa italica* 'Dropmore', winter-purpled fountains of columbine, lettuce-green paddle-shaped leaves of shooting star (*Dodecatheon meadia*), and even daylily spears and tussocks of hollyhock.

With luck, January should also bring a smattering of blooms on Carolina jessamine (*Gelsemium sempervirens*) and, among the wildflowers, the magenta *Verbena canadensis*, false rue anemone (*Isopyrum biternatum*), and the occasional toothwort (*Dentaria* species).

February

February's capricious weather can lay low even the wily daffodil, sheathing the earth in an icy glaze from which only the irrepressible pansy (*Viola ×wittrockiana*) emerges with its original cheer intact. On frosty mornings we find them pitched forward on their faces like gay little tents stitched to the ground with a lacing of frost. But as the sun dissolves their bonds, they lift themselves up and seem to shake themselves off, their petals ruffling like feathers in the breeze.

Cut pansies make exquisite little arrangements to bring cheer to a winter day, for it is impossible to look a pansy in its sassy little pekingese face and be depressed.

In the South pansies are typically planted in the fall. October is good. But I wait until after a killing frost — some time in November or even December — because I can't bear to tear out the exuberant melampodiums, marigolds, or zinnias they'll replace until frost removes the need for guilt. No doubt my pansies would put on a fall showing and come on stronger and earlier in spring if I set them out before cold weather.

This year I have only Easter basket colors — sky blue, mottled pink, primrose yellow, lab rabbit white — except for a lone purple and orange 'Jolly Joker', which, fittingly enough, somehow sneaked into the flat when no one was looking. Most years, however, I can't decide on a color scheme, and I come home with a couple of flats of bright, mixed colors, heavy on the golden yellow and mahogony.

A flat of pansies costs no more than a flat of impatiens and gives an easy six months — at least — of jolly companionship. Pansies fizzle out around here by June, when the weather gets really hot.

The Maxim hybrid pansies are dainty, profuse bloomers with personable expressions and good heat tolerance. 'Maxim Marina' is crisply refreshing, with dark blue features displayed against a background of white and shades of blue — no two blossoms exactly alike.

Pansies like loose, rich soil and sunshine. They won't take drought — important to remember over winter if you happen to have them in a raised bed which dries out quickly. A loose — not suffocating — mulch of pine straw or chopped leaves retards dehydration and gives protection against temperature extremes.

CROCUS

Crocuses by the doorstep are supposed to bring good luck. Crocuses take up very little room, come and go rather quickly, and, since we can all use the luck, we should definitely adhere to this convention. Besides, it's heartening to step out on a raw February day and look into the garish throats of a crowded clump of crocuses demanding attention like a nest of hungry infant birds.

Crocuses are also divine to scatter — naturalize — for they do multiply though don't expect the offspring of hybrids to match the parents. Clusters planted in the lawn beneath deciduous trees give the lazy homeowner a valid excuse for leaving the mower crushed beneath a tangled nest of bicycles at the back of the garage far into the spring: "I can't possibly mow yet; I've got to let the crocuses set seed." Or, at least: "I'm afraid I must allow the crocus foliage to mature." Hopefully, the neighbors share such a gardener's appreciation for the beauty of sunlight sparkling on the dew-dipped tufts of wild onion by now dotting the lawn. (Do your neighbors behave sometimes as if *your* yard is somehow *their* yard, and, yet, *you* should mow it?)

There are some six dozen species of crocus, native to a vast arid or seasonally arid band of the Old World. Depending on the species and the site, the six-petaled, goblet-shaped flowers emerge from the corm before, during, or after the appearance of the grass-like leaves. Some species bloom in late winter or early spring; others typically bloom in fall. The true crocus is in the Iridaceae, or iris, family, while the colchicum, the more costly "autumn crocus" encountered in many catalogs, is actually a lily family member. The difference becomes obvious when one notes its gracefully slender styles and lilylike, pollen-shedding anthers.

The silvery lavender *Crocus tomasinianus* and the golden *C. susianus* are among the year's first floral offerings, squat little harbingers of spring shuddering in the cold wind of early February. Later, into March, will come the larger *C. vernus* hybrids: the pristinely white 'Jeanne D'Arc', the lilac-striped 'Pickwick', and the satin-purple 'Remembrance'.

The daintier species crocus like *C. chrysanthus* 'Blue Bird' or *C. tomasinianus* 'Barr's Purple' are good to combine on a moist, shaded bank with winter aconite (*Eranthis hyemalis*), snowdrop (*Galanthus* species), and hardy cyclamen.

One almost never sees winter aconite in the South, but Mike Gibson grows it along a steep woodland trail on nearby Green Mountain. Snowdrops are something of a southern rarity, too. Mike says they need sandy loam, and his snowdrops grow thicker and healthier than any I've seen in these parts. Mine dwindle away, probably because I keep insisting they naturalize in too-heavy soil.

I have far better luck with snowflakes (*Leucojum*), which persist and increase indefinitely with absolutely no effort on my part. These will bloom in March, when so much else is going on they'll hardly be noticed, for leucojum is an elegant but not showy little plant with dainty nodding white bells — dotted with green near the tips of the petals — suspended above narcissuslike (only greener) foliage. It will grow in dampish spots where narcissus and tulips won't.

NARCISSUS

February truly belongs to the narcissus, for at this color-starved time of the year our eyes can't get enough of their cold-banishing warmth and gaiety. By mid-month we are spotting bouquets of jonquils about town. By the third week of the month, 'King Alfred', the king of the big yellow trumpet daffodils, comes into bloom. My grandmother grew 'King Alfred', and, chances are, yours did, too. She (*my* grandmother, not yours) marveled once that the bulbs she had set out forty years before were still blooming. Daffodils are forever unless you flood them or pave over them or, as happened to a merry row of 'King Alfred' I left behind at a former residence, the next tenants construct a deck over them.

Though it violates convention, I find myself dividing clumps of narcissus immediately after bloom and distributing them to drab spots about the yard for next year. It works.

When we lived in Jacksonville, Alabama, we used to drive by an abandoned pre-Civil War era mansion whose walkway in late winter was thickly lined with large-cupped yellow daffodils, which fanned in a great wave into the long neglected lawn.

At our present home the backyard narcissus were all inherited from a couple of keen gardeners who lived here some years back. Most were arranged along the fence on the south side of the yard, but gradually I'm scattering them about — a few mingled with *Muscari* 'Blue Spike' beneath the apple tree, a few beneath the peach, a few mixed with ajuga in a corner by the creek. I don't know their names, but in February and well into March, I'm grateful for the sunny delight of their company.

On Ewing Street I grew 'King Alfred' and several other narcissus for sentimental reasons — they were dug from the yards of dear, departed relatives — or because I was lured by catalog hype into craving to be the owner of the only pink daffodil on the block (it was apricot, actually), but my all-time favorites have long been *Narcissus cyclamineus* 'Peeping Tom' and 'Jenny'.

'Peeping Tom' is a long-stemmed (to eighteen inches), bright golden early and long bloomer with a long, flaring, upward-facing trumpet behind which the reflexed perianth streams like a mane. When whipped by the wind, a clump of this rapidly multiplying selection reminds me of a herd of horses at full gallop.

March-blooming 'Jenny', on the other hand, is shy and quiet, about twelve inches tall with a sweetly scented light yellow trumpet and gracefully swept-back perianth. Day by day her trumpet fades to ivory and she gains in purity and sweetness. *Narcissus cyclamineus* 'Dove Wings' is very similar. 'Jenny' comes through early spring snow and ice with less damage than heavier, taller narcissus, and she is a peerless companion for pansies and early tulips.

A Foretaste of Spring

Over at the botanical garden the tiny lemon-yellow *Iris danfordiae* blooms in February, as does the little *I. histrioides* whose flowers are purple with a tinge of red. Mike Gibson says the trick to keeping *I. danfordiae* from dividing into myriads of tiny, bloomless bulbs is to plant it in clay (*not* sand) and to mulch it rather than bake it in summer.

Overhead the red maple (*Acer rubra*) flowers, a haze of orange and yellow. If the weather is warm, *Iris* ×*albicans*, the common early white iris, may bloom among the candytuft; and, if we are really lucky, a rose red *Camellia japonica* might enter the picture.

Spiraea thunbergii will muster a silver cloud of minute white blossoms along its wiry whiplike branches. It makes a stunning foil for the forsythia and quince now coming into bloom, and a striking partner for the red berries of nandina. This spirea has an airy grace and light green coloring seen in few shrubs. It seldom grows too large to set below a window, and, if it does, its slender branches are easily pruned (from the base, to preserve its graceful, wispy quality). Thunberg spirea holds its orange and bronze-tinged autumn foliage well into winter and, with the least encouragement from the weather, breaks into bloom sporadically throughout the winter.

Flowering quince (*Chaenomeles speciosa*) and the lower-growing Japanese flowering quince (*C. japonica*) do this, too, bursting into exuberant bloom with the slightest provocation.

I had a pair of scarlet quince on Ewing Street, but I let them gradually become absorbed into the burgeoning shrub border, making no effort to rescue them from total obliteration because I had become disgusted with the way their leaves were nearly eliminated by leafspot every summer. Still, the most breathtaking spring border I've ever laid eyes on was backed by pink quince and forsythia interspersed with conciliatory white clouds of *Spiraea prunifolia*.

For a taste of spring after the winter holidays, the thorny branches of quince are easily forced into bloom. The same is true of other fruits such as apple, cherry, pear, and peach and those of forsythia and the early-blooming spireas and magnolias. Just cut a couple of deep slits in the bottom of the stem with your hand pruners and slip the stems into a bucket containing several inches of water. (You can add a packet of floral preservative if you want.) Cover the branches with a large plastic bag and secure it snugly around the bucket. Set the works into a chilly garage or other unheated room. Change the water about once a week, and, when buds begin to open, bring the branches indoors and arrange to your heart's content.

Flowering quince is to be had in a versatile color range. *Chaenomeles speciosa* 'Texas Scarlet' is a compact spreader, flame-red in bloom. 'Nivalis' has icy white flowers on upward-reaching branches and is surprisingly effective in a crisp white-on-white scheme against a white gazebo or picket fence. *Chaenomeles japonica alpina* is a low, orange-flowered creeper, interesting to mix with cotoneaster or orange-berried pyracantha.

DECIDUOUS MAGNOLIA

We hold our breath when we see the buds on the deciduous magnolias swelling with color, for in how many years do we actually get to behold the rumpled pink blossoms of *Magnolia ×soulangiana* against a clear blue sky? With so many of our early-flowering magnolias, the usual sequence is as follows: The weather warms (it could be February, it could be March); the magnolia wakes and stirs; the weather warms still more; the magnolia unfurls a few blossoms as if to test the air; the weather stays "unseasonably" (ha!) warm; the foolhardy magnolia, having absolutely no recollection of what happened last year, decides to go for broke and untwists every downy bud — just as a cold front with an attitude sweeps down to turn every swollen bud and newly opened blossom on the tree as brown as a can of rusty nails. Perhaps the breeders should stop concentrating on giving us cold-hardy material and work on coming up with a magnolia with a memory. What breeders try to do, actually, is to develop beautiful, large-flowered hybrids that bloom a bit later, when freezes are fewer and farther between, yet before the new leaves pop out to obscure the extra-large, colorful blossoms.

Of course, occasionally, we have a magic year when *M. stellata* and *M. ×loebneri* 'Leonard Messel' bloom and bloom and the North Wind, evidently preoccupied with giving the Russians or the Scandinavians fits, fails to intervene.

Still we would be wise to consider such tardy bloomers as *M.* 'Betty', a shrubby April-blooming cross between *M. liliiflora* 'Nigra' and *M. stellata* 'Rosea', with rosy-purple tuliplike buds which relax to reveal a near-white, pale interior as broad as a salad plate. Or perhaps the treelike *M.* 'Galaxy' with luminescent magenta blossoms. 'Jon Jon', one of the Todd Gresham hybrids, is a high spring bloomer with foot-wide white-tinged-pink blossoms borne on a handsomely proportioned, rapidly growing small tree.

The yellow-flowering magnolias are gaining in vogue. 'Miss Honeybee', a selection of our rare native yellow cucumber tree (*M. acuminata* var. *cordata*), unfurls flowers with narrow, twisted, soft yellow petals. They appear as the leaves emerge. 'Butterflies', a small hybrid magnolia whose parentage I do not know, is spangled with double yellow blossoms, which open before the leaves.

Magnolias are displeased with drought and do best in fertile, moist, well-drained but retentive acid soil in either sun or light shade.

NANDINA

By late February the resident mockingbird (with a bit of help from the robins) has polished off the berries of the hollies and pyracantha and is, with apparent reluctance, resorting to those of the nandina (*Nandina domestica*), which has given such welcome color all winter.

Nandina stems are stiff, unbranched canes. This posture partially accounts for the shrub's other common names: heavenly, sacred, or celestial bamboo, though it's no more a bamboo than you or I, but a member of the barberry family. The delicately divided frondlike leaves are concentrated at the tips of the stems, giving the plant a legginess that induces revulsion among its critics. I find this habit agrees with either oriental or modern architectural styles. At any rate, the complaint is easy to remedy by intelligent pruning or by skirting tall nandinas with lower-growing shrubs, even with certain dwarf nandina cultivars like 'Harbour Dwarf', a dense, spreading three-foot version of the type.

A healthy southern nandina may reach ten feet in height, but, even so, the canes rarely grow too thick to be easily removed at the base with loppers. It's probably the easiest of shrubs to keep in bounds without the use of electric shears. Pruning should be done just at the tail end of winter so that you and the birds can enjoy the hefty trusses of glistening red berries as long as possible, but before the new flower clusters begin to take shape. Pruning away the spring flowers eliminates the prospect of fall berries. In 1992, however, we had such an unusually wet summer that our nandinas rebloomed in the fall and set a second crop of berries.

Mercifully, nandina is one of the few shrubs, along with the mahonia and, to an extent, the aucuba, which can't be sheared into a ball, though the excessively popular dwarf 'Atropurpurea Nana' comes distressingly close in its natural form. (This cultivar, in fact, never needs pruning, but then it never, as far as I know, has berries anyway.)

By pruning in a stair-step fashion nandinas can be persuaded to bush out down low and cover their skinny legs with new leaves. Starting a foot above the ground, cut off the outer canes just above an old leaf node (one of the swollen areas along the stem). Go a bit deeper into the shrub and cut off the next row of canes about two feet above the ground, and so on. Or you can simply remove the tallest canes to encourage growth at ground level.

Nandinas sucker and self-sow a bit, but they never become as unmanageable as, say, a runaway forsythia. Birds carry the seeds about, so it's not unusual to encounter a nandina, an Asian native, in the local woods.

I once proposed to an editor that I write an article on nandina for her magazine, but she rejected the notion on the grounds that nandina is "too common." Well, sure it's common, though not necessarily because it's popular, but because every nandina planted in the South since its introduction in 1804 is still alive today (except one that once belonged to my friend Pat Gardner, but I wish he hadn't told me). Certainly nandina is troubled by no pests or diseases worth mentioning and is extremely adaptable. I've even seen it grown as a ground cover under *Magnolia grandiflora*.

The great cone-shaped flower clusters begin with pink buds that open into small white flowers with prominent yellow anthers. The weighty panicles of vivid berries which follow are loosely draped outside and/or above the foliage, last for months and are ready-made Christmas decorations. Nandina foliage has been described as "warm-toned" and yet, even in winter, when it's apt to be splattered with rust, purple, orange, or even pink, its sheen may reflect the cool blue of the sky.

Some winters the berries and foliage are singed brown and fall off after sudden extremely sharp temperature drops, but last year's mild winter left my back porch nandinas sporting both white flowers and red berries together in spring. I know of no other plant that gives more year-round color. I suppose its only "dull" time of the year is early fall, when both foliage (except in certain cultivars) and berries are predominantly green.

Among the larger *N. domestica* cultivars available at present, 'Royal Princess' is noted for the delicacy of its fernlike foliage. The best of the dwarfs includes 'Nana Purpurea', a mounded two-footer that turns stark raving red in winter, and 'San Gabriel', with such finely divided ocher and rust leaves that a planting of this cultivar goes all blurry, making you want to rub your eyes in a useless attempt to focus. This one's winter hardiness is doubtful above Zone 8. Most nandinas are wholly hardy throughout Zone 7 but may be killed to the ground in Zone 6.

MAHONIA

The mahonias have nothing to do with either hollies or grapes, so we'll not call any of them Oregon grape-holly (though, much to my surprise, I see some of them do come from Oregon). They share a leggy, canelike habit with their cousins the nandinas and can be used in the landscape in much the same way. The compound leaves are far tougher, however, and the leaflets, arrayed in direct opposition along the rachis, are uncomfortably spiny. The flowers are yellow and in most species appear in late winter. Those of *Mahonia aquifolium* are tightly clustered like popcorn on a stick and are showy against the shrub's stormy purple winter coloring, though coloring at all seasons varies with cultivar and exposure. Grapelike bunches of blue fruit appear in summer. This species is seldom more than waist-high and tends to sucker about.

The more familiar *M. bealei*, leatherleaf mahonia, and the very similar *M. japonica* boast broad, spraylike racemes of yellow, fragrant flowers, which burst, starlike, among the exceedingly coarse, glossy leaves. These shrubs have a rigid, upright posture and are the mahonias we are apt to receive as gifts from the birds, who relish the frosty blue fruits.

Chinese mahonia (*M. fortunei*) is perhaps the most refined of the lot, with almost inviting leaves divided into narrow, gracefully tapering leaflets and often a full, compact habit. It blooms but seldom sets fruit.

Taken as a whole, mahonias are fussier than nandinas, expecting moist, acid soil and protection from strong sun and wind in order to be their best. Sicklier, too, for they play host to an assortment of small insects and unsightly diseases. But then *everything* is fussier and sicklier than nandina except, perhaps, Japanese honeysuckle.

Odds and Ends

Winter pruning must be finished quickly now. The ajuga patch is purpling and the sweetautumn clematis is starting to stir. It's no longer pitch dark at suppertime, and we have more days when we can set the pelargoniums and Boston ferns out on the porch. (But we must leave ourselves a prominent reminder to bring them back in by nightfall!) There's no sense in dragging out the big old waxy-leaved houseplants — they're too tropical for all but the nicest weather anyway — but geraniums (genus *Pelargonium*, that is) and ferns grow dry and pale and drop their leaves in dreary, overheated houses and greatly profit by a stint on the porch on those sixty-ish days. And, if it's raining, all the better. Rain water has an acid pH which counteracts somewhat limey tap water. (Huntsville's water, I've read, has a pH of 8.3.) And rain isn't chlorinated and fluoridated.

CLIMBING ONION

If you've an old climbing onion or Zulu potato (*Bowiea volubilis*) stuffed into a dark corner somewhere you might want to check it for signs of life. My Aunt Mary Lee Johnson gave me one of these mysterious lily family members some years back. The plant grows from a translucent bulb which sits on top of the soil and looks like a green tomato. From the bulb's top emerges a sinuous, tubular green stem which snakes about up and down the plant stand and weaves through the ponytail of its neighbor the ponytail palm (*Beaucarnea recurvata*). The stem is accompanied by a flurry of excruciatingly thin, wavy, stemlike leaves which serve to give the whole a nervous, disheveled demeanor. Last summer it bloomed — the first time I've ever noticed it, but then the small, green and cream starlike flowers would hardly stop traffic. It used to "die" occasionally, and I would set it in a cool, darkish bathroom and forget about it for a few months. Finally it would send up a new tendril as if in search of the light switch, so I would water it well and set it in a sunny window, where it would proceed to thread itself through the curtains until the weather was warm enough for it to move outdoors. *Hortus Third* says it is dormant in summer and blooms in autumn, but mine hasn't had a dormancy in several years now, though I water it sparingly. It is propagated by seed and by separation of new bulbs which periodically split away from the original.

New Beginnings

Back when I had a small greenhouse, I started my tiniest, most dustlike seeds in February, for minute seeds produce minute seedlings, which typically take two months or more to reach sufficient size to set out. Though the four-by-six-foot corrugated fiberglass greenhouse was unheated (my husband, who built it, called it "a tall cold frame"), it was cozy during the day and held enough warmth at night to incubate small seedlings. Damping off (stem rot at the soil line) was not a problem as long as I used sterilized soil. The greenhouse drew slugs and snails in winter like Florida draws Cadillacs, so eventually I replaced the easy-access wooden slat shelves with hardware cloth.

Now, lacking a greenhouse, I wait until March, and then I'm in no hurry, for every flat of seedlings that sprouts — with only a few ultra-hardy exceptions like larkspur, calliopsis, or American bellflower (*Campanula americana*), which can go out to a cold frame or into the ground immediately — must somewhere, somehow be given plentiful light and protected from cold until setting-out time in mid-April. This takes up considerable space indoors.

Like many southern ranch-style homes, ours has broad, awninglike eaves which cause windowsill seedlings to lean toward the distant light and grow leggy. Rotating their container a half turn or so daily takes care of the leaning but doesn't address the legginess.

By far the best indoor seedling nursery is a metal or wooden stand with height-adjustable wide-spectrum fluorescent lights. You might even want to include an electrically heated grow mat to hasten germination and keep your babies' roots toasty. These come in handy for rooting cuttings, too. I've never had one of these, but our first winter here I kept cuttings of vitex and azaleas under a desk lamp in an old aquarium out in my garage darkroom. They rooted nicely, and I supposed that I had the only combination greenhouse-photographic darkroom in town.

By March the days are often mild enough for the infants to go out on the back porch, where they either grow strong and tough in the sunshine or dry up in the wind — or damp off or freeze when I forget to bring them in at night.

Many years ago I wisely invested in a dozen or so plastic silverware trays, the long, skinny kind that fit on a windowsill. I trowel roughly an inch of soil into each tray, sow my seeds according to package directions, more or less, often reserving a few in case disaster overtakes the first batch, water lightly, and cover the tray with plastic wrap. Some seeds germinate with startling rapidity — within two or three days — when the tray sits in a warm spot. The top of a warm appliance, like a refrigerator or badly insulated water heater, works well. This year I lined up my trays on two shelves of an old aquarium stand and set them near a heat vent in the den, and they germinated promptly. Once they've sprouted, the seedlings should be uncovered, since excessive moisture encourages fungus. On the other hand, once uncovered, the seedlings must be carefully watered every day lest they perish of thirst. A liquid detergent bottle delivers an acceptably fine stream for the job. A shot of diluted liquid fertilizer will spur the babies into growth. Too much fertilizer can be deadly, however, particularly in such a nondraining flat, where the excess can't be washed away. Damping off is always a danger with small seedlings. It helps enormously to use a sterile planting medium. There are wonderful starter mixes on the market which are clean, weed free, fast-draining yet moisture-retentive, and even fortified with essential nutrients. But compared to good old discount store potting soil, they are expensive. You can use vermiculite or plain sand, too. I use the cheapest potting soil I can find and most years I go to the trouble of at least semisterilizing it.

I used to bake great pans of potting soil in the oven, but this is slow. (You know it's done when you insert a toothpick and it comes out clean. Just kidding.) I tried microwaving it, but microwave ovens heat unevenly. Afterward I still had spiders running around in the corners. I think pouring a couple of pots of boiling water over a colander of dirt works reasonably well but it's hazardous if you're the clumsy type.

Temperature plays a role in damping off. This year I have several cellpacks of sesame (in unsterilized soil, I confess). Those which spend evenings on the back porch have suffered casualties; those which come in at night are hunky-dory.

Once the seedlings are up and doing, they can be transplanted into cellpacks, where they'll grow ever so much faster. Or you can use inexpensive plastic drinking cups or single-serving yogurt containers with a hole punched in the bottom. This is a tedious task if you've hundreds of seedlings, and some years I sow the seed directly into the cellpacks and later thin the seedlings. This is painful, of course. You feel guilty. But seedlings really won't grow well if they're crowded. Even self-sown annuals like cleome will be spindly and small if they come up in a bed too thickly and are not thinned.

Most cellpacks fit into either a single silverware tray or two trays side by side and can then be watered from the bottom, which eliminates the risk of accidentally toppling the thin-stemmed infants with a strong squirt. Small seedlings often tolerate overwatering more readily than their adult counterparts. Sometimes I line a nursery tray with newspaper, pour water onto the paper, and set cellpacks of seedlings inside. The paper holds water surprisingly well and transmits the moisture to the seedlings.

Cellpacks and flats dry to a crisp so rapidly that it might be prudent to overwater a bit. Though I've seen *Salvia splendens* seedlings shriveled and prostrate with thirst spring back to life when watered, such stress is hardly beneficial.

When we moved to our present home, I built two cold frames; that is to say, I dug a pair of rectangular pits, lined them with bricks and topped them with fiberglass sheets, which I weighted with more bricks. (I'm no carpenter, obviously.) I reasoned that the frames would be a fair substitute for the greenhouse, but, like the greenhouse, they rapidly filled with slugs and roly-polies, too, as the kids call pill bugs. My seedlings vanished, all but the columbine, which the bugs and slugs never touched. True, I could have used poison, but I don't *like* snail and slug bait. The smell makes me sick, and it isn't safe to use where children, birds, or pets may find and eat it.

So I constructed (I use the term loosely) an "elevated cold frame" — a flimsy table, really — consisting of a window screen suspended above the slug-infested earth by a pair of spindly wire tomato cages. The seedlings are snuggled into a nest of pine straw, and the apparatus is set close to (but not quite touching!) the east wall of the house under the eaves. Now my seedlings are safe until slugs sprout wings. They might get cold, but they won't get eaten. Believe it or not (we are talking hardy seedlings here, not impatiens, tomato, and the like), the seedlings of coreopsis, evening primrose, and bachelor's buttons left out on this frame during the Blizzard of '93 (March 12), when the temperature fell to 12 degrees Fahrenheit, were as cheerful as ever when their eight inches of insulating snow finally melted away a few days later.

Recently, the kids' last fish, an unnamed tetra of some sort, finally passed away (disproving my friend Cindy Baier's contention that the *last fish never dies* and you always eventually break down and buy more to go with it). When I had overcome my grief, I emptied the ten-gallon aquarium and set it among the crowd of houseplants that press against the sliding glass door that lets onto the back porch. It has made a wonderful, humid home for the baby ferns my pal Wade Wharton started from spores and for cellpacks of tender new seedlings. In fact, seedlings that pass their days on the back porch protected from the chilly, drying wind by the aquarium's warmth-trapping walls were well ahead of their siblings. The aquarium's height and width (roughly ten and a half by twenty and a half inches) match those of a standard nursery flat, so I stack a flat of seedlings on top when I bring the whole kit and kaboodle in at night.

I have another old aquarium with a corrugated fiberglass lid held down with a rock. It lives out back against the house in the shade of the old juniper, where it serves as a propagating chamber for cuttings. I fill a cellpack or other container with sand (or potting soil, but I could use vermiculite) and wet it, dip the moistened stem of the cutting in rooting powder, make a hole in the sand with a pencil, and insert the cutting. Some things root quickly; some things never root. Lily bulbils are easily started in this rig, too. A very cheap, low-tech substitute for a mist bed.

I filch cuttings and seeds wherever I perceive I can get away with it. One must try to act nonchalant: "My, what a lovely *Jasminum nudiflorum*! Oh, dear! How clumsy of me! I seem to've broken it. May I have this itsy little piece?" And there's no finer memento of a vacation well spent than, say, a thriving stand of white-flowered penstemon, started from a slip snitched from a pile of thinnings bound for the compost heap at a botanical garden and kept wrapped in moist paper towel in a plastic bag in the ice chest until one gets home. Seeds travel well in a film canister or envelope and should be promptly labeled (always carry a fine-point permanent marker) unless you enjoy trying to recall what the heck they are when you discover them months later in the bottom of your purse. Though it's a well-documented fact that stolen plants enjoy greater health and vigor than plants obtained by honest means, one should certainly not go waltzing out of public gardens with entire display specimens under one's raincoat. But to rescue a dying plant, ah, that's not thievery but rather a laudable act of mercy. So now if Washington, D.C., is suddenly wiped off the map, at least the National Arboretum's wild white penstemon will have been salvaged.

Of course, there are states that threaten to hang on the spot anyone caught smuggling in potentially disease- or varmint-ridden plant material. If you encounter this situation, it helps to pretend not to understand English.

Rescue is also one of the few ethical ways (we must wear our ethics like a crown, in case we decide to run for public office some day) of obtaining many wildflowers, particularly rare wildlings, which are fair game only when they are sitting squarely in the path of a bulldozer.

When setting any rooted cutting or new plant into the garden, always water it in well to settle the dirt around its roots, even if you hear thunder and the western horizon is growing dark. If the first day or two in its new home is sunny, give the plant shade: an inverted paper sack split halfway up the sides and the resulting flaps weighted with stones or bricks works nicely to keep the sun and wind from drying out the newcomer before it develops sustaining new roots. Holes or silly cut-out faces can be added for ventilation. Berry baskets and light-colored plastic containers work well for small plants. It's best to set out all rooted cuttings or divisions in spring or fall. Even toughies like *Verbena stricta* or sundrops (*Oenothera*) will wilt to a crisp on the 90 degrees Fahrenheit plus days of high summer, shade or no shade.

Even more precious than my silverware trays are my four-inch plastic pot labels. Long years ago I ordered a box of a thousand from A. M. Leonard, Inc. With postage they cost eleven dollars, which appalled me. I recently ordered my second box: twenty-three dollars. These pot stakes can be had in various sizes and colors, but I'm partial to the four-inch white ones, which can be used over and over again as long as you write on them with pencil rather than permanent marker.

The four-inch size is perfect for labeling pots and flats of seedlings. Out in the garden you may prefer larger, perhaps fancier labels, but I stick to the four-inch model. They're fairly unobtrusive, though, as another writer has observed, they bear an often fitting resemblance to tiny tombstones.

Popsicle sticks are cheaper and can be had by the thousand from craft and school supply shops, but they decompose rapidly. You can cut your own markers from vinyl window blind scraps and assorted other plastics, even milk cartons, but the cost of having fingers reattached makes all the bother less than worthwhile.

While I'm on the subject of indispensable paraphernalia, I might mention that no gardener should be without a red wagon, a Radio Flyer or its equivalent. Unless, of course, you can afford or have storage space for a two-wheeled garden cart. I used to trundle about the yard with a wheelbarrow, an awkward, treacherous vehicle. But the kids' wagon was already under foot. Unlike the wheelbarrow it was never stored away behind the lawn mower and a barricade of forty-pound potting soil and cat litter bags, and thus it became the conveyance of choice. It holds all but my long-handled tools and is a great little mulch hauler.

As winter wanes, everything is eager to grow; dying is the last thing on a plant's mind. Trees and shrubs set out now will suffer minimal setback. Divisions can be dug from suckering shrubs such as spirea and kerria and transplanted elsewhere in the garden or shared with friends. It isn't necessary to prune top growth to compensate for "root loss"; experts now advise that we leave the top growth alone. But go ahead if it makes you feel better.

There is a similar perpetual debate about how best to dig a hole. Deep planting holes filled with amended soil was the preferred method. Lately I've read that when planting a tree one should set the roots into a hole just deep enough to accommodate them and then loosen the surrounding soil to a depth of twelve inches over an area at least five times their diameter. The problem with the old approach was that roots set into a virtual clay "pot" hollowed out of heavy soil and filled with fluffy new dirt tend to grow round and round within the planting hole, rarely venturing into the heavier soil outside. Defenders of this method charge that trees planted in the new way develop shallow rooting systems and are thus less resistant to wind and drought. It seems we could easily settle this dispute with comparative field tests, but I suppose it's more fun to argue.

March

In March life reasserts itself. Sparrows brawl and wrens shop for housing. Silver-lined clouds race across a freshly rinsed blue sky. Only in March may one glimpse a frothy white pear tree sporting a single perfect cardinal like a boutonniere.

But though the daffodils dance, the southern red oaks are tasseled with catkins, and the maples are crisp with samaras, we may still awaken to hard-frozen, frosty mornings and even a sifting of snow.

Of Peaches and Apples

The March lamentations of the peach growers are as familiar as the shrill chatter of the blackbirds that have wintered on our lawns and in our red cedars: Either the winter has been too mild for the peach trees to set buds, or, having set buds and proceeded to bloom, the trees are now at risk of losing their crops to a freeze. This is a matter not to be trivialized. We Southerners eye with loathing the grocery chain's traitorous attempts to deceive us with rosy-hued, pie-apple-hard California substitutes with gritty flesh as white and tasteless as newsprint. For a peach to be worthy of its cream and sugar, it must have taken an ever-so-short ride nestled inside a wire-handled basket in the back of a pickup truck — a ride just rough enough to stir its juices, yet not so violent as to bruise its tender flesh. It must have a fragrance that induces swooning and a tartness, when bitten into, that brings tears to the eyes.

We have an elderly, fallen-over peach tree in the backyard, which, while seemingly near death when we moved here, now appears to be enjoying renewed youth. The trunk is basically hollow and splits into several branches, most of them sinuously rotted stubs. The bark that remains is crusty with lichens. The surviving limbs sprawl on the ground, giving rise to a forest of upright sprouts. Our younger daughter, Rachel, planted her now-abandoned wildflower garden near the base of this tree, so that *Trillium cuneatum* and shooting star emerge, refreshed, among the violets and new grass as the pink peach blossoms fade. Last year I scattered daffodils among the toppled branches, and I fantasize about unleashing a clematis.

I don't spray this tree. It would be futile anyway unless I dealt somehow with the squirrels and birds who make off with the crop long before it ripens.

We've an aged apple tree, which seems to be perking up as well, cloaking itself with pale pink blossoms between the peach's bloom time and that of the dogwoods. When we moved here the apple was shrouded by the shinglelike leaves of a wild grape. The garter snakes treated the ropy vines as a hammock of sorts, a cozy spot to sun safely out of reach of the dog and the lawn mower (but too close to the bird feeder dangling from the apple's lowest limb for my comfort).

Eventually I began to snip and pull at the grapevine veil, and after years of pruning I brought it under control. The apple, now that it sees the sun, makes small, speckled fruit for our birds and squirrels and for the nighttime visitors: raccoons, possums, and skunks. The snakes have taken to warming themselves in the mulch pile, where we occasionally scare the soup out of one another.

CRAB APPLE

Crab apples should be grown for fragrance as much as for the beauty of their flowers and fruit. The roselike scent of a crab apple in bloom carries for considerable distance and makes being outdoors in early spring all the more exhilarating. Years ago I foolishly planted a 'Hopa' crab, assuming that all crab apples smelled like the deliciously fragrant southern crab apple (*Malus angustifolia*). Wrong. Most modern *Malus* hybrids smell like wire flyswatters, though 'Dolgo' and 'Copper King' (both white-flowering), 'Sugar Tyme' and *M. toringoides* var. *macrocarpa* (both with pink buds, white flowers), and 'Maria' and the double 'Prince Georges' (both pink) are among the exceptions, with a measure of disease resistance to boot. 'Dolgo', 'Sugar Tyme', and 'Maria' offer an abundance of showy fruit, too.

Crab apples need full sun to fill out properly and, like other members of the rose family, have a lot of enemies. Most will be defoliated by summer's end unless regularly sprayed. After bloom you might just plan on using the tree as a trellis for nonaggressive or annual vines and never mind the shortage of leaves.

I no longer grow forsythia, though I welcome the sunny cheer of its countless bell-like blossoms and admire the grace of its far-flung, whiplike branches. Our present yard lacks this vigorous shrub, and I won't be introducing it (though a stem just stuck in the wet ground this time of year would soon strike roots and make a sizeable bush), for I grew weary of trying to control it at our previous home. Border forsythia (*Forsythia ×intermedia*) only blooms satisfactorily where it gets plenty of sun, but it makes a tall, ever-widening thicket in either sun or shade. I can't think of another shrub that requires more maintenance to prevent its taking over a place. Thank goodness it doesn't have babies all over the yard like euonymus. I don't know why, because the seeds are winged and fertile, even on the polyploids, as far as I can tell.

I'm partial to the paler-flowering cultivars like the graceful 'Spring Glory' or the weepy 'Densiflora' rather than the richer gold of the popular 'Lynwood'.

'Northern Sun' and 'New Hampshire Gold' are among new selections resulting from crosses involving species noted for bud resistance to cold, though forsythia hardiness is not something we're overly concerned with here in Zone 7. We take it for granted that forsythias will start to flicker into bloom even before February is out. The flower buds on most cultivars are hardy to at least Zone 6.

Forsythia, like spirea and scarlet quince, should be pruned soon after flowering by cutting out the oldest canes at or near ground level, if the shrub's natural grace is to be preserved. I chafe at seeing it sheared into boxes and inverted pyramids. And, yes, I confess I do miss having a forsythia at hand for winter forcing.

Leguminous Trees

March sees the zigzag stems of the native redbud (*Cercis canadensis*) erupt with cool pink blooms a week or more before the floppy, heart-shaped leaves appear. As if the type were not attractive enough, there are cultivars from which to choose, including 'Forest Pansy', whose claim to fame is a vibrant purple leaf color in spring; 'Flame', a double-flowering pink; and 'Royal White', an exceptionally flowery white form.

The larger-flowered Chinese redbud (*C. chinesis*) blooms at the same time and is showier still, though it is more a multistemmed shrub than a small tree. All of the redbuds make quite a picture in combination with thrift (*Phlox subulata*) and Virginia bluebell (*Mertensia virginica*).

Though unsurpassed for providing a patio with quick shade, either careful siting or constant pruning is required to keep redbud and other fast-growing leguminous trees from scuffing the shingles off a roof. On Ewing Street the north end of our house was shaded by a venerable black locust (*Robinia pseudoacacia*), a living umbrella whose deeply furrowed black bark was concealed by a cloak of English ivy. In May this majestic old tree foamed with racemes of fragrant, pealike flowers, which drove the honeybees wild (and made the children's playing beneath it temporarily hazardous). The rambunctious young black locust I planted to shade the kitchen and back porch, however, proved unmanageable, seemingly twisting itself about overnight so that I was constantly amputating lanky limbs that sought to hold the back door shut. Had I not lost patience and cut it down, it would have eventually developed into a calm, noble shade tree like its parent and saved us money on air conditioning. (It tried for a long time to regenerate from the roots, but I had hardened my heart.) I much prefer this stout, substantial tree to the common honey locust (*Gleditsia triacanthos*), landscape specimens of which always seem so pathetically puny by comparison. Both have compound leaves composed of small, oval leaflets that seem to vanish in fall without the gardener's assistance.

Prior to the black locust, I tried to shade the back porch with a mimosa (*Albizia julibrissin*), an often multistemmed, rather tropical-looking member of the pea family with fine, ferny leaves and fuzzy pink summer flowers that exude the aroma of Avon's Hawaiian White Ginger cream sachet. Unfortunately, this marginally hardy (to −5 degrees Fahrenheit) little tree is as delicate as it looks and is prey to a wilt disease that causes annual defoliation and dieback. A pity, since the tree's smooth bark and modest dimensions make it a great climbing tree for young beginners.

The redbud, mimosa, and the locusts all produce raspy seedpods in late summer (the yellow-leaved *Robinia psueudoacacia* 'Frisia' does not), and seedlings appear about the yard but not, I think, to an objectionable extent. Black locust tries to make a grove of itself, sending up suckers from its wide-ranging roots, but this is tolerable and occasionally even desirable.

One leguminous tree I've longed to try, though it resents the heat of the lower South and its use is discouraged below Zone 7, is the goldenchain tree (*Laburnum ×watereri*). I saw this small, green-barked tree blooming with a dark purple lilac in Ontario and was just bowled over. The long racemes of yellow pea flowers give way, however, to extremely toxic seeds which can prove fatal to a curious child.

Spring Changes, Spring Beauty

Though the tender, emerging leaves of hostas and daylilies may be turned to mush by a cold snap, and the first fern fronds may be nipped, most perennials prepare for spring impervious to the March cold: columbines spread ferny new leaf fans and pump up bloom stalks with the turgor of celery; false dragonhead (*Physostegia virginiana*) creeps about, fashioning a dark mat of glossy new crowns.

Our backyard, a monument to civic irresponsibility, becomes a fluffy sea of spring beauty (*Claytonia virginica*) and dead nettle (*Lamium maculatum*), flecked with the purple and gold of the common blue violet and dandelion. It is, I insist, what British gardening books refer to as "an informal flowering lawn."

Spring beauty's succulent, grasslike foliage emerges in winter from an edible corm which looks like a Ping-Pong ball. The narrow leaves turn purple with the cold. The dainty, five-petaled flowers with peppermint stripes and tiny pink anthers appear from January to April, but are borne in dazzling abundance in March, when, on sunny days, they hum with honeybees.

Spring beauty ranges throughout eastern North America and is generously scattered among northern Alabama's wooded hillsides, but nowhere on Earth, I am confident, does it grow in greater profusion than in our backyard. Since I've no crocuses out back, the spring beauties are my excuse for putting off mowing until April, for they must be allowed to set seed; and besides, they shade out the germinating crabgrass. Or so I claim.

TRILLIUM

By the first week of March *Trillium pusillum*, the least trillium, should be blooming at Beaver Dam Swamp, west of town. This trillium is unusual in that it is found in boggy ground in swamps and along floody rivers. It is nowhere really plentiful, I believe, and is almost unheard of in American gardens and yet, so I've read, enjoys a kind of vogue among English gardeners.

It is a tiny creature; I've not seen it get above six or eight inches tall, and its features are slender and scaled down. *Trillium pusillum* seems to come and go rather quickly, the dainty white blossom turning pink as it ages.

The Southeast is rich in trilliums, and there are said to be more species in Alabama than anywhere else in the world. Trilliums are lily family members normally featuring three — or a multiple thereof — of most everything: three leaves in a whorl atop a stem bearing a solitary flower with three petals, three sepals, and six stamens. The flower precedes a fleshy, triple-chambered berry packed with numerous (no doubt another multiple of three) small seeds which may be distributed by birds. Some trillium species (along with hepatica, Dutchman's breeches, and many other plants) are myrmecochores, that is, their seeds are dispersed by ants, who carry them off and later feast on the elaiosomes, or fat bodies, attached to the seeds' exteriors. This is as good a method as any, for there isn't a square foot of Alabama in want of ants.

The most plentiful species in our area is *Trillium cuneatum*, a tall (to eighteen inches), sturdy, umbrellalike plant with faintly mottled, outstretched leaves and a large, sessile (unstalked) flower with brown, maroon, or greenish (occasionally yellow) petals which never flare apart to reveal fully the flower's interior. The flower's typically rotten scent attracts the flies that serve as pollinators. (So now we know that ants and flies were not put on earth simply to louse up our picnics.)

Trillium sessile, known as toadshade or wake-robin, has more prominently mottled leaves and a smaller, reddish flower. Yellow, lemon-scented sessile trilliums are variously identified as *T. luteum*, *T. sessile* var. *luteum*, or *T. viride* var. *luteum*. Whatever, when struck by a shaft of sunlight, the flamelike blossom appears to be lit from within.

Another divinely fragrant trillium (pollinated by angels, I suppose) is *T. flexipes*, the bent trillium. It grows in mass profusion in a few isolated spots in northern Alabama, and the collective aroma is intoxicating. (Imagine if *T. erectum*, or stinking Benjamin, as it's aptly called, were to grow in such abundance!) *Trillium flexipes* is so tall (to two feet) and the nodding white flowers so large that it is sometimes confused with *T. grandiflorum*, which is seldom, if ever, seen here.

Trillium flexipes often shares a woodland neighborhood with *T. stamineum*, the twisted trillium, whose lightly mottled leaves resemble those of *T. cuneatum* but whose sessile, upward-gazing flowers have narrow, purple, curlicued petals that stick out around the stamens like the propellers of an airplane. A bit more compact than *T. cuneatum*, this is an exceedingly handsome plant for the shade garden.

The most striking foliage I've ever seen on a trillium belongs to my friend Inge Paul's *T. underwoodii* (Underwood's trillium), a species found along the coastal plains of Georgia, Florida, and Alabama. The leaves are splotched with multitoned camouflage markings as vivid as an ocelot's spots. Inge's leaf mold-over-limestone garden also supports the tiny, early-blooming dwarf white snow trillium (*T. nivale*) from west of the Appalachians.

Trilliums habituate moist, shady slopes and, given a suitable environment, require no care, their stubby, thick rhizomes gradually spreading about to form tight clumps. The foliage persists well into summer, particularly if the plants receive ample water. Some years wildflower lovers remark on the luxuriant size of the trilliums found in our woods, and I suspect this is due to an unusually wet summer the previous year. The foliage remained functioning to plump up the rhizomes all season. Inge mentioned that her bloodroot (*Sanguinaria canadensis*) stays green and lush all summer, too, if it receives plenty of water, and I imagine this promotes lavish growth the following spring.

On the Soapbox

The ethical acquisition of trilliums and other native wildflowers that are rare or extremely slow to reach maturity is a touchy subject (six or more years may pass between germination and a trillium's first flower). Collecting wild plants often places as much pressure on wild populations as loss of habitat. Some nurseries are not averse to selling dug-in-the-wild plants as "nursery grown," which simply means that plants have spent the time since they were collected sitting in a nursery pot. The magic words to look for are "nursery propagated," but even then it's wise to ask questions about the plant's origin.

Whenever possible, wildflower habitats should be preserved, but, where this is clearly not going to happen, the next best course of action is to move the plants at risk to safer quarters. The Huntsville Wildflower Society periodically conducts digs, or rescue missions, as we prefer to think of them, on property being cleared for new subdivisions. The treasures removed are shared with the group or transplanted to the Huntsville Botanical Garden's Nature Trail. Thus, with luck, plants otherwise doomed to destruction are preserved, and a bit of our potentially harmful collectors' lust is beneficially sated.

Similarly, teacher Sally Elliott and her special education class at Blossomwood Elementary School, my daughter Rachel's alma mater, have made a native plant garden consisting in large part of plants that the children themselves rescued from local construction sites. As they strive to duplicate the plants' original environment, the children are receiving a grounding (literally) in the natural sciences and have created in the process a delightful sanctuary for plants, animals, and people.

CHRYSOGONUM

Out at the botanical garden the *Chrysogonum virginianum* is swelling into bright green balls of scalloped leaves liberally dotted with cheerful yellow daisies the size of bottle caps. Known as either green-and-gold or goldenstar, this plant isn't found in the wild in northern Alabama at all, though it grows in mountainous regions to our north and east and in the pine forests of the Gulf coastal plain to our south.

There are said to be two botanical varieties of *Chrysogonum*: the clump-forming *C. virginianum* var. *virginianum* and the stoloniferous *C. v.* var. *australe*.

Chrysogonum is prettiest in the spring at this floriferous, globelike stage, but it continues to bloom sporadically until frost, gradually stretching into a prostrate groundcover. It needs a well-drained soil, as it is prone to annihilation by southern blight (*Sclerotium rolfsii*), yet it is intolerant of drought. A mixture of grit and organic matter and a sloping site in partial shade suit it best.

I'm afraid I may have lost all my chrysogonum this spring. When it plunged into sudden decline, I dug it from its formerly happy home by the driveway and divided it, carefully separating individual crowns and their sturdy white roots and setting them into various spots about the yard, even putting one into a pot. Alas, I don't believe a single one has survived. Whether I should attribute the loss to disease or inept gardening practices, I'm not sure.

Several years ago, as I was researching chrysogonum, I naively queried Allen Bush, proprietor of Holbrook Farm and Nursery in Fletcher, North Carolina, as to whether he knew of any named cultivars of this plant. Imagine my embarrassment when, shortly thereafter, I learned from another source of the existence of *C. virginianum* 'Allen Bush'! This selection is a rapid spreader, while *C. v.* 'Mark Viette' is less vigorous but more floriferous.

VERBENA

Verbena canadensis, or rose vervain, is a versatile plant, but it takes a bit of management. It spreads excitedly all about a sunny bed by rooting at the nodes of prostrate stems and lays down a thick mat of vegetation, much of which, over the following winter, will die and harbor moisture and disease to afflict the following year's comparatively puny show. In the wild we most often find this verbena peeking out of the woods at the edge of clearings, where it gets a bit of sun and air circulation. It resents heavy soil.

This colorful native can bloom from February to the first hard freeze of autumn, but the primary flush of brilliant magenta flower clusters, borne at the tips of elongating spikes, comes in early spring and is especially juicy in combination with the rich purple of the native dwarf larkspur (*Delphinium tricorne*), or with the *V. canadensis* selection 'Homestead Purple'. Its cascading habit renders it ideal for a planter or hanging basket.

Stiff verbena (*V. rigida*), a South American escapee, is very similar in habit, but the leaves are narrow and coarsely toothed, and the somewhat smaller, rounded flower spikes are deep purple.

Of far greater refinement is the moss verbena (*V. tenuisecta*), another South American immigrant found growing in gay profusion along roadsides near the Gulf. The finely divided leaves form a ground-hugging mat covered with a mad flurry of small, most often purple flowers. It is very like the *V.* ×*speciosa* 'Imagination' currently offered in some catalogs. I dearly love this plant, but I repeatedly lose it, as its hardiness is, at best, marginal above Montgomery or thereabouts, I'd estimate.

Verbena bonariensis is enjoying great popularity at present as a tall, well-behaved, self-sowing, airy, see-through perennial useful in back or front of a border. I'm growing it myself this year, but both this and its look-alike South American cousin, *V. brasiliensis*, have become common field weeds throughout the South.

Among the annual bedders, so good for poor dry soil in blistering sun, the aptly dubbed 'Peaches and Cream' is the belle of the ball at present, but there are many excellent and more vividly colored choices. *Verbena* 'Amour', for example, appeals to gardeners with an orderly mind-set, bubbling into neat mounds of pink, red, white, and purple. I, however, am partial to the run-together anarchy of *V.* 'Romance', which weaves itself into an impressionistic tapestry of similar hues. This tender sort, of course, must not be set out until after spring's last frost.

The violets come into their own in March, most notably the justifiably ma-ligned common blue violet (*Viola papilionacea*), perhaps the one weed all gar-deners eventually come to know intimately. The countless seeds, which find their way into every bed and border, are produced by both the purple flowers borne on separate stalks from those of the leaves, and by cleistogamous flow-ers — greenish, self-pollinated, unopened flowers borne at ground level. Ger-minating by the thousands, particularly in late spring, the seedlings quickly develop bulky, succulent, ground-gripping rhizomes which stubbornly resist being weeded out and may, in fact, reattach themselves to the ground and begin to grow anew even if they are uprooted.

Beneath the vast sycamore on Ewing Street, the violets came into bloom while the new leaves were just emerging, so that the ground seemed lost in a purple haze. The kids loved the "violet patch," as they called it, and brought me petite bouquets to admire on the kitchen windowsill and fed the leaves to their guinea pig, who preferred them to lettuce. (They are said to be edible, after all, and rich in vitamins A and C.) When I let them go unmowed, the toothy, heart-shaped leaves grew broad and beautiful and lushly carpeted this shady expanse of summer-dry clay, giving a cool, glenlike effect. The thick rhizomes stored water, and only during the longest or hottest dry spells did this rich green, foot-high groundcover resort to wilting. Daffodils, daylilies, hostas, and spring wildflowers — toothwort, Virginia bluebells, even *Phlox divaricata* — survived here, too, with no care on my part.

But near a flower bed, particularly an unmulched bed in full sun, the common blue violet and its attractive purple-on-white variant, the Confeder-ate violet (*V. p.* var. *priceana*), are a royal nuisance. At the botanical garden we volunteers spend many hours every year digging endless mats of violets out of our summer wildflowers, lest they shade out seedlings of annuals like *Salvia coccinea*. And I must do the same at home in lightly mulched beds where I depend on annuals like larkspur, cosmos, and cleome to seed themselves. Inge Paul, who presides over the finest backyard wildflower garden in town, is the most vigilant enemy this violet ever had, patrolling her garden with a wicked little knife with which she excises these resourceful varmints. You'd have to go to Antarctica to find fewer common blues than you'll see in Inge's garden.

Inge allows other, less rampant violets into her garden, though, includ-ing my favorite, the long-spurred violet (*V. rostrata*). With a fuzzy delicacy that calls to mind a miniature African violet, this demure habitué of mossy banks and damp hillsides is distinguished by its long spur cocked above the striated lavender or purple bloom like an elevated pinky. Given a moist, shady spot in the garden (preferably where its special elegance can be viewed at close range), this native violet will live for many years and never get out of hand.

I've a white violet in my garden that Margaret Vann, who has forgotten more about wildflowers than I'll ever know, assures me is *V. striata*. It isn't *V. blanda*, I know, because the flowers, which come in March and April, are borne on the same stalks as the leaves (not separately). And it can't be Canada violet, for, although the coarsely grooved, attractively tapered leaves are similar, the flowers are smaller and lack the characteristic pinkish tinge. The paper-white flower face bears a prominent white mustache, and the pollinator runway petal is conspicuously striped with purple. Though it's happy enough in shade, in full sun the plant has a wonderful, moundlike habit. In either case it likes a fair amount of water. It has seeded a bit downhill of its planting site, but I doubt the common blues have anything to fear.

This violet looks good in the wild garden in combination with lyre-leaved sage (*Salvia lyrata*), for the violet's white flowers set off the sage's purplish, almost black stems. It works well with thrift (*Phlox subulata*), too, for their habits are similar.

The showiest of our native violets — and one of the most difficult to retain in the garden — is the bird-foot violet (*V. pedata*), noted for its large, often bicolor velvety flowers and its deeply cut foliage. This violet needs well-drained, sandy soil and ample light (a half day of sun is good). One sometimes spots it in gravelly soil along steep road banks. I've repeatedly lost this violet, no matter how diligently I strove to meet its needs. We've had considerably better luck with it at the botanical garden, where we have a variety of specimens, including a spectacular bicolor brought to us by Willodene Mathews from her property in rural Cherokee County.

The Johnny-jump-up, or European wild pansy (*V. tricolor*), an ancestor of the garden pansy, has escaped from cultivation and become naturalized throughout the eastern United States. Sometimes it escapes from our flower borders and becomes naturalized in our lawns, an occurrence which alarms some folks and delights others. Its loose, rangy foliage is capped by crowds of rather gaudy, purple and yellow pansylike flowers with cartoonish faces. It can be grown in friable, well-drained soil — either moist or on the dry side — in sun or shade, but, though it seeds about a bit, it tends to dwindle over time.

TWINLEAF

When a wildflower enthusiast is at a loss to identify a yellow daisy, he or she is apt to shrug it off as just another D.Y.C. (damned yellow composite), for there are so many yellow members in the *Compositae* family (now more correctly termed the *Asteraceae* family) that it seems no one can possibly know them all. When I first began to study wildflowers, I wished for such a handy catchall for the plethora of spring wildflowers bearing solitary white flowers.

One such is twinleaf (*Jeffersonia diphylla*). It is a comely plant with large, unique leaves cleanly divided into an opposing pair of kidney-shaped leaflets, like a bean sliced through the middle and opened. The white flowers, borne singly at the tips of slender scapes, are smaller than those of bloodroot, less numerous than those of rue anemone, swifter to go by than those of hepatica. The seed capsule, carried atop a much-elongated stem, is unusual, resembling an old-timey shop whistle in appearance.

With only two species in its genus (the other is in Japan), this member of the barberry family is rare in Alabama, where it is found in small patches among limestone outcroppings. I've read that it is in decline over much of its range, which stretches north into New York and Wisconsin. It is favored by deer, and I suspect the exploding deer population may account for its diminished numbers. Yet twinleaf is long-lived in the garden. I've grown it easily under partial shade in clay mixed with leaf mold. It lends a touch of elegant simplicity until the pushier summer flowers take over.

COLUMBINE

I used to say that if I could grow but one flower (what an idea!), it would be the eastern wild columbine (*Aquilegia canadensis*), for I've long been enchanted with the grace and delicacy of its beautifully crafted, crownlike blossoms, which dangle with shy majesty from two-to-three-foot wiry stems. It is our first "tall" spring flower (discounting ragwort) and, with its long, nectar-filled spurs, is custom-designed to welcome the returning hummingbirds. This columbine blooms some weeks before hybrids like the dramatically long-spurred 'McKana's Giant' or the old-fashioned European granny's bonnet (*A. vulgaris*) and combines charmingly with the slender species tulip *Tulipa clusiana*, for, in my garden, at least, they share the same rosy-orange and cream coloration.

In the wild one often sees this columbine erupting from cracks in a sheer rock face, yet it adapts well to any well-drained garden soil in either sun or shade. Flowers are more numerous in sun. The compound leaves are divided into triple-lobed leaflets resembling chubby hands with fingers outspread and, collectively, appear as a soft tuffet of light blue-green (purple in winter). In summer the leaves are rather ornamentally disfigured by leaf miners, which hollow crazy patterns between the layers.

Columbine may bloom for six weeks or more, and afterward the pointy, upturned seedpods dry out and split, releasing hundreds of flealike seeds, which will quickly germinate in a flat. Seedlings stay small and neat until they are set out, even if you put it off for months. Seedlings set out this year will bloom *next* year. Since individual plants are seldom long-lived, it is wise to have a supply of fresh seedlings.

The hybrid columbines are equally easy from seed and, with their celebrated promiscuity, cross to produce offspring in astonishing combinations of floral style and color, which pop up serendipitously all about the garden. The refreshing, blue and white Rocky Mountain columbine (*A. caerulea*) does reasonably well in the South, too.

LUNARIA

Last year my mother in Birmingham sent me an envelope of pressed leaves and flowers and asked if I could identify this strange wildflower that had appeared along her back fence. I had to smile as I recognized money plant, or honesty (*Lunaria annua*), a southern European native that has decided to see the world. The lunaria in my own yard, in fact, had come from Germany, as seeds brought back by a friend. Though lunaria's silvery, disklike seedpods are often seen in dried arrangements, many people are not familiar with the plant in its blooming state.

Lunaria is a biennial (so why it isn't *L. biennis*, I know not). It finds its way into nooks and crannies in any soil that isn't under water, in sun or shade, and self-sows thickly, forming a squat groundcover of sorts with coarsely hirsute, dark green (purplish in cold weather) leaves with scalloped margins, which may persist over winter. The following spring most of these plants, so lackadaisical heretofore, will suddenly shoot up two or three feet and sprinkle themselves with half-inch, four-petaled purple (or sometimes white) flowers.

Lunaria annua variegata 'Stella' has white flowers and leaves strongly spattered with cream. Judging by her photo in the Thompson & Morgan catalog, I'd say she looks diseased, but British garden authority Christopher Lloyd, in his book *Foliage Plants*, credits variegated lunaria with providing stimulating undercoverage to a boring deciduous shrub (a lilac, in his case). This plant, he says, will come true from seed as long as it's segregated from the purple sort.

Lunaria's big draw, of course, is the silicle, or coinlike (or moonlike, given the Latin genus name) seed capsule, so cherished for dried arrangements. If left too long in the garden, these are apt to mold or self-destruct. I've rarely succeeded in drying them to the desired degree of whiteness, in fact. If not used indoors, they can be shredded into out-of-the-way spots where a smattering of purple or white might be welcome in succeeding springs.

AJUGA AND FOAMFLOWER

Ajuga (*Ajuga reptans*) and our native foamflower (*Tiarella cordifolia*) are lovely in combination with our earliest azaleas. Both do well in moist shade, but ajuga is most floriferous in sun, where it is also less prone to debilitating fungal disorders. It is more heat- and drought-resistant than you might think and even takes moderate foot traffic.

Ajuga becomes an avid cascader when placed in a planter or window box. It is shallow-rooted, and, though it lays down a frilly carpet of purplish stems and leaves, it tolerates company. The common variety is generally more vigorous than most of the fancier, variegated or curly-leaved cultivars. Some have spikes of pink or white flowers rather than the typical blue.

A while back I was given a start of *A. pyramidalis* 'Metallica Crispa', an ajuga with glossy, near-black, radically curled leaves. I nursed it along for a couple of years, first in shade, then in sun, before it vanished. But the common sort ramps unrestrained about the premises in several places.

Foamflowers are either clump-formers or spreaders depending on the variety you choose. *Tiarella cordifolia* var. *collina* is clump-forming, while *T. cordifolia* var. *cordifolia* spreads about by runners. The tiny, white, starlike flowers stand out along the raceme like bristles on a bottle brush. The fuzzy, medium-green leaves are shaped like those of a sugar maple. Wherry's foamflower (*T. cordifolia* var. *wherryi*) is clump-forming and has smaller leaves and pinkish flowers. All three are impossible in other than moist, humusy shade.

HEUCHERA

The heucheras, or alumroots, are more reliable. Very like the tiarellas in leaf and habit, their feathery, wandlike inflorescence comes a bit later, is taller than a foamflower's, and persists in beauty long after the minute flowers themselves have faded.

Heuchera sanguinea, the garden coralbell, is native to the American Southwest and is perhaps most familiar to us in the 'Bressingham Hybrids' series in shades of carmine, pink, and white. *Heuchera sanguinea* 'Mt. St. Helens' looks positively incendiary — showers of hot red sparks rising from "almost evergreen, ivy-shaped foliage," to quote the Wayside Gardens catalog.

"Almost evergreen" is probably right. My *H. micrantha* 'Palace Purple' holds its bold, glossy leaves but looks mighty rough by winter's end. Still, I would cheerfully nominate this durable, versatile heuchera as World's Finest Perennial. The foliage is a strong, bronzy, reddish purple when grown in sun (sort of a coffee and beet juice mixture), greener and less shiny in shade. In either situation it sends up long-lasting, airy, greenish plumes that are especially effective en masse.

For some time I've used a single chunky plant of 'Palace Purple' as a rich accent at the base of a similarly red-purple Japanese maple in a bed that bakes in summer. This isn't the ideal for either plant, of course, but they take it reasonably well, particularly if I water conscientiously.

TROUT LILY

Long ago I gave up trying to dig trout lilies, for *Erythronium americanum* and related species, or fawn lily or dogtooth violet, as it is as often called, is deeply and stubbornly rooted, often beneath rocks, so that one may accidently separate the beautiful gray-green and soft chocolate, speckled leaves from their corms. Yet I do have a trout lily, though it is still too young to bear the nodding, lilylike yellow blossom of the predominant local species (trout lilies take four or more years from seed). Mine came up in soil around a Christmas fern I had liberated from the middle of a trail used by off-road recreational vehicles (yes, I know I could simply have relocated the fern off the trail, but we are in need of moral justification here).

There are some twenty-five species of trout lily, three native to Alabama, I've read. Being well under a foot tall, our native erythroniums are not individually showy, but they are often found in sheets of thousands on moist, shady hillsides, so that it is impossible to be unimpressed.

For the garden one might prefer a more flamboyant hybrid like E. ×'Pagoda', whose airy, knee-high, rain-slicker yellow blossoms hover like butterflies over broad, vaselike leaves of great substance. *Erythronium* 'White Beauty' features extra-large, cream-colored flowers over sleek, marbled foliage.

VIRGINIA BLUEBELL

The Virginia bluebell (*Mertensia virginica*) is achingly beautiful. The foliage emerges cautiously in late winter: purple-green shoots that expand and flatten ever so gradually into a rosette of soft, paddlelike leaves surrounding a tightly held clutch of purplish flower buds. As March draws to a close, these buds, along with a few of the now bright green leaves, are propelled upward on tilting stalks where the limply nodding cymes of pleated pink buds flare into downcast, sky blue bells. When found growing en masse along steams and in damp meadows or on moist, wooded hillsides, the effect is overwhelming.

In the garden Virginia bluebell is a surprisingly adaptable and reliable perennial, enduring summer drought in sun or deciduous shade without complaint as long as it receives ample water in spring. Though in our area it's usually found in sandy soil, it survives and blooms beautifully (but does not increase appreciably) in heavy clay. Since it goes dormant in May as the seeds mature, it should be overplanted with ferns or perhaps a groundcover or shallow-rooted annual, such as impatiens, to avoid accidental injury to its deep, thick roots.

DUTCHMAN'S BREECHES

Near the end of March, when the Virginia bluebells and trout lilies are at their peak — or perhaps just a few days before — the Dutchman's breeches (*Dicentra cucullaria*) blooms. With its low, finely cut, ferny foliage and its diminutive blossoms like puffy white pantaloons hung out on the line to dry, it is far daintier than its stout, rosy-flowered cousin the bleeding heart (*D. spectabilis*).

I admit I've not had great good luck with this plant. Inge Paul says it's because I planted mine too deeply. Apparently they like to be barely underground and yet cool and moist, but not under such a blanket of mulch

A sunny winter's day spurs hepatica to grant us a glimpse of spring.

PHOTOGRAPH BY
CAROL B. HIPPS

Impervious to cold, winter jasmine lights up a winter's day.

PHOTOGRAPH BY
CAROL B. HIPPS

*Florida anise tree,
here seen festooned
with maroon spring
flowers, is a calm,
cool, collected
evergreen shrub that
belongs in more
southern gardens.*

PHOTOGRAPH BY
CAROL B. HIPPS

*Eastern red cedar,
dangerously weighted
with a picturesque
glaze of ice. This and
other trees with near-
vertical branches are
particularly prone to
ice damage.*

PHOTOGRAPH BY
ELSABE HOLST-WEBSTER

*The diminutive
majesty of a single
perfect crocus.*

PHOTOGRAPH BY
PAT GARDNER

January
⁂
February
⁂
March

A stampede of N.
cyclamineus,
'Peeping Tom'.

<small>PHOTOGRAPH BY
CAROL B. HIPPS</small>

*Nandina berries look
good enough to eat,
but aren't.*

<small>PHOTOGRAPH BY
PAT GARDNER</small>

Mahonia aquifolium *contrasts sunshine-yellow winter flowers with brooding purple foliage.*

PHOTOGRAPH BY
CAROL B. HIPPS

Forsythia and redbud let the neighborhood know that it's time to stop taking winter so seriously.

PHOTOGRAPH BY
ELSABE HOLST-WEBSTER

*Small but elegant,
spring beauty
delights in seeding
itself into a lawn.*

PHOTOGRAPH BY
PAT GARDNER

Bird-foot violet is a temperamental charmer.

PHOTOGRAPH BY
PAT GARDNER

January

&

February

&

March

*A bit of sky brought
down to earth,
Virginia bluebell
nods modestly.*

PHOTOGRAPH BY
PAT GARDNER

that they rot, which they are prone to do. One encounters occasional vast patches on the north side of mountain ridges and along streams, but *D. cucullaria* is nowhere overly plentiful. The foliage vanishes after bloom, while that of bleeding heart persists through summer, if the plant is kept moist and shaded.

GRAPE HYACINTH

The grape hyacinths are native to the Old World, particularly the Mediterranean region, but have made themselves at home here to such an extent that they are as plentiful as dandelions in many a lawn. The musk hyacinth (*Muscari racemosum*) has skinny, round leaves resembling those of wild onion, while *M. botryoides*, the common grape hyacinth, has a thin, flat leaf. Both bear stubby racemes of tiny, grapelike purple flowers.

Because *M. racemosum* bloomed rampantly in our lawn and formed tight mats of nonblooming foliage in my flower beds, it never occurred to me to *buy* a grape hyacinth, though I flirted with the notion of ordering the rather novel feather or tassel hyacinth (*M. comosum* cv. 'Monstrosum' or cv. 'Plumosum'). Then in with a bulb order I received a complimentary supply of *M. armeniacum* 'Blue Spike', which I scattered beneath our apple tree. What a difference! The ten-inch spires of chilly, China blue stood head and shoulders above the naturalized "commoners" and mingled deliciously with the pink and white spring beauties. Now it remains to be seen if this splashy newcomer persists and increases like its runaway cousins. There is a cultivar of this muscari, 'Heavenly Blue', on which each little bell-like blossom is brushed with white.

Muscari azureum, often listed as *Hyacinthella azurea*, bears comparatively broad, straplike leaves and conelike racemes of very bright blue flowers in early spring. Its height is comparable to that of *M.* 'Blue Spike'.

Muscari botryoides 'Album', pearls of Spain, is a small white version of the plentiful blue sort, with flowers like crowded grains of puffed rice.

TULIP

By month's close the fiery red 'Apeldoorn' tulips are goblets of light. Cindy Baier gave me these bulbs, and, for the last three years we lived on Ewing Street, they put on a splendiferous show near the back doorstep. The first year their bowllike blossoms could have held a softball, and each year thereafter . . . maybe a baseball.

When we bought the Ewing Street house, I planted cool red and white 'Merry Widow' tulips in a ring around a dogwood in the front yard. (Oh, how plebeian, you scoff.) I thought they were lovely with my azaleas, but every year I lost a few, marked the spot with a label reading "replace tulip," and attempted to fill each vacancy in the fall. Usually I used 'Merry Widow', but, if I didn't see them in the catalogs, I ordered 'Lucky Strike', *Tulipa clusiana*, or some other tulip that seemed to carry on the color scheme. This never worked well, for the replacements bloomed slightly before or after the others and tended to be the wrong size or color. (This is how I discovered that *T. clusiana*, or at least *my T. clusiana*, is rosy-orange and cream, not candy-stripe red and white as catalogs depict.) Such unpredictability is probably the best reason for planting tulips in masses rather than geometrical patterns. Casualties won't ruin a display.

Terrible things can happen to tulip bulbs. They can be eaten by rodents, and are often planted in wire baskets to prevent this. Old gardening books suggest controlling insects around the planting site to discourage moles, whose tunnels provide mice and chipmunks with access to the bulbs. Summer heat may roast and dehydrate dormant bulbs. The small, early-blooming species tulips, like *T. kaufmanniana*, are considered more likely than larger hybrids to function as perennials, but culture affects longevity. In the South no tulip should be planted less than eight inches deep, and a foot or more is even better. If drainage is doubtful, amend the soil with organic matter and grit, placing extra sand or fine gravel in the bottom of the planting hole. Mulch to further insulate the bulbs from heat.

Deep planting and light fertilizing minimize bulb-splitting, a situation in which bloom-sized bulbs divide into (or simply produce) multitudes of small, bloomless ones. Bonemeal, long regarded as the ideal fertilizer, is harmless but unnecessary, as it is mainly phosphorus, an element seldom lacking or unavailable in most moist, acidic soils. As they decompose, organic mulches slowly and safely release most of the nutrients bulbs need. (Still, I admit, I give my tulips a shot of liquid fertilizer at some point, usually when I'm feeding the pansies in March or April.) Newly purchased bulbs should be stored at 40 degrees Fahrenheit until planting out time (late October through January). Snap off developing seed capsules if it makes you happy. Always allow the foliage to die down naturally after flowering.

At tulip time (March through early May) decide where the garden could use a spot of color and make a note on your September calendar, so when the bulb catalogs arrive in fall (if you haven't taken advantage of the early-bird spring specials), you will remember what to buy and where to put it. You may realize, for example, that you're in need of a planting around the mailbox to echo the dogwood's gentle shade of pink.

If you're the impulsive sort (as I tend to be), you'll probably toss a pack of bulbs into your grocery cart in October and plant them *somewhere*, so that when spring comes both you and the neighbors will be startled by the sight of a pack of flaming orange parrot tulips knocking heads with the cluster of delicately tapered, mauvish 'Lilac Time' you'd forgotten you had. Life, for some of us, is full of surprises.

My backyard beds are primarily summer-blooming, and last year, determined to alleviate their drab look in spring, I ordered dozens of 'Rembrandt' tulips. These are supposed to be long-lived, and indeed, year after year I had admired an ancient planting of 'Rembrandts' in an utterly neglected yard near the Ewing Street house, where they meandered along a walkway bisecting a lawn that had been allowed to revert to woods. These were such *interesting* tulips, no two alike, all appearing to've been dipped in one color and striped with a feather in a contrasting hue. But mine were a disappointment, each one basically rose-red with a smidgen of white on the petal edges and a blocky lack of grace. They bloomed for weeks, though, and if they come back, I'm sure I can learn to love them.

If it's grace you want, the lily-flowering tulips, with their long-waisted, vaselike shape and pointed petals, should suit, and the color range is impressive. I've especially enjoyed 'West Point', a clear yellow, though one is a bit less thrilled by yellow once the daffodils have done their bit and the azaleas are opening pink and fuchsia buds. The tall 'White Triumphator' goes with anything and brings regal splendor to a cut arrangement. The petals of 'Ballade' are a soft red-violet edged with white — very classy with 'Imperial Pink' pansies. For years I allowed the elegantly tapered 'Lilac Time' to be rudely shoved about by a burgeoning throng of 'Peeping Tom' narcissus, until I took up the tulips and gave them roomier quarters in odd spots about the yard. This curvaceous tulip is a subdued, frosty amethyst and needs a pink or light yellow companion to set it off. The most common, glaringly pink shade of thrift, or moss pink (*Phlox subulata*), will do, or perhaps a late-flowering narcissus like *Narcissus triandus* 'Hawera'.

This year I had a blazing clump of 'Aladdin' lily-flowering tulips, with skinny, flamelike, fire-hydrant red petals singed at the base and along the edges with yellow. In need of a touch of warmth, I had plucked them off a rack at the grocery store last fall, brought them home, and dumped the whole pack of ten or so bulbs into a single eight-inch-deep by six-inch-wide hole in an elevated front yard bed, so that some of them were actually on top of others. They made an alarming bouquet in March and early April, clashing as anticipated with the lavender *Phlox subulata* and my pastel pansies. Sometimes I wonder about my deep-seated aversion to good taste.

I witnessed a comparable example of perversity elsewhere in the neighborhood this spring: a brooding violet smokescreen of *Berberis thunbergii* fronted by a score of what I took to be the burgundy-black Darwin tulip 'Black Pearl', or perhaps the profoundly maroon 'Queen of the Night'. It was an angry scene that seemed to say "Bah humbug!" to spring.

The prettiest tulip displays I saw this spring were on McClung Avenue, almost across the street from one another, and both included the Darwin or cottage tulips now collectively known as single late tulips. One planting was a ribbon bed of diminutive clipped box lapped by a stream of blue pansies and punctuated at precise intervals by stately pink tulips. The other lay beneath a flowering dogwood and featured a profusion of low-growing, pale pink azaleas interspersed with towering white tulips — perhaps the thirty-inch 'Maureen'.

Better Living Through Chemistry?

Somewhere between the flowering of the forsythia and the dogwood — that is to say, March — is the prescribed time to apply preemergent herbicide for crabgrass. I've done this only once. One year on Ewing Street I decided to do the neighbors a favor and deal with the crabgrass that shot up around our knees faster than we could mow it in the sunny parts of the yard.

As I broadcast the greasy little pellets, I was surprised at the strength and unpleasantness of their smell; somehow I had expected the product to be more like a hormone than an outright toxin and therefore "safer" to use. The next day our dog, Johnny, who typically passed much of his day sunning in the very spots I had treated with the herbicide, suffered repeated bouts of retching. And to top it all off, the crabgrass came up just the same.

If you feel you *must* use herbicides and pesticides (and when your grandmother's favorite rose, which you raised from a cutting, is being denuded by little green caterpillars, you feel you must), read and follow all the boring instructions on the label and take the warnings seriously. It wouldn't hurt to invest in an assortment of masks to filter the air you breathe when you resort to chemical warfare.

A few squirts of Roundup (glyphosate) now, while the poison ivy and Japanese honeysuckle are pumping out new growth, may save pain and labor later, when the vines will otherwise have added yards to their tangled dimensions. This is perhaps the most environmentally friendly herbicide, but it may have to be reapplied every other week or so until the unwelcome intruder has exhausted the reserves in its roots. Even kudzu can be eliminated by persistent defoliation, but our determination is apt to sag once hot weather sets in, so the more accomplished during the gardener-friendly days of spring the better.

A Pound of Prevention

Years ago I foolishly cleared infestations of poison ivy bare-handed and bare-armed because I "wasn't allergic to it." Then one year I was covered up each side and down the middle with maddeningly itchy blisters. That's when I learned that one can become sensitized to poison ivy by repeated exposure. Sometimes even in winter I break out in blisters if I unwittingly come into contact with dormant vines. And I've gotten the rash on my hands from handling the roots of plants newly dug from poison ivy-infested woods. The irritating oil in poison ivy, urushiol, is somewhat like carbolic acid and can be transferred from one object to another by touch. There is a new product on the market, Tecnu, which can be rubbed on the skin before or after exposure to minimize the risk of reaction.

Otherwise, keep Benadryl and a hydrocortisone/anesthetic spray on hand for poison ivy and, while you're at it, lay in a supply of antiseptic, insect repellent, and sunscreen. It's a dangerous world out there.

The Mower the Merrier

A well-maintained lawn presents a perfect setting for an equally well-groomed bed or border. Still, for me, tax day (April 15) excepted, the unveiling of the lawn mower is the most dreaded event of spring. I put off mowing as long as possible, for I hate it with all my heart.

Though I am encouraging an assortment of groundcovers to extend their coverage into some of the areas we now mow, my husband and I (and occasionally our older daughter Anna) must still put in several hours a month shoving our five-horsepower walk-behind mower about the yard. It is loud, it vibrates, and it drinks gasoline like a 1958 Cadillac. Mowing a large yard, especially when the temperature and humidity are high, is exhausting and potentially hazardous both to the one doing the mowing and to pets and other innocent bystanders as well.

High, moisture-heavy grass often clogs our mower's discharge chute, stalling the machine and necessitating a series of shoulder-wrenching restarts. This tempts the impatient operator to take risks, like propping open the safety guard on the discharge chute or, as a three-fingered acquaintance of mine once did, attempting to clear the chute while the engine is running. Raising the cutting height helps. (I suspect that cutting the grass before it's halfway up my shin would help, too.) I've read that a new breed of eerily quiet, battery-powered mulching mowers is being sent down from heaven to ease our travails. We'll see.

March Tidbits

Quick-growing annuals and perennials can be started indoors from seed now. They can be ready to fill in when the pansies burn out. We have a long growing season and there's no need to get in a panic over this, but it is nice to have our seedlings up and doing before the hot, dry weather arrives in June. Then in July I start a batch of marigolds for fall and perennials for next year's bloom.

If you kept any impatiens, pelargoniums, coleus, and the like over the winter, cuttings can easily be rooted in water for setting out after frost. But it's more fun and a lot easier to go to a garden center, have a good browse, and buy new bedding plants when the time comes.

March is like Christmas all over, as the UPS truck groans to a halt out front and the neighborhood dogs frenetically broadcast to all who can hear the happy news that the plants we ordered have come. Set them out promptly, but, if this can't be done, set them temporarily into loose earth or mulch and keep them moist and shaded. Don't let them sit around and dry out in their shipping box.

Most perennials and suckering shrubs can be divided now, if need be, without serious setback. And everything save the azaleas and rhododendrons can be fed. (We don't want to encourage our azaleas to put forth new leaves until after we've enjoyed their blooms.)

Chrysanthemums tend to play out if not periodically rejuvenated. Take cuttings as soon as the new shoots are four to six inches long.

If March came in like a lion, there's a good chance it'll go out the same way.

April

Ah spring! True spring, the incomparable days of high spring! The brooding air holds just the faintest touch of the chill that settles into the hollows after dark, tracing the leaf litter with frost. Pastures glow with the warmth of golden ragwort and the lustered yellow of buttercups. Redbud and Carolina jessamine shower neon green lawns with spent blossoms of cool pink and yellow-gold. Lumbering clouds pile high in the sky once again, briefly shadowing spring's sparkle, shattering its song with the sudden violence of their passage, ultimately enriching its colors with their cleansing rain. Our freshly mowed backyard is spangled with low-lying dandelions, like myriad tiny suns, which beckon great flocks of matching goldfinches to a seedy feast.

DOGWOOD

I've often thought that if every yard in the South weren't already generously supplied with dogwoods and azaleas, that perhaps the law should mandate it, for surely there can be no more glorious sight than this April blizzard of pastel bloom. Once Rachel and I took a ride over Huntsville in a small plane. It happened to be the peak of the dogwood season (early- to mid-April), and we were amazed at the sight: The city virtually frothed with dogwoods—pink and white fluffiness everywhere we looked.

The flowering dogwood (*Cornus florida*) is no doubt our most beloved small tree, and, unlike its nearest competitor, the imported crapemyrtle, is native to the entire eastern United States. The specific epithet "florida" simply means "flowering." The flowers appear before the leaves and are rather insignificant. What fills us with rapture are actually the four bracts surrounding each crowded flower head, the "petals" of pink, near red, or white.

There are many cultivars from which to choose. One would do well to shop and consider carefully, for, with luck and good care, the tree you select should last for decades. It's also a good idea to purchase a tree grown either in your own climate zone or a region further north; the flower buds of trees born and raised in the lower South may not prove winter hardy further north.

Prepare your new tree's planting site well. Dig deep and wide (especially wide) and work in lots of organic material. Dogwoods like moist, acid, well-drained soil. Sun or shade is okay, but mulch the root zone well and *never* let it go dry until the tree is well-established—at least two years. Don't bother to transplant even a pot-grown tree in summer. If there is the slightest root damage, the heat will draw moisture from the leaves faster than you can pour it back in with the hose, and the tree will die, embarrassing you in front of the neighbors. The rest of the year works fine.

Dogwoods are plagued by a host of varmints and diseases, and lately we hear less about borers and more about an anthracnose caused by a fungus of the genus *Discula*. This begins as a dark-rimmed brown leaf spot and eventually expands to consume and kill the leaf, which may then cling long after normal leaf drop in fall. Twig and branch dieback and eventual death may follow. The disease responds to fungicides, but the best defense is to plant resistant varieties and to keep dogwoods well fed and watered.

We've heard over and over that dogwoods, which naturally inhabit the woodland understory, don't like full sun, but, of course, we see healthy specimens growing in practically Mediterranean circumstances almost every day. True, in strong light dogwoods fold their leaves a bit so as to lessen the angle of photonic attack, but, except perhaps when the thermometer approaches 100 degrees Fahrenheit, they are as happy as any other dogwood *as long as they are kept watered*. There are exceptions, of course. Certain of the variegated sorts—'Welchii', for instance—may scorch in strong sun; but even many of these are touted as sun-safe. The white-flowering, green-and-white-leaved 'Cherokee Daybreak' and the red-bracted 'Cherokee Sunset', with its pink new growth and yellow-edged mature leaves, are two examples. 'Cherokee Sunset' is a veritable kaleidoscope of color in fall and enjoys a reputation for resistance to anthracnose, too.

'Cherokee Chief' has long been the leading red-flowering dogwood, though the bracts are prone to an unattractive spotting. Michael Dirr suggests instead 'Junior Miss', with extra-large, disease-free, ruby-pink bracts that pale toward the center.

Hot pink bracts take on real urgency against a rain-blackened trunk, but I prefer a softer shade of pink, like that of the cultivar 'Apple Blossom'. And, of course, to mix with the many shades of pink or lavender azaleas, one must have a white dogwood or two: perhaps the ever-so-showy 'Cloud Nine', which is said to have particularly cold-hardy buds, to boot.

A flowering dogwood is stunning when set against a deep, dark *Magnolia grandiflora* or into an overstory of pine. A striking combination I noticed this year is that of flowering dogwood with purple leaf plum (*Prunus ceracifera* 'Atropurpurea') or red-leaved Japanese maple, both of which leaf out just as the dogwood breaks into bloom.

The Ewing Street house came equipped with a pair of dogwoods, both white, one in front and one out back, but I longed for a pale pink one, envisioning it dreamily entwined with a fully blooming *Clematis* 'Barbara Jackman', whose blue-with-violet-striped saucers age to a smooth, almost silver lavender. Being rather broke at the time and stingy under any circumstances, one fall I cajoled a nurseryman into selling my husband and me, for a mere five dollars, a spring leftover, a little pink-flowering (we were assured) tree which had slipped a few roots out of its burlap and worked them into the ground. Despite the rude interruption, the little tree grew and prospered, though it took a couple of years for the intended floral show to gain momentum. Some years the magic worked; others, Barbara ignored her assignment until the dogwood shed its bracts and leafed out. Still, I was satisfactorily enchanted.

Meanwhile, in the backyard, the wild corner paved in violets beneath the sycamore became well-populated with seedling white dogwoods, a few of which I allowed to grow into something of a thin copse, and one of which I let shade my little greenhouse (as if the sycamore weren't enough to keep the summer sun from baking it). It seemed to take them surprisingly little time to reach blooming size—well under the five years or so I'd expected—and most were quite appealing in form and flower. The one by the greenhouse was especially worthwhile, for it bloomed earlier than all the rest and its flowers were much larger. Of course, its location could have been the factor sparking its exceptionality, but I chalked it up to the wonders of genetic diversity. I once heard Tennessee nurseryman Don Shadow expound on the virtues of growing shrubs and trees from seeds rather than relying exclusively on clones of established varieties; it's the only way (apart from serendipitous branch sports) to discover something brand new. Seedlings are not always inferior to their pedigreed parent.

The alarmists among us would have us plant kousa dogwood (*C. kousa*), an oriental species, in place of our beloved *C. florida*, for, so far at least, the kousas show resistance to the *Discula* form of anthracnose (though not, entirely, to borers).

Their buds are hardier than those of *C. florida* and, opening two or more weeks later, after the tree has leafed out, are virtually never ruined by a late freeze.

The flowers are sometimes very large (up to eight inches across in the cultivar 'Moonbeam') and float above the leaves on short stalks at the tips of twigs along the markedly horizontal branches. The prominent bracts surrounding the tightly clustered true flowers are pointed at the outer tips rather than notched like those of *C. florida* and persist for weeks. The fruit, resembling a shrunken golf ball suspended by a peduncle, cherry-style, reddens in late summer. It is marginally edible.

Kousas are a relative rarity here, but when I was in Washington, D.C., in early June of last year, they bloomed everywhere, all but outnumbering the pigeons.

There are a host of cultivars, including 'Summer Stars', whose profusion of white bracts persists almost summer-long, even until the fruit ripens, according to Wayside; then in autumn we are treated to luscious maroon foliage.

Cornus kousa is a fine addition to a garden but never, to my mind, a replacement for *C. florida*, for who can bear to put off spring?

Luckily, the newly introduced Stellar series of dogwoods combines the kousa's resistance to borer and anthracnose with the flowering dogwood's earlier bloom time to produce a disease-resistant hybrid with a bloom period that falls between that of its parents. There is even a light and lovely pink, 'Stellar Pink', in the series.

AZALEA

Now we need some azaleas to go with our dogwoods. Azaleas and dogwoods need ample water year-round to be their best, and, while nothing is more splendid than a crystalline morning in high spring on an old southern street where ancient azaleas all but hide the front porches and the dogwoods' trunks are as big around as beach balls, the five-year drought the latter half of the 1980s made us wonder if we shouldn't be growing cactus instead. There was mounting anxiety that the drought signified a permanent change in our climate. Was it ethical, we wondered, to lavish water on purely ornamental plants when wells were running dry in nearby communities and the Tennessee River, Huntsville's major source of water, was running so low and so warm that there was concern that the reactors at Brown's Ferry, the neighborhood nuclear power plant, could not be adequately cooled? Perhaps not, in such an extreme case, but during our normal summer dry spells I feel it is okay to water flowers, trees, shrubs, corn, okra, tomatoes, pets, and livestock, but it's immoral to water lawns and lima beans or to wash cars.

Many of us own azaleas purchased from the discount stores, and some of these are satisfactory. The spring after we bought the Ewing Street house I made the rounds of the Kmart and Handy Dan's discount stores and bought azaleas whose colors I happened to like, although, admittedly, they didn't combine quite as harmoniously as I later came to wish. But there were other problems, too. The fuchsia-colored Kurume hybrids bloomed a week or more ahead of any of the others, which was fine except that, by the time 'Delaware Valley White' hit stride, the kurumes were headed into the shaggy brown stage where they needed shearing or—at the very least—sweeping to rid them of their unsightly, spent blossoms. The long overpopular 'Coral Bells', another kurume, shares this annoying trait.

'Delaware Valley White', on the other hand, a Glenn Dale hybrid, lightly tosses off its big, sugar-white blossoms as quickly as they are done with, as neatly as you please.

I'm also inordinantly fond of the frilly and bright 'Pink Ruffle', one of the Rutherfordiana hybrids, I believe (this appellation is applied in the trade to several different plants, I'm afraid). These hybrids are listed as hardy only to 20 degrees Fahrenheit, though obviously mine can do better than that or I'd have lost them long ago. I do, however, throw a blanket or heap pine straw over all my azaleas if a hard freeze is predicted once the buds have begun to show color. Winter before last I allowed my neighbors to bundle their azaleas and camellias on an exceedingly bitter night, while I lazily left mine to fend for themselves. *Their* azaleas went on to bloom; mine, on the other hand, reproved me with their cold-stunned, copper leaves and ruined flower buds every time I set foot out the door, like the damning stares of the Ancient Mariner's dead shipmates. If the temperature plunges to zero at any time during the winter, though, I am apt to lose some buds no matter what precautions I've taken.

Tucked into a sheltered corner on either side of the front door on Ewing, I grew a matched pair of what my Aunt Thelma claimed were 'Formosa' azaleas, a cultivar of the rather tender southern indica type. I've never been sure of their identity, for the parent plant, which graced my aunt's creek-bottom yard in upstate South Carolina, bore large, floppy blossoms of a lovely lavender rather than the magenta described by Dirr. Nonetheless, for all it bloomed its head off in South Carolina, it habitually lost its buds to cold in North Alabama. If I were shopping for store-bought azaleas rather than mooching cuttings, I would make cold hardiness a priority. The indicas are a risk above Zone 8. Here is where buying azaleas from a well-run nursery or mail-order concern beats opting for discount store bargains. And a good nurseryman or -woman should be familiar with the plant's ultimate habit, so, if you are looking for a filler to front a low hedge of dwarf Burford holly, for example, he or she may prescribe the cherry-red creeping spreader 'Joseph Hill', or perhaps the extra-hardy, low-mounding Robin Hill selection 'Hilda Niblett', with her neat puff of tiny green leaves crowded with broad blossoms in multiple shades of peachy-pink.

The Robin Hill azaleas, by the way, are late bloomers—from May even into June—so with them late frosts are not likely to be a problem.

'Robin Hill Gillie' slips into step with summer's hotter colors with its flaring, five-inch blossoms of the pinkish orange we called "pank" when I was a child. The buds are reportedly safe down to –10 degrees Fahrenheit.

As much as I love the solid sheet of color presented by a hybrid azalea, I admire the rangy informality and simple grace of our tall and airy native azaleas. Widely known as bush honeysuckle (though they are heath family members, far-removed from the true honeysuckles; the resemblance lies in the long-trumpeted blossoms, with their thin, outswept stamens and pistils), a number of species are scattered across the southeastern woodlands. Some, like our lovely piedmont azalea (*Rhododendron canescens*), present loose clusters of sweetly scented funnel-form blossoms of white to deep pink just as the leaves emerge. Others, like the vivid orange-red plumleaf azalea (*R. prunifolium*), withhold their fireworks until mid- to late summer.

Breeder David G. Leach has mixed assorted native azaleas into his Madison group and July series of summer-blooming hybrids. He describes the flowers of his Madison hybrid 'Coloratura' as "probably the most barbaric color combination of any azalea in cultivation," with an upper corolla lobe of "emphatic orange" and the other four "an incandescent bright red."

Some years back I was smitten by a magazine photo of the Florida flame azalea (*R. austrinum*) and could not rest until I owned one. So intense was my longing that I actually bought one, mail order, rather than snooping around town for a cutting to filch. This tale has a sad ending, though. Perhaps I had grown lazy or overconfident and didn't take time to adequately prepare my soil. Perhaps the soil was contaminated with root-ingesting microbes. Perhaps the drainage was lousy (no doubt the most common cause of azalea mortality). Whatever. For a couple of years my flame azalea grew statuesque and brought forth the exquisite clusters of lemon-orange, honeysucklelike blossoms I had envisioned, and they glowed like lamplight when backlit by the sun. But then the stupid thing died. I replaced it with an azalea mollis (*R. molle*) seedling, whose apricot-tinged blossoms never quite fit the bill.

Azaleas prefer at least partial shade. Whenever you set out an azalea, work in all the organic matter you think the soil (whether clay or sand) can hold, then work in some more. Leaf mold, aged grass clippings, wood chips, peanut hulls, chicken feathers—whatever you can get, thoroughly mix it into the nice wide hole you've prepared, as if you're tossing a very unsanitary salad. Then be careful to set the plant into the hole so that the crown of the rootball is level with or even a bit above the soil line. Good drainage is absolutely critical; I've even seen azaleas growing in heaps of pine straw or bark with no soil at all. Azaleas are shallow-rooted and moisture-loving, so keep them mulched with pine straw or other leaves, and never let them parch.

Right after bloom is the best time to prune. It's an excellent time to fertilize, too, and add a bit of iron sulfate or iron chelates to prevent chlorosis, an iron deficiency caused by too-high pH or insufficient water, either of which renders the iron in the soil unavailable to the plant. Yellow leaves with green veins are the symptom.

Several years ago I was visiting Inge Paul and remarked on the deep green coloring of the foliage on her azaleas, rhododendrons, and mountain laurel. The secret, she responded, was Epsom salt. From time to time she worked a bit into the soil around each plant. Epsom salts, a hydrated magnesium sulfate, acidifies the soil and provides magnesium, a critical ingredient of chlorophyll (all this, and it relieves constipation, too!).

There are fertilizers on the market designed specifically for acid-loving plants. And there are complete fertilizers. These contain not just the usual nitrogen, phosphorus, and potassium found in most fertilizers, but also the other essential macronutrients—calcium, magnesium, and sulfur—as well as the eight essential micronutrients: boron, iron, manganese, copper, zinc, molybdenum, cobalt, and chlorine.

I find that azaleas are easy to propagate from four- to six-inch cuttings taken in June on wood that has begun to harden but is still flexible. I remove all but the newest leaves, wet the cutting and dip the stem in clean rooting powder, and insert it into a pencil hole in moist sand or potting soil. A quick squirt of water will settle the soil around the stem without washing away the powder. Constant high humidity is essential, and, lacking a mist bed, I keep the cuttings either in an old covered aquarium or suspended from a shrub or fence in a closed plastic bag in the shade. When new growth appears (after a few weeks) the cutting is presumed rooted and transferred to a partially covered, shaded aquarium to begin acclimatization to the real world. The leaves of plants grown in high humidity lose their protective waxy coating and will dehydrate rapidly if they are abruptly exposed to dry air.

RHODODENDRON

The azalea, of course, is really a rhododendron. We typically say "azalea" when we mean the evergreen, semievergreen, or deciduous sort with funnel-form flowers having five stamens, and "rhododendron" when we refer to the evergreen kind with more bell-like flowers containing ten or more stamens. But since the temperate regions of the Northern Hemisphere contain close to a thousand species, and there are Lord-knows-how-many hybrid cultivars in circulation, there are enough exceptions to scuttle any attempt at strict separation.

The first time I saw *Rhododendron catawbiense* in the wild, I was amazed that such *huge* trusses of bloom occurred in nature, outside of the tropics (conveniently forgetting for the moment wisteria, paulonia, and catalpa). But then the leathery, broodingly dark green leaves are somewhat larger-than-life, too. This is a fine, fine plant, with a commanding presence even when not adorned with grapefruit-sized clusters of luminous purple flowers.

There are countless Catawba rhododendron hybrids and cultivated selections, but I'm partial to the type, having grown one on Ewing and purchased another when we moved here, after my attempt to propagate cuttings failed. In general, rhododendrons are tougher to root from cuttings than azaleas. Dirr recommends taking cuttings in mid-August.

Leach has produced a colorful line of summer-blooming rhododendrons derived in part from the native rosebay (*R. maximum*) and noted for bud-hardiness. The rather columnar 'Summer Summit' features frilly pink-fading-to-white blossoms with a touch of mellow green on the upper corolla lobe. 'Red River' has flowers of crackling red. The upper lobes of the cool white blossoms of 'Summer Solace' are freckled with chartreuse. All are excellent additions to the shady shrub border.

Rhododendron yakusimanum, a compact, low-growing species from Japan, has deep rose buds that break open into pure white blossoms. The popular Tony Shammarello hybrid 'Yaku Princess' unfurls rosy pink buds which flare into pale pink ruffles. Similarly, Leach's 'Mist Maiden' opens deep pink buds to soft pink blossoms, which age to white. 'Anna H. Hall', an *R. yakusimanum* ×*R. catawbiense* cross, exhibits the same enchanting transformation.

VIBURNUM

It is a shame that so many of the viburnums choose April in which to bloom, for, though some of them are lovely enough in their own right (and others are frankly dingy), it is hard for even the sensational Chinese snowball (*Viburnum macrocephalum* 'Sterile'), with its great globes of florets as white and unscented as typing paper, to compete for attention with the flurry of azaleas and dogwoods.

And then there is the matter of the strong resemblance some viburnums bear to certain of the hydrangeas when in flower. Much confusion results, which no doubt hinders the viburnum's popularity.

I would be tempted instead to choose my viburnums for their fall display of leaf or berry. Withe-rod viburnum (*V. cassinoides*), for example, has dull white, disklike cymes of flowers in summer that produce fruits in a rainbow of colors as they progress from green through pink to red, blue, and finally black. "Often all colors are present in the same infructescence (fruiting cluster)," writes Dirr. In fall the foliage undergoes a similar transition, from muddy green to subdued orange, crimson, and smoldering purple.

Linden viburnum (*V. dilatatum*) is a bit coarse of leaf, but in autumn is so painfully weighted with clusters of long-lasting, glowing, scarlet drupes that all is forgiven.

Tea viburnum (*V. setigerum*), too, is a bit rough and ungainly, but the autumn display of glossy red fruit earns it a spot in any shrub border.

European cranberry bush (*V. opulus*) has much to offer, if you like a bit of spectacle. *Viburnum o.* 'Roseum', the old-fashioned European snowball, is hung with great spherical masses of cool white, sterile flowers in April and May, much like those of the Chinese snowball, while *V. o.* 'Compactum' is touted as a tidy, low-maintenance shrub with a dense habit and a mature height of, perhaps, five feet. Its crisp, lace-cap flowers make way for large, persisting, brilliant red fruit. Fall color is said to be exceptional.

Fall color in the viburnums is, I believe, greatly influenced by exposure: The more sun, the earlier and more inflammatory the show is apt to be, as long as water is adequate. Viburnums don't take kindly to drought.

If the oldest growth is cut out from time to time, the doublefile viburnum (*V. plicatum tomentosum*) lends both a softening effect and one of neatness, as the leaves and stemlets are arranged in a herringbone pattern along its multitude of widespread, faintly furry, horizontal branches, which in April are thickly strung with cymes of white flowers. The effect is a bit like that of kousa dogwood. Wayside's catalog, in fact, enthuses that the exceptionally large flower clusters of the cultivar 'Shasta' rival those of flowering dogwood in beauty. Dirr also waxes rhapsodic over 'Shasta's' superior-to-the-type flowers but warns us to beware of cheap imitations, as, apparently, they abound in the trade. Doublefile viburnums' fruits turn red and finally black by late summer. Toward the end of October the leaves begin to turn purple and red, and unless, as occasionally happens, we have an early freeze, they go on to join the maples' end-of-season visual tumult.

I confess, the closest I've come to growing a viburnum of my very own is the cutting I've kept out back in the old aquarium for six months now without visible signs of progress. (Ah, here's the problem: Dirr says I should have taken my cutting in June or July, not in fall.) It is a cutting of Judd viburnum (*V. ×juddii*), a versatile cross between *V. carlesii* and *V. bitchiuense* noted for the fragrance of its pink-tinged, white flowers, full, bushy habit, and resistance to bacterial leaf spot. I had especially admired its orange and purple autumn foliage as I came and went through the east entrance to Morrison Hall at Alabama A&M. (If you must steal, steal from something that can regenerate the missing part.)

FRINGE TREE

Our native fringe tree (*Chionanthus virginicus*), is a shrub or small tree with long (to eight inches), bright green leaves and a comfortable spreading, open habit. Also known as Grancy gray-beard or old-man's beard, fringe tree can best be appreciated when planted where early morning or late afternoon sunlight streams through its translucent, fringelike blossoms in late April and early May. It is not encountered with great frequency here, but it was evidently done-to-death in Elizabeth Lawrence's part of North Carolina, for the late author resented its tedious inclusion in almost every garden and likened the limp, shredded panicles of fragrant white flowers to slaw. Perhaps we should drop its bevy of common names and just call it "slaw tree." I rather like the name.

Fringe (or slaw) tree is late to leaf out, so one should not be quick to assume that a newly planted specimen has failed to survive its first winter. It seems to be very adaptable as to soil, but it does need full sun to show to advantage, and it grows slowly no matter what, though it blooms while very young and small.

Like other members of the olive family (Oleaceae), fringe tree is difficult to propagate vegetatively (and seeds are no picnic, either), which no doubt accounts for its rarity in the nursery trade.

The fruits, dark blue, olive-shaped drupes savored by birds, are likely to be more plentiful if multiple trees are planted in close proximity. Individual trees are predominantly male or female, though both bear at least a sprinkling of perfect flowers (flowers containing both male and female parts). Males have flowers with longer petals and are slightly more ornamental in bloom, but predominantly female plants produce far more fruit. Fall color is a pleasing yellow.

BUCKEYE

It is wonderful to watch the buckeyes (*Aesculus* species) come to life in spring. The great, tumescent, rosy buds break forth from the slick gray bark with a seeming cognizance of their surroundings that is almost unnerving. At Beaver Dam Swamp and scattered along the moist, shady hillsides dipping down to touch the Tennessee River, the red buckeye (*Aesculus pavia*) lifts torchlike trusses of tubular blossoms blending tones of warm brick and cool coral dabbed with yellow. Though the fanlike, compound leaves are substantial, red buckeye makes a rather skimpy small tree, particularly in shade.

Aesculus p. var. *pavia* is rigged to accommodate hummingbirds, according to Dirr, while the yellow-flowering *A. p.* var. *flavescens*, with a campanulate floral design, can be pollinated by bees.

Buckeye seed is poisonous, by the way, and loses viability rapidly. Seed should be started promptly in a bed or container deep enough to allow development of the seedling's taproot.

One shrub I lust after with regularity is the bottlebrush buckeye (*A. parviflora*). This is among the most impressive of shrubs in bloom, generously spiked with enormous brushy wands of white flowers in June. Dirr notes that the selection 'Rogers' boasts inflorescences eighteen to thirty inches long. In moist, humusy soil it will sucker to fill an awkward corner in either sun or shade and provides an effective counterpoint to the creamy panicles of oakleaf hydrangea (*Hydrangea quercifolia*). Unlike *A. pavia*, which drops its leaves with a weary sigh at the first hint of autumn, *A. parviflora* takes on a bright yellow fall color.

SPRING BLUES

Just fleetingly, in April, the triangular bed beneath the two front yard dogwoods becomes a multitextured carpet of cool blue. Along with the little spurred violet and Virginia bluebell are dwarf larkspur, wild sweet William, Jacob's ladder, Spanish bluebell, blue star dogbane, and wild hyacinth.

Dwarf larkspur (*Delphinium tricorne*) is by far the sturdiest and most reliable of the delphiniums I've tried, though perhaps the least showy, being only a foot or so tall. One finds scattered colonies in the local woods. The word "delphinium" is from the Greek word for dolphin, an allusion to the flower's dramatically tapered outline. To me there's something just a bit sinister, however, about its looks; with its flared brim and pointed peak, it reminds me more of a witch's hat. Colors range from white to deep purple.

The tall larkspur (*D. exaltatum*) is showier but, for me, shorter-lived, perhaps because its slender, fibrous roots lack the durability of the stout, tuberous roots of its shorter cousin. Locally we find it in gravelly hillside clearings, a graceful wand of startling blue, three or four feet high.

A pale haze of wild sweet William (*Phlox divaricata*) sweeps across the woodland floor in April. This delicately beautiful native is equally at home in the garden, where, if it finds conditions favorable, it expands into great cushions of airy lavender stars about as tall as a house cat. The dark green oval leaves are glossy yet faintly fuzzy; they remain attractive all summer.

This plant grows naturally in the unmowed corner of our backyard, by the creek, but I've had difficulty establishing it in the front yard bed. The first year I peppered the bed with wild phlox dug from a construction site, and by the following spring I'd lost every one. Perhaps the clay soil was too hard, or quite possibly the plants resented the pine straw mulch with which I enwrapped them (I can't recall having found blue phlox under pines in the wild). But I've made great strides in limbering up my soil, and the new plants I have out front this year look as happy as clams.

Phlox divaricata is shallow-rooted and stoloniferous and appreciates loose, humusy soil with fast drainage, which, no doubt, is why it favors slopes and precipitous siting. Surprisingly, I've seen it flourish where its deciduous canopy has been bulldozed away.

Jacob's ladder (*Polemonium reptans*), another phlox family member, is usually found in moister situations, along streams and the like. The small pointed leaflets are arranged pinnately along the rachis of the leaves like the rungs of a primitive ladder, giving the plant a ferny look. The flowers are clusters of tiny, five-petaled dangling bells of blue, carried at the tips of both primary and axillary stems. By root and by seed Jacob's ladder spreads into broad, foot-high swatches, which remain presentable even when the plants lapse into a midsummer sprawl. Fresh foliage emerges for winter interest, too.

I've never learned to appreciate the garden hyacinth (*Hyacinthus orientalis*), though I love the fragrance. It looks too artificial, too rigidly perfect, at least when new. But after it's been in the ground a few years it limbers up a bit and takes on a looser, friendlier aspect.

I am, however, partial to the wood hyacinth, or Spanish bluebell, which is listed variously as *Endymion hispanica*, *Scilla hispanica*, *Scilla campanulata*, and, lately, *Hyacinthoides hispanicus* (and they tell us that binomial nomenclature eliminates confusion!). Whatever, Spanish bluebell's blue, pink, or white bell-like blossoms chime in concert with the April-flowering azaleas and dogwoods. I particularly love the extra-large, blue-flowering version with the wider, straplike leaf, for it makes a planting of 'Pink Ruffle' and 'Delaware Valley White' azaleas into a pastel dream.

Spanish bluebells multiply prodigiously from bulbs that look like dirty Ping-Pong balls. They can be divided and tucked around the feet of shrubs or used as a precursor to annuals all about the estate. The foliage conveniently disappears after bloom.

Wild hyacinth (*Camassia scilloides*) makes broad swaths of graceful, yet erect racemes of soft lavender-blue inflorescences reaching two feet or more in moist, even low-lying ground. It is one of the most impressive flowering plants for shade but is content in sun as well. Longtime wildflower gardeners tell me this lovely bulbous native member of the lily family can get out of hand. Good. I rather look forward to that. But since it vanishes without a trace after bloom, I doubt this will be too worrisome.

Bluestar dogbane (*Amsonia tabernaemontana*) is an interesting companion for camassia, for they bloom at the same time, at the same height, and in the same delicate shade of blue. Amsonia, however, bears its starlike blue flowers in loose cymes at the ends of strong, upright stems. The flowers come and go quickly, but the smooth, attractively tapered leaves remain handsome all season and turn yellow in fall. They are intermediate in texture between those of the hostas and ferns we rely on so heavily in shade. The foliage forms a slowly expanding vase-shaped clump capped by vertical pairs of stringbean-thin fruits resembling those of the milkweeds. The sap is blue and milky.

Amsonia is a tough, reliable perennial in either shade or sun. It is adaptable to most any soil, so long as it drains. I have, however, seen this plant severely marred by rust in a hot, dry site.

For some reason, one doesn't see pulmonaria, or lungwort (*Pulmonaria* species) very often in the South, and yet it does reasonably well here as long as it's kept moist and shaded.

Several years ago I did a bit of plant-swapping with Mrs. Val Burnside, of Indianapolis, Indiana, and wound up with a start of pulmonaria. I'm not sure which species; my guess would be *P. officinalis*, known as Jerusalem cowslip and sometimes Jerusalem sage (though it hails from Europe). Much to my surprise, it has increased moderately in a foundation planting in which it must compete with English ivy and yet has died out in the bed beneath the front white dogwoods, where it is pampered relentlessly.

It mats around to make a pretty little groundcover of scratchy, heart-shaped, dark green leaves with lighter speckles. In bloom it's like a junior Virginia bluebell—they're both members of the borage family, after all.

Another borage family member—this one blooming a bit later in April and needing more sun—is anchusa. I've grown *Anchusa italica* (*A. azurea*, really) 'Dropmore' off and on for years. With me it is a rather short-lived perennial, and I never quite manage to save the seed. Eventually, after I've done without it for awhile, I order more seed, for there are few tall plants in bloom at the end of April, and this one's intense ultramarine is particularly welcome. It is marvelous with the pink native penstemon (*Penstemon hirsutus*) or with pink bearded iris. The batch I have at present is of a paler, dustier blue than usual—not as pleasantly startling. There are dwarf and annual cultivars, too.

There are several species of spiderwort (*Tradescantia*) in our area, but we tend to think that there are only two: one short and one tall. The short (to twelve inches) is *T. hirsuticaulis*. It blooms as early as March. This one we find on wooded hillsides, often clinging to cliffs. The flowers are as likely to be rosy pink as blue, and occasionally, white. It goes dormant in summer. I prefer the tall (to three feet), summer-blooming spiderwort (*T. virginiana*), for its chilly blue flowers mix deliciously with the sunny yellow of the prairie coneflower (*Ratibida pinnata*), yellow daylily, or the cheery pink of purple coneflower (*Echinacea purpurea*). Each blossom in a cluster is open only in the morning and consists of three round petals, three sepals, and six stamens conspicuously marked by yellow anthers. The foliage has a rangy, awkward look, with stiff, canelike stems interrupted by long, skinny, clasping leaves. It is one of those most valued gardening commodities: a tall perennial that performs well in shade. But then this plant is showy in sun, too, as long as it's kept moist, and is not fussy about soil.

There are many cultivars, some of which are shorter and more compact than the average wildling. *Tradescantia virginiana* 'Red Cloud', for instance, limits its dimensions to compact, eighteen-inch stems capped by hot pink blossoms. *Tradescantia v.* 'Iris Pritchard' has petals as white as Ivory Snow, framing feathery purple innards.

The dayflower (*Commelina erecta*) is very similar to tradescantia in appearance, though the flower is a sharper blue and the foliage is thinner. This is a profusely seeding annual, which easily becomes a pest, even crowding out such stalwart perennials as physostegia. It is a pretty weed from a distance, but I would keep it well away from my flower beds and instead banish it to the fence I shared with my least congenial neighbor or perhaps a creekbank.

One last April blue, which I *wish* I'd successfully established in my garden, is phacelia, or scorpion weed (*Phacelia* species), two or three species of which are native to Alabama. The most common species locally is *Phacelia bipinnatifida*, which has leaves that are twice-divided and beautifully spotted. These shade-loving annuals or biennials spring from the leaf mold atop limestone boulders. Many Huntsville residents who live on the rocky mountainsides have this plant in profusion in spring. Surprisingly, along our botanical garden's nature trail, where it was introduced to the alluvial sludge, it has increased abundantly. It sets seed and dies away promptly after its generous bloom.

Despite its unsavory moniker, it does not harbor scorpions, but the inflorescence is a cyme, which starts out coiled like a scorpion's tail or like the fiddlehead of a fern and unrolls to display numerous five-petaled, bell-shaped, small blue flowers, which teem with bees.

The western *Phacelia* species were used to create dwarf, summer-blooming strains, like the indigo blue 'Tropical Surf' offered by Thompson & Morgan or Park's vivid, heat-resistant *Phacelia campanularia* 'Blue Wonder'. *Phacelia tanacetifolia* is a tall, loose westerner with a worldwide reputation as a honey plant.

A TRIO OF YELLOW

I've come to admire yellow star grass (*Hypoxis hirsuta*), though, with its dime-sized, six-pointed, starlike (if stars were yellow) blossoms, borne a mere eight inches or so above the ground, and wispy grasslike foliage, it isn't the sort of plant that brings traffic to a screeching halt. But it is a superb rock garden plant, and, if it is watered regularly, it will bloom until frost. It asks only that it not be shaded out by less mannerly neighbors.

April gives us the first coreopsis in the dwarf eared coreopsis (*Coreopsis auriculata* 'Nana'), a perfect little edger or rock garden plant with golden, ragged-edged daisies over dark green, tear-shaped leaves. Though it can take some shade, this shallow-rooted dwarf is easily overrun by taller, more avaricious companions and can be lost in the process.

Only a true aficionado of wildflowers would want the bellworts (*Uvularia* species) in his garden, for they make the gardener appear inept, as if he hadn't sense enough to water. With their dishrag-limp leaves and drooping, anemic-yellow blossoms, as twisted and limp as if they'd been wrung out, bellworts are a sad sight. No doubt it is in ironic jest that they are also known as merrybells.

We evidently have some five species of bellwort lurking about our woodlands in Alabama, the one coming closest to garden-worthiness being, perhaps, the large-flowered bellwort (*Uvularia grandiflora*). With arching, zigzag stems piercing relaxed, five-inch-long, almost oval, soft green leaves, and a pale, two-inch-long blossom resembling an upside-down lily-flowering tulip, this plant contributes a touch of novelty to the scene, if not exceptional beauty or function.

TRUE AND FALSE SOLOMON'S SEAL

For a stronger foliage effect in the shade garden, midway between that of the ferns and hosta, one might consider Solomon's seal (*Polygonatum biflorum*) or false Solomon's seal (*Smilacina racemosa*). Both have arching stems lined with prominently grooved, gracefully pointed leaves. The flowers of Solomon's seal, however, are practically hidden, suspended like pale lanterns in a line beneath the stems. Those of false solomon's seal are showy—creamy, plumose panicles at the stem tips—and evolve into clusters of waxy, dull-red berries by fall.

The variegated Japanese Solomon's seal (*P. odoratum thunbergii* 'Variegatum') is considered more choice than the native Solomon's seal. The young stems are red, and the six-inch-long leaves are brushed with yellow along their edges. In moist, humusy soil this plant will colonize by rhizomes.

SHOOTING STAR

Perhaps April's most endearing wildflower is the shooting star (*Dodecatheon meadia*). With its stamens fused into a "beak" protruding from a dark "mask," its reflexed, twisted petals, and its crook-necked stem, it resembles nothing so much as a swan, or rather a flock of swans, for the single scape that rises above the rosette of apple-green, paddlelike leaves bears an umbel of flowers in various stages of maturation. After fertilization the petals drop, and the ripening capsule straightens up like a small chalice. The leaves soon shrivel away, leaving the dry scape, which stands like a tidy candelabra into winter and, occasionally, until the following spring's bloom stalk begins its rise to glory.

The shooting stars in our area are practically all white-flowering, though pink or purple predominates in some regions of the country. Locally they are usually found along the narrow channels carved by hillside runoff, where the soil is moist and sticky and relatively free of leaf litter, but in the garden they are highly adaptable and dependable. I have a shooting star in full sun which has returned for three seasons now. Though the leaves go wilty on hot days (it *can* get hot in April), this plant consistently produces the biggest, strongest seed stalk of any shooting star on the premises.

The seeds, I've read, need a period of cold in order to germinate. Up the hill from our house is a vacant, shaded lot, home to an especially dense colony of shooting star, made that way, I suspect, by an occasional mowing, which scatters the seed more efficiently than the normal method of dispersal.

I used to assume that shooting star was named for its aerodynamic good looks, but now I have another theory. If you stroke the flower's "beak" of fused stamens, a puff of pollen will erupt like smoke from a fired revolver. You can do this over and over, causing the same flower to eject puff after puff of pollen.

FIRE PINK

Unless you're dead set on a pastel color scheme, you might want to set a few shooting stars against the taller fire pink (*Silene virginica*), a common but showy woodland catchfly that comes into bloom while the shooting star is at its peak. The fire pink's raving red crackles alongside the stark white of the shooting star.

Fire pink is as difficult for me as shooting star is easy. Though it's naturally distributed throughout the eastern two thirds of North America, it's hard to please. Twice I've thought I'd successfully adopted it only to have it turn into an aster or a sesame plant. Now I'm growing it in a pot in part sun on the back porch, and I dare it to pull that prank again.

Though the red flowers with their five notched, or "pinked," petals are distinctive, resembling brilliantly colored starfish, the foliage is not—a rosette of paddlelike, roughly fuzzy, deep green leaves giving rise in spring to stiff, sticky, slender stems bearing one or more opposing pairs of leaves below the terminally borne flowers.

My friend Charlie Higgins, whom we fondly regard as boss of the wildflowers at the botanical garden, notes that in the wild fire pink is usually found in comparatively exposed spots bereft of leaf litter and where it gets a good daily splash of sunlight. It favors slopes and is sometimes found in abundance along logging trails.

My potted fire pink appears to be bursting with health and vigor (perhaps due to a popular brand of fertilizer advertised on TV by celebrities). I think it enjoys the sunshine and instant drainage its home in the pot affords. I have every confidence it will survive the winter just as it is, for it's hardy into Canada.

CELANDINE POPPY

If you don't mind a spring display that takes on the rowdy exuberance of high summer, you might want a celandine poppy (*Stylophorum diphyllum*) in your garden. When given an environment comparable to the moist woods in which it grows, this gay perennial, with its bowl-shaped, buttercup-yellow blossoms, will slowly increase and persist indefinitely, sending up a shin-high clump of coarse, hairy, gray-backed, deeply lobed leaves resembling those of oakleaf hydrangea. The sap is a brilliant orange and makes a fine warpaint. The root is as solid and hard as a block of wood and is vivid orange inside.

Inge Paul tells me that removing the spent flowers prolongs the period of bloom. I'm ashamed to admit that I have difficulty distinguishing the developing seed capsule from the kitten's-paw-fuzzy flower buds. For a cool yet cheerful effect celandine poppy also combines spectacularly with *Phlox divaricata*.

VALERIAN

Another seldom-seen native which puts on a good show in April is *Valeriana pauciflora*. From a distance it could be taken for an allium in bloom, for the funnel-form pink blossoms are bunched into a ball atop a strong two-foot stem, which shrivels as the winged seeds form. Meanwhile, on the ground, rhizomes stretch about to weave a loose mat of ankle-high, light- to medium-green leaves shaped like those of violets. *Valeriana pauciflora*, in fact, makes a becoming deciduous groundcover in light, moist soil in either sun or shade and is easily torn out if it ventures where it isn't wanted.

Sedums are so versatile and long-lived and so easily cultivated that there's no wonder there are scores of species in cultivation. I regret I've grown so few. At the moment I have on the premises only three. One is *Sedum ternatum*, a low, spreading stonecrop which slithers over the limestone boulders in the local woods and is frosted with starry white flowers in spring.

I don't think *S. ternatum* favors sun, but the increasingly popular blue spruce sedum (*S. ochroleucum* subsp. *montanum*) seems relatively happy anywhere, though it raises more diminutive towers of butter-yellow blossoms in full sun. The real attraction is the foliage, curvaceous ropes of succulent, needle-like, glaucous leaves.

As with other jade plant relatives, sedums are easily started by tucking broken-off bits into soil for rooting. Though live-forever is another appropriate common name for the sedums, it is possible to lose them, and quickly. I've had the much-touted *S. spectabile* 'Autumn Joy' (lately relegated to the genus *Hylotelephium*) for many years, moving it from site to site as the notion grabbed me. Last year I plunked it into a brick planter and, the next time I noticed it, it was riddled with holes about the roots and only a single stem was left standing. The only varmints at home when I knocked were pill bugs. Similarly, the creeping red sedum (unlabeled and marked down to sixty-seven cents at Kmart) I put beneath the Japanese maple, too, harbored pill bugs and disappeared despite desperate, belated applications of bug-killer. Whether the pill bugs actually perpetrated the crime or were merely innocent bystanders, I can't say for sure.

'Autumn Joy' has made a stunning recovery, however, in a sunny new spot. It is a sturdy upright plant and reaches about knee-high. By July the fat, rubbery leaves are capped by wide, flat clusters of small flower buds, like broccoli florets, which open milky pink and gradually go rusty-bronze by summer's end.

It puzzles me that such a fuss is made over 'Autumn Joy' in the magazines and catalogs. No doubt it is a neat, sturdy, uncomplaining plant whose muted colors seldom clash with those of its neighbors. And it is decent to look at almost year-round. So I should shut up and not gripe about its lack of pizzazz and just be grateful that it's willing to put up with me at all.

IRIS

In the South there is some species of iris trying to bloom at virtually every time of year. In the middle and lower South *Iris unguicularis* 'Marginata' unfolds its starkly beautiful purple-striped-with-yellow blossoms amid spiky foliage in the very heart of winter, so this low-blooming Mediterranean beauty may come and go without notice unless placed by a frequently traversed walkway. Soon after, the diminutive *I. reticulata* and *I. danfordiae* stand at attention amid the first of the crocuses.

In early spring we have the native dwarf iris (*I. verna*), emerging like a small miracle from the woodland floor, and the fancier though less fragrant dwarf crested iris (*I. cristata*). I've encountered this one most frequently on sandy, shaded hillsides and along streams where the skinny rhizomes seem barely to skim the earth. This iris must be transplanted ever so shallowly and in the garden may make a mat of itself. The flower forms a triangle of three lavender-blue sepals identically blotched with yellow, white, and violet, and reminds one of the scene inside a child's dime-store kaleidoscope.

The butter-and-cream (eighteen-inch-high) blossoms and lush leaves of *I. bucharica* come next, followed in April by the Dutch iris, hybrids drawn, at least in part, from the bulbous Spanish iris (*I. xiphium*). Just as dainty as the dwarfs but taller (to around two feet, usually), they dwindle with me, but they are always smashing their first year, showing to greatest advantage when planted in generous clumps. The color range is impressive, and, though I'm partial to the clear yellow, I'm intrigued by the novelty of 'Frans Hals'. I can't decide if his honey-bronze falls and purple standards are pretty or ugly.

The equally graceful Siberian iris (*I. sibirica*), to three feet, thrives indefinitely on sheer neglect and can be had in white and shades of blue and violet. The clumps spread ever wider with the years, the narrow rhizomes deftly feeling their way over, around, and through the competition.

At four feet the copper iris (*I. fulva*) is a lanky, brick-colored denizen of southern swamps but adjusts to typical garden conditions. Yellow flag (*I. pseudacorus*) is even taller (to five feet), with long, graceful leaves that can be mistaken for those of cattails when the plant is not in bloom. The April flowers are normally yellow.

The double form 'Flore-Plena' is particularly showy. We have a white form which once belonged to my husband's grandmother, who called it duckbill. It looks like a giant Dutch iris. It's happiest in or near the water but is willing to settle for a sunny corner of the garden. On Ewing Street I used a curtain of *I. pseudacorus* to hide the air conditioner's compressor from view. There is a form with variegated leaves.

Another moisture-loving iris is *I. kaempferi*, the Japanese iris, whose large, flattened blossoms stretch their season of bloom into summer. Moist, acid soil and plenty of sunshine all but guarantee success with this plush, velvet-flowered plant.

At the botanical garden whenever I see members of the Iris Society toiling away in the hot sun, extricating the roots of invasive weeds from the rhizomes of their charges, I'm so glad I work in the wildflowers, where we can always find enough weeds to pull in the shade. But for the bearded hybrid irises to bloom their best, they must be grown in full sun, preferrably in raised beds of well-drained, friable soil. They should be planted so that the spindly roots go down, while the burly rhizomes straddle the ground. I associate the oppressive perfume of bearded iris with uncomfortably hot, childhood Sunday mornings in church. And yet, when iris time comes around (late April into May), I always find myself wanting more, though, as with pansies, I can never decide which colors. One year I go with rich rusty browns and yellows, the next I long for frilly pinks and soft blues. Only fire engine red is absent from the vast palette of choices.

In all iris groups, but especially the beardeds, there are rebloomers which put on a second performance in fall. 'Baby Blessed' is pale yellow and rated the best of the reblooming dwarfs. The cream-colored flowers of 'I Bless' are said to appear summer-long, while 'Queen Dorothy'—a tall white, edged in violet—blooms almost year-round.

A different sort of fall display is to be had with the gladwin, or scarlet-seeded, iris (I. foetidissima), the lavender spring flowers of which make way for gaping pods brimming with glossy, orange-red fruit in autumn. This iris does well with a bit of shade and is best kept on the dry side.

Even if they never flowered, irises should be planted for the bold distinctiveness of their foliage. The swordlike leaves of bearded iris in midsummer make just as daring a statement in the landscape as yucca. The cream-streaked fans of I. pallida 'Albo-variegata' are luminously emphatic.

Busy, Busy, Busy

April 15, tax day, is also our customary frost-free date (usually) in this part of Zone 7. I would as soon see income tax come due on Christmas Eve, there is so much to be done in the garden in April. I suppose that there are well-organized individuals who, having mailed in their tax forms *months* ago, are ready to hop into the car and toodle over to the garden center for a few flats of half-grown bedding plants to fill their previously prepared, weed-free beds. And then there are those of us whose would-be bedding plants are either still in the seed packs or so pathetically small and spindly that they'd never compete with the explosion of common blue violet and *Rudbeckia triloba* seedlings that have taken over the beds.

But it is time to get moving, for, with any luck at all, we should have two solid weeks of ideal growing weather before the stultifying heat sets in.

Nights should be warm enough to leave even the tiniest seedlings outside, and, as time permits, we can set them into the ground. I like to mix a bit of compost or other well-weathered organic matter into each planting hole, to help feed the infant and aid in the gradual improvement of the soil. Survival rates are higher if the youngsters are surrounded by a cutworm collar; a paper cup with the bottom cut out works fine. I mulch around a small plant only lightly, to prevent its drying out. Once the seedling gains size and strength, it is less likely to succumb to the pests and diseases a heavier mulch may harbor. Water the newly planted infant well to settle the dirt around its roots, and give it a shot of liquid fertilizer. Later, when the weather gets hotter, it may be necessary to shade newly set-out plants until the roots have become established.

Summer- and fall-blooming perennials, such as physostegia, Maximilian sunflower, and chrysanthemum, can still be divided now without serious setback. I prefer to keep tall late-bloomers, like physostegia, silphium, asters, and ironweed, cut back to below knee-high until midsummer. This keeps them from visually obstructing earlier-flowering plants, forces them to form axillary branches and, consequently, more flowers, and prevents them from flopping over for six feet in all directions. It makes them bloom a bit later, perhaps, but that is fine. Of course, if you prefer, rather than cutting them back you can pin flopped-over branches to the ground, and each node along the stem will send up a flower stalk.

Wait until they've finished blooming to fertilize your azaleas and rhododendrons. Otherwise, feed everything in sight if you didn't get around to it last month. Roses should be nourished well in anticipation of next month's extravagant display. And it's not too early to spray them with fungicide, if you take your roses seriously.

If I don't grow another vegetable (and often I don't anymore), I have to have a tomato plant or two. A rich, constantly moist growing medium, lots of fertilizer, a little lime, full sun—that's what it takes to have tomato sandwiches so good they make you shudder. This year, inspired by the giant tomato vine billowing out of Wade Wharton's enormous compost heap last summer, I'm growing a 'Park's Whopper' in a bushel basket of pure leaf mold on the back porch, but it dries out fast, and it's a struggle to keep it watered. I suppose I should set the basket into a pan which I could keep constantly full of water. You can't overwater a tomato, a fact which makes it such a dandy crop for hydroponics. Later in the season I'll snap off a couple of shoots and root fresh plants in plain water, for a continued supply.

(Actually, I suppose you *can* overwater a tomato for, if you let the soil go dry first and then water the plant well, the fruit may swell rapidly and split its skin.)

Tomato plants stuck in ordinary yard dirt against the back fence dry out rapidly, too. Mine are happiest in my nice, fluffy flower beds, for, like the rest of us, they secretly long to be regarded as beautiful, rather than merely functional.

When I first began the rock-lined bed in the backyard, it became overrun with salad tomatoes and potatoes, for all the preceding winter I had slipped my vegetable peelings under its mulch layer for disposal. The fruit of the tomato plants I allowed to survive had the tough, vinyllike skin of their store-bought parents. I ripped out all the potato plants, since I didn't know what chemicals had gone into the grass clippings that comprised a portion of the mulch, nor what unsavory ingredients had been transmitted to the soil by the heavy layer of newspaper beneath the lawn clippings and chopped leaves. Root crops are more likely to take up such unwelcome contaminants than fruit formed higher on the plant.

Organic mulches "burn up" rather quickly and must be constantly replaced. Grass clippings are gone in no time; leaves take a bit longer. Wood chips are marvelous; they take a long time to decompose, and they come closest to making a permanent improvement in the soil, leaving behind a rich, loose, black residue in which plants positively frolic.

Still, you have to go easy on the mulch in beds where you hope to see self-seeders like cosmos, cleome, and American bellflower (*Campanula americana*) reappear. A mulch is as adept at keeping down choice annuals as it is at keeping down weeds. By the end of April, we should be seeing these annuals and more.

May

M ay is for roses. Just now, briefly, while the ground lies heavy with spring rain and the air edges day by day from merely warm to frankly hot, the roses throw out their grandest display. The scattered blooms of April are mere practice for the explosive beauty of May, but by June, though the blooms will be numerous, their span of perfection will be shortened by the thickening heat, and the insects and diseases, too, may be gaining the upper hand.

My only complaint with roses (apart from their vicious, ensnaring thorns) is that most are susceptible to a throng of diseases (most notably blackspot) and all are magnets for both sucking and chewing insects. Serious rose fanciers, therefore, must go around in a perpetual fog of insecticide and fungicide. I would be interested to know how the lifespan of the average rosarian compares to that of other horticultural hobbyists. Those who hope to live long enough to be a nuisance to their children suit themselves up for protection like a combination beekeeper–skin diver, though the heat inside the costume presents its own hazards. What rose growers need is a suit that circulates ice water, like the ones stock car drivers wear. But with a respirator.

Unless you're intent on producing exhibition-quality blooms, you might do well to consider one of the rugged species roses. Lady Banks' rose (*Rosa banksiae*), a favorite in the middle and lower South since before the Civil War, has changed little since it left its native China, and, knock on wood, still exhibits few problems with pests or diseases. (I don't know how she gets along with Japanese beetles.) Graceful, far-ranging, virtually thornless, and flushed with umbels of mildly fragrant, pale flowers throughout spring, 'Lady Banks' is found in several forms, all perfect to be trained along a porch rail, or onto an arbor or fence, or up into a tree. The form most commonly seen is the double yellow 'Lutea'. 'Lutescens' is the single yellow form. 'Albo-plena' is a double white, 'Normalis' the single.

The Cherokee rose (*R. laevigata*), a Chinese climber thoroughly naturalized across the South, is a less fortunate choice for the landscape. Though it clouds its prickly, spreading branches with a froth of single white blooms for a couple of weeks in late April and May, this spectacle is soon followed by a similarly grand display of mildew, or at least that was the case with the specimen that scampered over, under, and through the 'Hopa' crab on Ewing Street. And the birds seed this rampant sticker-vine everywhere, which is how we came by ours, come to think of it. (But I should not malign the state flower of Georgia.)

The cultivated double-flowering roses, by the way, have sacrificed this ability to reproduce sexually (for the most part) in exchange for their surfeit of petals.

Another species rose—this one grown strictly for its smoldering bronze-purple foliage—is the redleaf rose (*R. glauca*). With judicious pruning this upright European native can be an exclamatory accent in the border. Single pink flowers and red hips add interest, too.

Rosa moyesii, a species rose introduced from China in 1894 by the legendary plant explorer E. H. Wilson, has brilliant red flowers in summer and drips with lacquered red, bottle-shaped hips in fall. 'Geranium' is a compact form with lighter foliage than the type and extra-large hips.

Much excitement has been occasioned in recent years over the introduction of English hybridizer David Austin's series of English roses. Derived from crosses between old shrub roses and floribundas, they are touted as disease-resistant shrubs for the smaller landscape (most mature at five feet or less). The color range is expansive, ranging from white and palest pink and apricot to yellow, rich pink, crimson, and purple. Some, like 'The Prince' whose blossoms open crimson and age to purple, change color as the blooms mature. Some have blossoms with crinkled or rather squashed faces, like peonies that have been sat upon; some have globose, cabbagelike blooms (the pink-faced 'Bibi Maizoon' looks as if she could give birth to a Cabbage Patch doll at any minute). A few are semidouble. Little pruning is required other than the occasional removal of old wood to foster fresh growth.

Alabama's climate is nothing like England's, of course, so I was a bit surprised to see many of these English roses thriving and blooming at our botanical garden in mid-July. 'Graham Thomas', named for the famed English horticulturist, is depicted as caution-light yellow in the catalogs, but the plump blossoms of our specimen were of a subdued, almost tan, yellow. The cup-and-saucer blossoms of 'Heritage' were of an exquisite shell pink and released a pleasing—and unusual—scent with an overtone of citrus. 'Abraham Darby' was bursting with vigor, broad and tall and thickly cloaked with healthy green leaves and generously spangled with mottled blossoms of yellow over pink. This one can be trained as a moderate climber, to ten feet or so.

The only disappointment was the white, barely double-flowering 'Windrush', which looked a bit tired and bug-bitten, but then Wayside's rose catalog describes its foliage as "pale green," so maybe it's supposed to look anemic.

Of the floribundas 'Iceberg' was liberally frosted with crisp, cool, white flowers. Huntsville rosarian Terry Lee rates this extremely hardy evergreen rose one of the best white roses for the South. 'Ginger', meanwhile, seemed almost to revel in the heat, all but hiding her lush foliage with coral blooms.

The miniatures were in fine form, despite temperatures in the nineties. 'Minnie Pearl', named for the grande dame of the Grand Ol' Opry, was a cushion of pink and white. And my favorite, 'Starina', veritably simmered with dainty scarlet blossoms.

It was especially gratifying to see so many hybrid teas still gamely forcing out bloom, though the petals of many were sun-singed. The delicate, light-catching pink blossoms of 'Touch of Class' discharged their wonderful "tea" scent. Fewer-flowered but nonetheless bewitching, 'Voodoo', another of Terry's recommended cultivars, adorned robust, dark foliage with richly hued blossoms of yellow-over-orange-red. The vigorous, coralflowered 'Camelot' filled the air with an exaggerated rose scent, like a potpourri. The clear yellow of 'Limelight' and the soft apricot of the lusty 'Summer Dream' added a touch of romance to the scene, while 'Double Delight', a bicolor confection of strawberry and cream, radiated pizzazz. The delicately scented 'Dainty Bess' drew attention to herself by her comparative modesty, her light pink, single blossoms centered with stark red, spidery anthers.

Among the great red hybrid teas the exceedingly red 'Grand Masterpiece' gave forth its heady old-rose smell, while 'Olympiad', whose vigor on this sweltering day could only be reported as "moderate," was almost scentless.

'American Spirit' managed a show of bright red splendor, and my father-in-law's pet rose 'Mister Lincoln', the heavy-scented, deep dark red offspring of the immortal 'Chrysler Imperial', remained impressive despite a few bug bites.

Oh, and I mustn't forget the wonderfully tea-scented blazing yellow of 'New Day' and, of course, the venerable grandiflora 'Queen Elizabeth', who, as claimed, does indeed provide a spring-to-fall display of beautifully formed blossoms of truest pink.

Hybrid teas and grandifloras should be cut back by a third or more in early spring. Using sharp (bypass, not anvil-type) shears, remove old or weak canes and prune all others to just above an outward-facing bud to preserve an open form. Pruning low removes buds of potential blooming branches but results in larger flowers. Major fall pruning is discouraged, as it deprives plants of needed food stored in the canes.

So much is made of the hybrid teas and grandifloras, I suppose, because these elegant roses with their long (at least under greenhouse conditions), graceful stems and high-centered blooms have dominated flower shows and the cut-flower market for generations. Yet beautiful as they are, their contribution to the landscape is hampered by their upright, lanky habit and their reputation as high-maintenance prima donnas.

The Meidiland series of landscape roses is tailored to respond to these shortcomings. Shrubby, long-season bloomers resistant to powdery mildew and blackspot, these roses are suitable for use as hedges, groundcovers, or simply as bright accents in the mixed border. Pruning is limited to a light shearing in early spring.

The raging red-flowerd 'Sevillana' is probably the showiest of the lot. Even in winter it won't shut up, but commands attention with its persistent orange-red hips. 'Bonica' covers itself repeatedly from spring until fall with plump, double, light pink blossoms, which are replaced by scarlet hips. 'Alba Meidiland' and 'Scarlet Meidiland', being spreaders, are recommended as tallish groundcovers (from two to four feet high). I don't think either gives a showy display of fruit.

The rugosa shrub roses (*R. rugosa* and hybrids) are rough customers, able to withstand salt spray, poor soil, and the bitterest of winter temperatures, yet I've read conflicting reports of their ability to tolerate the long, hot, and often dry summers of the lower South. They are bushy plants and take pruning well (in late winter) and so are useful as hedges and bank covers.

The flowers of the rugosas, while colorful and attractive enough, seem a bit unkempt compared to Austin's elegant English shrub roses. Still, they've much to commend them. 'Blanc Double de Coubert', an exceedingly fragrant hybrid, yields nonstop double or semidouble white blossoms resembling those of gardenia. It is resistant to powdery mildew and blackspot. Unlike the single-flowering 'Alba', it lacks showy hips.

Wayside's catalog waxes eloquent on the virtues of its yellow-flowering rugosa hybrid 'Topaz Jewel', which, it claims, blooms season-long with clusters of large, fragrant blooms that drop neatly away as they wither. We are promised disease-resistance. 'Linda Campbell', another Wayside introduction, is a blazing scarlet repeat-bloomer.

Michael Dirr's invaluable *Manual of Woody Landscape Plants* recommends 'Fru Dagmar Hastrup' above all others for its constant profusion of fragrant, clear pink, yellow-stamened single flowers, its phenomenal display of large red hips, and its exceptional disease resistance. Fru Dagmar has a tidier, more compact form than other rugosas.

Of the rather shrubby hybrid musk roses I would give my vote to 'Kathleen' for her extreme vigor and disease resistance. She will gallop over an arch. Not everyone can be content with a single-flowering rose, unwittingly convinced, I suppose, that a rose is not a rose without a congestion of petals.

But the aromatic 'Kathleen' is a charmer, with her pittance of five soft-pink petals surrounding a golden profusion of stamens so that she exudes a peachy warmth. Like all musk roses, she should be pruned back in late winter and old canes cut out to yield a longer season of bloom.

All roses are voracious feeders, and exhibition growers feed their roses as heavily as most of us stuff our tomato plants. Many rose growers use slow-release or granular fertilizers coupled with instantly accessible liquid plant food or homebrewed "teas" containing manure or other organic delicacies. Some growers provide magnesium in the form of a product called K-Mag or even Epsom salt.

Without abundant water roses may lapse into a near dormant condition during the long, hot, dry summer—a tendency some southwestern growers exploit, nursing their plants into a second season of glory when temperatures moderate and rainfall increases in autumn. Deep weekly watering will encourage all but strictly one-shot bloomers such as damask and most climbing roses to remain in bloom to some extent all summer.

In the real world roses make do with all sorts of soil situations. People pick up a bare root rose for $3.99 at the supermarket and take it home and plunk it into a hole pinched out of the hard ground with a posthole digger. It may live; indeed, it may never die, but chances are its performance would be vastly improved if time were taken to better prepare its soil.

Ideally you should dig a hole some twenty or more inches across and deep. (In truth, I've never dug a hole this size, not even to bury a cat.) Place a thick layer of gravel in the bottom if drainage is poor. Thoroughly mix the backfill with copious quantities of organic matter (compost, peat moss, pine bark, etc.) and sharp sand, too, if your soil is heavy. Rejoice if your soil measures a pH of 6.5 or so, for this is what roses like.

My sources disagree as to the correct distance above the soil line to place the graft, if the rose has been grafted onto the rootstock of a more vigorous kind of rose. At any rate, place the roots into the hole so that they fan downward and water the soil in carefully around them to eliminate hollow spaces. Mulch the plant deeply. The roses at our botanical garden are not planted exactly this way but are grown in raised beds equipped with a drip irrigation system and mulched with pine bark. Appears to work nicely.

While it's true that aphids and certain other insects can be controlled to some extent merely by hosing down the plant with a strong spray of water, rampant fungal diseases like blackspot are best prevented in the first place by spraying every seven to ten days with a fungicide—two fungicides, actually, should be alternated. An electric mist-type sprayer accomplishes the task using far less chemicals than a pump sprayer.

Planting disease-resistant varieties will drastically cut down on exposure to dangerous products. I have two completely disease-free roses. I wish I knew what they are (they came with the house). One is a white floribunda, the other a pink hybrid tea that I pretend is a climber and never cut back. The floribunda gets aphids, which I eliminate with the hose. They both get assorted caterpillars, which I control with Sevin. But neither ever has a drop of blackspot, which decimates the 'Pink Radiance' I bought as a "match" for the tea.

It's wise to remove leaves and petals which drop around the plant, for they may contain fungal fruiting bodies which, when they mature, erupt to propel their spores right back up on the plant.

It is not necessary to grow roses in day-long sun in the South. Three or four hours will do. My white floribunda blooms its little head off with about two hours of sun a day.

CLEMATIS

You need a clematis or two to get tangled up with your roses and complicate your pruning efforts. The word "clematis" calls to mind the tomāto-tomăto controversy: some folks say "clĕm´-a-tis," some say "clē-măt´-is." Both the kids' encyclopedia and my husband's fairly modern dictionary insist that "clĕm´-a-tis" is correct, while my good old-fashioned college dictionary lets us choose from among "clĕm´-a-tis," "clĕ-măt´-is," "clē-măt´-is," and "clĕ-mät´-is," though one should probably strive for consistency, at least within the same spoken sentence.

People who accent the second syllable can get away with adding *es* to form a plural; the rest of us just sound dumb, or, at best, drunk when we try this. The authors of *Hortus Third* write, "*Clematises* do best in fertile, light, loamy soil that is well-drained..." while those of the current Wayside Gardens catalog say, "*Clematis* prefer a rich, loose, well-drained soil...." Well, at least we know what kind of soil they like.

For years it was assumed that clematis needed a bit of lime in their soil, but lately I've read that this isn't necessarily so, though convention still holds that the large-flowering hybrids, at least, should have their feet in the shade (a mulched root zone is recommended) and their heads in the sun. They are thus ideal to set among shrubs, where they twine away to their hearts' content, clinging to their supportive companions with clasping leaves.

When we moved to this house, I decided it would be charming beyond words to have a clematis with bold blue blossoms the size of salad plates threading through the branches of the oversized pink hybrid tea rose I was coaxing in and out between the bars of the back porch railing. I selected 'Will Goodwin', who, according to Burpee's catalog, would thrill me with eight-inch, golden-anthered blossoms of purest blue. I prepared his home well in advance, fluffing up a piece of ground by the back porch with leaf mold and sand and a handful of fertilizer and lime. Spring came. Will arrived, a skimpy, threadlike crown dangling wormlike, naked roots. Into the ground he went, never to be seen again. I waited probably a month and finally dug down to find not a trace of my ten-dollar investment.

The next spring I again fed and fluffed the planting site and set 'Ramona' by the porch, a Languinosa hybrid noted for its lavender-blue, saucer-sized blossoms with bewitching dark-anthered eyes. 'Ramona' came twining out of the earth like a plant with a mission—for a day or two—and then she, too, magically disappeared.

That summer I watched and waited as Wal-Mart gradually marked down its clematis. When they hit two dollars and had still not died of dehydration, I brought home a wiry little vine marked "Clematis-blue."

By this time I had read an article by a very smart lady who suggested that a new clematis be pampered in a pot all summer and set out in the fall, by which time it should have gained sufficient size to be at less risk of instantaneous annihilation.

I took her advice, and my unknown blue-flowering clematis (it's actually a purple *Clematis* ×*jackmanii* of some sort, I believe) has prospered in the home I'd prepared for Will and Ramona. Had I read her article beforehand, I'd have known to set my young clematis more deeply in the soil so that if the top growth were eaten, surviving underground buds could have generated more.

I'll probably never know who ate Will and Ramona, but clematis are prey to nematodes (particularly in the South), borers, and stem rot—all of which can cause most or all of even a large, vigorous plant to wilt—as well as blister beetles (also prevalent in the South), spider mites, scale, whiteflies, and leaf spot. Plants stressed by drought are most likely to be victimized.

I have a new clematis on the opposite side of the porch, one which I'd craved for quite a while, but which had never survived the final cut on my order list (since, for the price of a clematis I can afford two ordinary perennials). But when I saw a shipment of healthy *C. montana* var. *rubens* left out to bake on the hot asphalt of a discount store parking lot, I indignantly snatched up a lively specimen and paid full price for it, right then and there. Sometimes called anemone clematis, this rapidly growing (some would say rampaging) vine hails from the Himalayas and the mountains of China, not Montana. In early summer it is crowded with pink two- to two-and-a-half inch, vanilla-scented flowers that remind me of those of flowering dogwood, for the four sepals are arranged in a cross like the dogwood's bracts. New foliage is tinged purplish-red. Dirr maintains that this clematis is easy to start from cuttings. He lists the richer pink cultivar 'Superba' and a bronzy-foliaged tetraploid, 'Tetrarose', which has slightly larger (three-inch) flowers. 'Elizabeth' has three-inch flowers of a pastel pink. *Clematis montana* is available in bluish and white versions, too. *Clematis m.* 'Grandiflora' is perhaps the most vigorous, growing to forty feet (though how one goes about measuring such a snarl I can't imagine, unless the entire tangle is forty feet long). The stark white, extra-large blossoms have creped edges and are spritzed at the center with sunshine yellow anthers. *Clematis m.* 'Perfecta' has large flowers of palest blue.

Now all I need to balance the pink rose and blue clematis on the opposite side of the porch is a blue rose!

Proper pruning of clematis is a confusing topic because some bloom on new wood in summer, some bloom in spring on old wood, and some start blooming in spring on the previous year's growth and continue on the current year's. Both Dirr and *Hortus Third* attempt to sort the hybrids into groups based on growth and bloom profiles.

Those of the Florida and Patens groups bloom in spring or summer on the previous year's wood and, if desired may be pruned back after bloom to encourage the growth of new wood for next year's flowering. My long-lost Ewing Street 'Barbara Jackman' belonged to the latter group (rather than the Jackman group, oddly enough), while the popular double lavender-blue 'Belle of Woking' and the double white 'Duchess of Edinburgh' are Florida group hybrids.

The Jackman and Viticella groups bloom on new wood in summer and fall and can be cut back to within inches of the ground in spring. The long-blooming 'Hagley Hybrid', with silken pink sepals accented by long purple anthers, and 'Star of India', whose plum-colored sepals are bisected by a streak of red, are Jackmans, as are the floriferous rich pink 'Comtesse de Bouchard', and the lusty, clear blue 'Perle d'Azur'.

Viticellas include the luminous, magenta-flowered 'Ernest Markham', so good for scrambling over and through dark green shrubs, and the fall-blooming 'Lady Betty Balfour', whose spidery, golden anthers contrast sharply with her deep, vivid blue sepals.

While *Hortus Third* lumps the *C. lanuginosa* hybrids into the Jackman group, along with the hybrids of *C. viticella*, Dirr assigns them a group of their own, explaining that many Lanuginosa group hybrids will bloom in late spring or early summer on growth of the previous season and will go on to flower again after pruning on the current season's growth. Some, he says, produce double flowers on old wood, single flowers on new. This group includes the familiar 'Henryi', whose rigid saucer-sized white blooms festoon many a mailbox and lamppost, and the beautiful two-toned pink 'Nelly Moser'—both repeat bloomers—and my ill-fated 'Ramona'.

It is only after we've quelled our appetite for the large-flowering hybrids, when every fence and trellis on the property is plastered to the point of tackiness with veritable stop signs of extravagant bloom, that we mature to an appreciation of the less flamboyant species clematis. Our native leather flower (*C. viorna*), for example, is a graceful twiner whose brownish-purple, bell-like, inch-long flower can be taken in only at close range.

The small scarlet bells of *C. texensis* are showier, but no more than an inch long. (You'd expect Texas to produce a really *BIG* clematis, wouldn't you?) *C. t.* 'Duchess of Albany' has slightly flaring, pink bells, supposedly from early summer until frost. Dirr notes that this species is tough to start from cuttings.

Clematis alpina, from Europe and Asia, sprawls or climbs to six feet or more and is graced in late spring with pink-centered, powder-blue, bell-like blossoms calling to mind Virginia bluebell. Noted for toughness, it can be left to scramble about rocky, exposed sites but is especially lovely threaded through silver-leaved plants like artemisia or Russian sage (*Perovskia ×atriplicifolia*).

Clematis alpina 'Pink Flamingo' bears nodding, rather columbinelike, pink flowers flushed a deeper pink at the base. It blooms for many weeks in late spring and early summer, primarily on old wood.

Clematis tangutica is a clematis with a difference, being yellow-flowering. This tough Asian native boasts buttery, nodding bells of what appear to be inverted tulips in midsummer, followed, as in most species clematis, by ornamental seed heads with the disheveled wispiness of Troll doll hair. The new foliage is pubescent, giving it a silvery softness.

Armand clematis (*C. armandii*) is a leathery, evergreen, rapidly growing vine with dramatically long, narrow leaflets. In spring it is sprinkled lavishly with loose panicles of starry white or pink flowers that occur on the previous year's growth. It is better used as an accent against a fence or on a lamppost than as a screen and needs a protected site in Zone 7, where its winter hardiness is occasionally tested to its limit. My current sources list three cultivars: 'Snowdrift', which is white-flowering, 'Farquhariana' with pink flowers, and 'Apple Blossom', whose white flowers are suffused with pink.

Perhaps the easiest, most reliable clematis to grow is sweetautumn clematis (*C. maximowicziana* nowadays, but until recently it was just good old, pronounceable *C. paniculata*). It is a handsome, fast-growing (I don't consider it rampant, though some do) vine with leaves composed of three to five crisp, roughly spade-shaped leaflets. In August it is thickly blanketed with small, frizzy-centered, starlike, white flowers. An introduced species which now runs wild in North American fields, sweetautumn clematis closely resembles the native virgin's bower (*C. virginiana*), which has a bit more tooth to its three-per-leaf leaflets. It is not particular as to soil and will completely swaddle a chain-link fence within a few years if not pruned back.

Clematis maximowicziana is at home in either a formal or informal setting. I've observed it used as a garland of sorts along a wall backing a positively Victorian color bed, and yet in Inge Paul's very natural garden it sweeps across her woodpile and in August foams along the retaining wall like summer snow, gleaming against the shadowy woodland background and lending sparkle to the stately silphiums and sultry *Lobelia cardinalis*. On Ewing Street my sweetautumn clematis rose from a cloud of four-o'clocks to enwrap our pedestaled mailbox. (I'm sure our mail carrier hated it when it bloomed, for it throbbed with bees, but the sweet fragrance was dizzying.) In winter I cut it to the ground to prevent its engulfing the mailbox—an easy task, no more difficult than removing a frosted morning glory, but I've read that some people are sensitive to the sap.

After bloom the seeds are embedded in fluffs composed of the long, feathery styles to which the seeds are attached and which eventually take flight on the wind, seeds and all. Seedlings often pop up where they're not welcome and should be promptly rogued out.

HARDY GERANIUM

Although in springtime the woodland floor is illuminated by the light-catching pink blossoms of the wild geranium (*Geranium maculatum*), I had always assumed that we in the steamy South could not grow the cultivated hardy geraniums (cranesbill) seen grinning out at us from every British gardening book. We simply never saw them here. And though catalogs bubbled with *G. endressii* 'Wargrave Pink' and *G.* ×*cantabrigense* 'Biokovo' ("prolific display from May until July"—likely translation: blooms in April) and even included us in their zone recommendations, it never occurred to me that they were really talking to us. Then one morning last May I pulled up in front of my pal Barbra Taber's house and blurted in amazement, "What is *that*?!" and pointed at a pair of what appeared to be clouds—one blue and one white—seemingly holding in suspension a white-flowering peony.

Well, Barbra didn't know what they were, but she'd had them for years and they always looked like that in the spring, she said. I'll go out on a limb and say that the blue one was *G.* 'Johnson's Blue' (crack!), described by Wayside as "heat tolerant and adaptable." Who knows, maybe the white one was simply *G. sanguineum* 'Album' (crash!). At any rate, Barbra's hardy geraniums were absolutely lovely and perfectly content in their bed on her sloping, boulder-strewn lawn, where they received afternoon sun.

The native *G. maculatum*, of course, is delighted with life in any southern garden, sun or shade, and romps about with gleeful abandon and thus must be thinned with a vengeance.

CALADIUM

The caladiums go out in May. Tender and tropical, they'll not do diddly until the soil is warm enough for their liking (65 degrees Fahrenheit or so). Though you might pot them up or start them in a flat of peat moss or leaf mold indoors, there's nothing to be gained by starting them early in the ground. Fancy-leaved caladiums (*Caladium* ×*hortulanum*) should be planted shallowly (a mere two inches is fine) in shade in light, humusy, constantly moist soil. With frequent fertilization (and *water*) the tuber will broaden and form new eyes capable of sending up more fountains of brightly veined and speckled aroid leaves.

Radiating a cool luxuriance, caladiums look best in masses, rather than dribbled along in skimpy rows, and are effective in mixtures as well as displays of a single cultivar. They combine stunningly with many other plants. Their thick, arrowhead-shaped leaves contrast with the delicately pinnate fronds of ferns. Those with crisp white leaves like 'White Queen' or the venerable

'Candidum' make an eye-stopping foil for red impatiens or geraniums (pelargoniums).

My longtime favorite caladium is 'Red Flash', which has huge, shieldlike leaves splashed with the vivid and varied coloration of a paint-ball target in shades of green, pink, red, and white.

Caladiums are dandy and impressive houseplants as long as you accept the fact that the tuber must occasionally rest. When the leaves die down, the tubers can be stored or the pot set aside for a couple of months before watering is resumed.

For years I heard that I should snap off the flower-bearing spadix so that the manufacturing of seed wouldn't "drain" the tubers. But lately I've read that the leaves actually last longer if the flowers are left uncut, and this does seem to me to be the case. I'm glad, because I've always admired the exotic beauty of the slightly menacing, hooded inflorescence.

Books suggest storing dormant tubers in peat moss, sand, or sawdust, but I've yet to find a foolproof way to store caladiums over winter. Stored too dry, they dehydrate; stored moist, they rot. And I've even had them arrive from the most reputable companies shriveled to the point of no return or oozing with slimy vermin.

The storage technique that seems to work best for me is, first, to mark the plants in late summer, just before they go dormant, so that the tubers can be located. Then, when decline is evident, dig and thoroughly wash the tubers and lay them out to cure for several days until the foliage has completely withered. Multieyed tubers can be divided now. Cut off the leaves, dust the tubers with a fungicide (certain foot sprays or powders seem to work nicely), wrap each individually in a strip of newspaper, and store the lot in a *ventilated* plastic bag in a cool closet. You will likely still have some molding, but it shouldn't be fatal, and some of the tubers should be showing tips of new growth when you retrieve them next May. Plump them up with a few hours' soak in a pan of water before you set them back out.

My mother-in-law's method is simpler and works just as well. She simply stores the unwashed tubers pointy side up in a bucket in a cool storage room. Caladiums have no enemies of consequence other than, perhaps, basketballs and Labrador retrievers.

AMARYLLIS

The amaryllis (*Hippeastrum* species and hybrids) is hardy outdoors here (not so, farther north) and should be blooming any minute. I like the pseudotropical, Florida-without-the-grit-and-glare look it imparts to the landscape. Each year the clump of bold, straplike leaves grows wider; each spring more and more almost ludicrously huge trumpets rise up on stout scapes as hollow and round as a shower curtain rod.

Amaryllis needs full or partial sun and rich, moist, humusy, well-drained soil. A near neutral pH is best.

Alas, when we moved from Ewing Street I left the wonderfully gaudy yet superbly photogenic clump of amaryllis, which bore enormous trumpets of bright red streaked with white. I've none at present, but I confess I'm very interested in the rather orchidlike (and allegedly more tender) "butterfly amaryllis" (*Hippeastrum papilio*). The broad white petals are pointed at the tips, and dark red stripes of varying width curve outward from the green-flushed throats. The foliage is said to be evergreen.

S M O K E T R E E

The American smoketree (*Cotinus obovatus*) comes into hazy bloom the latter half of May, when it becomes enshrouded with puffy, smokelike inflorescences the color of Pepto-Bismol and chocolate syrup stirred together. The hairy blur of filamentous panicles persists for much of the summer, bearing, at first, insignificant flowers and, later, insignificant fruit. This small (to thirty feet), spreading, native tree has broadly oval leaves, which are narrowed at the base and wear a bluish cast in summer. In fall they burst into conflagrant hues of red, orange, yellow, or purple.

Local legend has it that this tree is the chittamwood of the Bible and that, apart from the Holy Land, the species is found only on the limestone hills of the immediate vicinity. I have no idea what the biblical chittamwood is, but the American smoketree is found in limited areas (principally over limestone) in several southern states, from Tennessee and Missouri to Alabama and Texas. In the last century, it was harvested almost to extinction, for the wood yields a yellow dye.

Far more common in both home and commercial landscapes is *C. coggygria*, from Europe and Asia, particularly the purple-leaved cultivars. This species is shrubbier than *C. obovatus* and is effective either massed or as a specimen. Best color occurs in full sun. The selections 'Nordine', 'Velvet Cloak', and the long-popular 'Royal Purple' give a rich, summer-long display of smoldering purple leaves, blazing into brighter hues for fall's finale. Purple smoketree is occasionally seen in a mixed border with herbaceous perennials, where it is cut to the ground yearly to induce a flush of vividly colored juvenile growth.

The green-leaved cultivar 'Daydream' decks itself out in airy panicles that fade to the color of coffee with lots of cream and capture the morning light in a dreamlike glow. Similarly, *C.* 'Grace', one of the new Dummler hybrids, is noted for the great size of its inflorescent panicles and presents a phantasm of cottony softness and light.

I've noticed, however, that any panicles still attached to the tree as summer draws to a close have taken on the decidedly messy look of caterpillar webs.

Smoketree responds to pruning by throwing up vigorous but often isolated, asymmetrical new growth. I would situate it where it can develop naturally, so that the only pruning required will be the removal of dead or diseased wood. Unfortunately, smoketree is susceptible to *Verticillium* wilt.

FOXGLOVE

I've never seen prettier foxgloves (*Digitalis* species) than those which bloomed about town this spring. Perhaps they were encouraged by the mild winter capped by the surprise blizzard, but, more likely, by the cool spring.

Foxes do not wear foxgloves. A likely explanation of the name has it that it is derived from the Anglo-Saxon words for "folks music," folks meaning the little folks, or fairies, and their music being that which they had created on an instrument composed of bells of assorted sizes attached to an arching support.

For me, foxgloves impart an almost medieval (and somewhat ominous) aura to a garden, probably because I'm frightened by their advertised toxicity (the cardiac stimulant digitalin is derived from the leaves of some species, and the plant has been used medicinally—and dangerously—for centuries). The rosettes of thick, felted leaves persist over winter and do bear an unsettling resemblance to collards and, perhaps, other edible winter greens, so it is conceivable, I suppose, that tragedy could result from mistaken identity. (Perhaps, if I were a writer of murder mysteries, I could do something creative with this possibility. I remember once on a TV soap opera a doctor tried to do in his wife by giving her increasingly higher doses of digitalin—"What!" my victim could declare. "Collards again tonight?")

Foxgloves are native to much of the Old World and have naturalized in northeastern North America. I've heard that *Digitalis purpurea*, the common garden foxglove, has escaped in the South, too, but I've not run across it.

I suspect foxgloves are so seldom seen in southern gardens in part because they detest our hot, often droughty summers and thus must be grown in at least light shade, which allows the bloom stalk to gain sturdiness without letting the leaves scorch. And foxgloves pass so quickly from magnificence to rattiness that we tend to remove the flowering spikes before they've reseeded.

I've grown foxgloves in wet, acid clay, but all the books recommend well-drained, humusy soil, and I'm sure they're right, as usual, for mine dwindled away. If allowed, foxgloves spill dustlike seed from whence new plants will spring to heighten next year's show, though *D. purpurea* hybrids will likely revert, year by year, to the common purple type with flowers arranged along a single side of the raceme unless only the choicest specimens are allowed to set seed.

Some foxgloves are rumored to be perennials, at least in cooler parts of the South, if their needs are met. *Digitalis lutea* (to three feet) forms dense clumps bearing graceful wands of dainty, sharply flaring pale yellow flowers. In nature it prefers alkaline soils. Merton foxglove (*D.* ×*mertonensis*) has deep green, heavily textured leaves and a floral color repeatedly described as "crushed strawberry." Looks pank to me. The individual blossoms hang down like bells and are very large—two and a quarter inches long—but the plant stands only thirty or so inches high. It is a tetraploid hybrid, a cross between *D. purpurea* and the yellow *D. grandiflora*, yet reportedly will come true from seed. Perennial foxgloves, I've read, should be divided every two to four years. Mine should live so long.

Digitalis purpurea hybrids, like 'Apricot Beauty' and the massive 'Excelsior' strain, are treated most often as biennials. Seed is sown in spring or summer, and the seedlings are transplanted in fall. 'Foxy', the so-called annual foxglove, can be sown outdoors in fall or started indoors shortly after Christmas and hardened off in a cold frame and set out in March.

'Foxy' is a stocky, three-foot plant with multiple, densely packed racemes of tubular flowers with liberally spotted interiors. Colors range from white and yellow to rose and purple. The tubular blossoms of *D. purpurea* 'Giant Shirley', another three-footer, stand out from their stalks in varied and brightly colored abundance, their throats splashed with spots of brown and crimson. *D. p.* 'Alba' is a lovely white form, sans spots, reaching four feet.

Other *Digitalis* species worth a try include the Grecian foxglove (*D. lanata*), with pubescent, two- to three-foot stems and finely dappled blossoms with rudely protruding, pale lower lips, and the shrubby, eighteen-inch willow-leaved foxglove (*D. obscura*) from Spain, whose hot-colored bell-like blossoms crown narrow, leathery foliage. This one can do with more sun and needs perfect drainage. The rusty foxglove (*D. ferruginea*) bears a dense inflorescence of small, yellowish blossoms embedded with rust atop a slender, solitary, six-foot stem.

PENSTEMON

Of the roughly 250 *Penstemon* species in the world, all but one are native to North America, most to the western states. I am aware of, perhaps, seven in Alabama. (Incidentally, educated folks, at least those with a dictionary of plant names on their desk, say "pen-stē´-mon" when they're trying to speak Latin and "pĕn´-ste-mon" when they lapse into the vernacular. For example, it is correct to say, "*Pen-stē´-mon smallii* is the showiest pĕn´-ste-mon in my garden.") The name is from the Greek *penta*, meaning five, and *stemon*, or stamen. The four incurving stamens and singular staminoid—all with hairy tips in some species—account for the common name, beardtongue.

One could make a delightful hobby of collecting the various *Penstemon* species, for most are easy to grow (even from seed), undemanding, long-lived plants of considerable beauty, in and out of bloom. Taken altogether the color range is unlimited.

Like the foxgloves and snapdragons, the penstemons belong to the Scrophulariaceae, or figwort family. They bear panicles or racemes of tubular flowers on slender but sturdy stems arising from a basal rosette and crossed at intervals by clasping, opposing, narrow leaves.

The most common penstemon in our area is the three-foot gray beardtongue (*P. canescens*), which we find along roadsides and in gravelly clearings on the mountains. In full sun the May blossoms are a bright, lavender-pink; in light shade they are pale and washed-out. In heavy shade this species may or may not choose to bloom, though the puckered, paddlelike leaves are neat and tidy and not unpleasing in themselves. The rosy brown, panicled seedpods are ornamental all summer long and effective in dried arrangements. They have a faint, unpleasant odor, which I suspect somehow aids in the dispersal of the small, pulpy seeds.

Neighboring Georgia is home to one of the rarest of beardtongues, *P. dissectus*, the lavender-flowering, cleft-leaf beardtongue. West Texas and New Mexico give us one of the showiest: *P. wrightii*, with scarlet, trumpetlike blossoms on two-foot stems.

The smooth white penstemon, *P. digitalis*, has slender, evergreen foliage and tolerates winter wetness. The handsome, inflated, white (sometimes tinged with purple) flowers are borne on straight, four-foot stems. This abundant species is distributed throughout eastern North America. It is a very tough plant, pest and disease-free, in my experience.

Not all penstemons, of course, are of stately bearing. Mountainous regions of the West offer a number of low, mat-forming species. 'Claude Barr', for example, a selection of *P. caespitosus*, is a two-inch-high creeper, which is peppered with purple-throated, light blue flowers in summer. At the Denver Botanic Gardens it is used as a groundcover.

The deep rose flowers of *P. rupicola* are borne atop ground-hugging mats of tiny, rounded, glaucus leaves. A white form is available as well. The selection 'Diamond Lake' has vivid pink flowers and, at eight inches, towers over the species.

I think you can succeed with these western species in the South if you give them sharp drainage and good air circulation—don't let them sit around in a sopping wet mulch. Growing them in a rock garden or container with morning sun should work nicely. And save a little seed every year.

Come to think of it, catalogs also offer *P. hirsutus* 'Pygmaeus', a dwarf version of the widely dispersed lavender-flowering, eastern native hairy beardtongue.

GOATSBEARD

Goatsbeard (*Aruncus dioicus*) is a magnificent plant when in flower, with its great, cream-white feathers of bloom tossing about above toothy, mint green, pinnate leaves. It reminds me of a giant astilbe, though it's a rose family member, not a saxifrage. I have it in bloom in May, but one sees it clinging to rocky slopes along the Blue Ridge Parkway in June.

Unfortunately, it doesn't wear well over summer, accumulating bug damage, leaf spot, and the like, so that one comes to resent the considerable space it occupies so unattractively. It is an accommodating plant, though, and consents to being moved about. Goatsbeard is content in either sun or light shade as long as it has water. In shade it will strive toward the light, however. For me it has done nicely in a variety of soils, even heavy clay. There is a mini-goatsbeard (*A. aethusifolius*) from Korea that stands but a foot tall.

LYCHNIS

Lychnis coronaria, a catchfly native to far-flung parts of the temperate Old World, is seen in many gardens and has even managed to naturalize a bit in North America and yet few people know what to call it. The lady who gave me mine many years ago called it lamb's ears, but, of course, this appellation is usually reserved for *Stachys byzantina*. I don't have a lamb handy, but I can readily attest that the elongated leaves of both plants do, at least, have the felty resilience of chihuahua ears.

Mullein pink is another common name and probably an appropriate one for, when young, *L. coronaria* very much resembles a pubescent *Verbascum* seedling. And the genus *Lychnis* is, after all, a member of the pink family, *Caryophyllaceae*.

Rose campion is yet another name by which *L. coronaria* is known, and, most confusing of all, it is also one of the several unrelated plants known as dusty miller.

Whatever. In May the pale rosettes send up slender, silvery soft, three-foot stems bearing smaller, oppositely arranged leaves and crowned by cymes of flat, upward-facing, five-petaled blossoms of a positively lurid magenta, which throbs against the silver foliage.

This is an easy plant to grow and keep. Though it is a short-lived perennial or biennial, offspring appear wherever the seed capsules are broken, and it resists the rots brought on by too much rain or humidity far better than most silver-leaved plants. It does surprisingly well with some shade, too, and drought is the least of its worries.

After a few weeks of heavy bloom, the plant takes on a shabby appearance as stems exhausted by blooming and seed-making fade to light tan. *Lynchis coronaria* will bloom sporadically all season, however, but once the summer oranges and scarlets pop out to clash with its pulsating magenta you'll wish it would stop. (I *hate* it with orange daylilies but they seem curiously attracted to one another.)

I enjoy this lychnis with the dark red, brooding leaves of Japanese maple and with the sleek purple and pink of *Setcreasea pallida* 'Purple Heart'. It is pleasantly compatible with anything blue or white, too.

Lynchis coronaria is available in a white-flowering form, 'Alba', and in assorted shades of pink and red. *L. c.* 'Occulata' features white flowers with a pink eye.

Another lychnis I've enjoyed for many years is Maltese cross (*L. chalcedonica*), native to the northern reaches of the former Soviet Union. (I would have guessed the Mediterranean.) This is an altogether different animal, a very long-lived plant with stiff, faintly bristly leaves and stems a foot and a half or more in height. In late spring they are capped by rounded clusters of vivid scarlet blossoms, each resembling a cross, though having five petals, oddly enough. Removing the spent blossoms reportedly encourages another flush of bloom in late summer, but I've not tried this. This plant requires no maintenance at all, melting inconspicuously into the background after bloom. It does not seed itself about for me, though one respected source at my elbow claims that it is invasive and prone to various rots. I wonder if we're talking about the same plant. Certainly, however, I would give it excellent drainage.

In addition to flaming scarlet, catalogs offer *L. chalcedonica* in white and mixtures including shades of salmon and peach.

DIANTHUS

Gardeners in the South often fail with dianthus because our soil is too heavy or acid or we give them too little sun. Two parts sand and two parts compost to one part loam is recommended, and go heavy on the bonemeal or mix in a little lime.

Cheddar pink (*Dianthus gratianopolitanus* but sometimes listed as *D. caesius*), particularly the cultivar 'Bath's Pink', is considered one of the best perennial pinks for the South, tolerating heat and humidity and winter wetness better than most. Deadheading after the clove-scented pink blossoms have faded transforms the narrow-leaved, ten-inch, bluish foliage into an evergreen groundcover for a sunny site.

Dianthus deltoides 'Zing Rose' is a showy little thing, all but hiding its spiky, blue-green foliage beneath a glow of brilliant rose blossoms, which continue deep into summer.

The perennial pinks are said to profit by periodic division, which can rejuvenate a dwindling clump, particularly if soil conditioning is included in the operation. I regret to confess that twice I've allowed the cottage pink (*D. plumarius*), with its superb silvery foliage, to slip away from me. This dianthus I saw grown to perfection in southern Ontario, where it cascaded jubilantly over walls and sparkled with shaggy-edged pink and white blossoms. Here, I've seen it well-used in a hanging basket with blue and pink annuals. In a container, at least, it stands a fighting chance against winter wetness. Heat is another matter.

The annual pinks, bred primarily from *D. chinensis*, may falter as the mercury soars, though certain strains, like the All-America Selection 'Ideal Violet', are advertised as heat- and drought-resistant. It wouldn't hurt, though, to mix a few verbenas or catharanthus (vinca) into the scene for insurance.

The best-loved dianthus in the South is no doubt the biennial sweet William (*D. barbatus*), which, as a long-lasting, May-blooming cut flower, is included in many a Decoration Day cemetery arrangement. The tightly clustered cymes of bright-eyed blossoms are borne atop wide-leaved stems ranging in height from under a foot to two feet, depending on variety.

Sweet William can be started from seed in midsummer and planted out in well-prepared ground in fall, though most folks just purchase plants and set them out in fall or early spring. Sweet William is a thirstier plant than its narrow-leaved cousins and succeeds under average garden conditions in soil that is neutral or slightly alkaline. I've read that warm, wet weather encourages stem rot, so I'd go easy on the mulch. Full sun produces the strongest plants, but a dab of shade won't hurt much.

INDIAN PINK

Indian pink (*Spigelia marilandica*) is a vivid, May-blooming native plant deserving of greater use. Despite the common name, it is not a pink but a member of the rather large but relatively unheard-of logania family (Loganiaceae), along with the Carolina jessamine and the buddleia, or butterfly bush. Some members of this clan contain poisonous, strychninelike alkaloids, particularly in the roots and nectar. The roots of *S. marilandica*, so I understand, were once used as a treatment for parasitic worms, the notion being to dispatch the parasites without quite killing the host. I suspect the idea was merely a trick deployed by the Indians to rid the continent of its pesky white intruders.

Nonetheless, Indian pink is a lovely plant with a rigidly upright carriage, just the sort of plant (naturally beautiful, graceful, and perfectly proportioned) that the breeders love to take hold of and mess up. The stems, bearing opposite pairs of nearly sessile (attached to the stem directly, without a stalk) oval leaves, are crowned by clusters of vivid red, up-facing trumpets, which flare open, starlike, at the top to reveal a yellow interior.

I've read that keeping the spent blossoms removed prolongs the period of bloom, but I've always been too lazy to try this. It is happiest in light shade but will slowly form long-lived, deep-rooted colonies in almost any well-drained soil.

PRAIRIE CONEFLOWER

The graceful prairie coneflower (*Ratibida pinnata*) carries its long, skirtlike, drooping, yellow ray flowers atop stiff, four-foot stems rising from fountains of deeply divided, rough, toothy leaves. In northern Alabama this wide-ranging native isn't a prairie flower at all but a denizen of the rocky hillsides, particularly along roadsides, where it gets a peek at the sun.

Easy from seed, prairie coneflower is long-blooming (from May until midsummer) and long-lived (for years and years) in any well-drained garden soil, and it takes shade better than most daisies. The conelike seed heads give off a pleasant anise scent when broken.

The splashier though shorter-lived Mexican hat (*R. columnifera*) is a western native that is becoming naturalized in the East in large part through its inclusion in wildflower seed mixtures. The flower does indeed resemble a tall sombrero. The high, narrow cone is skirted with broad, reflexed ray flowers (functionally, if not technically, petals) which are hotly streaked with red and edged with yellow. I would give it full sun and treat it as an annual or biennial.

COREOPSIS

Now we see the tall coreopsis break into radiance. Lance-leaved coreopsis (*Coreopsis lanceolata*) holds such brightness in its golden, shell-like blossoms, upturned like a shallow bowl and deeply pinked at the edges, and displays such delicacy in its smooth, slender, deeply lobed leaves and two- to four-foot pipe-cleaner-thin flower stalks that it is welcomed with ardor, even by those who may have hoped to preserve a less summery blend of colors just a bit longer.

This shallow-rooted perennial seems to move about, its semiprostrate foliage skimming the ground, while the ever-swaying flowers stretch for the sky. It needs a light soil, strong sun, and protection from more aggressive spreading plants if it is to persist reliably from year to year. Lance-leaved coreopsis paints an especially gay picture when accompanied by flaming scarlet *Lychnis chalcedonica* or fronted by blue pansies.

Much later, in June and July, we will begin to see the popular thread-leaved coreopsis *C. verticillata* 'Moonbeam' sprinkle its dainty, pale yellow, starlike daisies above a puffy green cloud of willowy leaves. I have three plants which are supposed to be 'Moonbeam' but are more likely the stockier, rowdier-yellowed dwarf 'Zagreb'. (Switched at birth!) Whatever. They are hard-working, first-rate little plants. I've read that shearing back *C. verticillata* after flowering induces a new flush of bloom, but, really, if they're not allowed to go dry, they bloom naturally from midsummer on without letup.

The tall, wispy, golden-flowered *C. verticillata* found in our woods is more difficult—a frail thing, easily shoved aside by less restrained neighbors.

I'm surprised that whorled tickseed (*C. major*) is so rarely found in gardens. Even when not covered with cymes of boldly cheerful, sunshine yellow daisies (as it is much of the summer) its sleek, rich green whorled foliage, reminiscent of that of many lilies, is handsomely engaging in itself. This is an easy, long-lived plant in sunny, sharply drained soil (it is partial to sandy banks). It is susceptible to the same (or very similar) stem rot that plagues rudbeckias hereabouts when they are stressed by hot, dry weather. Just clip off affected stems, water the patient well, mutter a few appropriate incantations, and chances are it will recover.

Coreopsis rosea is unusual in that it requires constantly moist soil and the small blossoms, frilly as a ballerina's skirt, which dance at the tips of two-foot stems rising from clumps of grassy-thin foliage, are *pink*. In our state this eastern North American native is reported to haunt piney wetlands and cypress swamps. A white form is listed.

Calliopsis (*C. tinctoria*), or garden coreopsis, as it's sometimes called in books, is seldom seen in southern gardens, though it's plentiful enough—sometimes for miles and miles—along highways. The dark-eyed flower heads—produced by the hundreds—are no wider than a half dollar and are two-toned yellow and mahogany. While this hard-blooming annual usually doesn't exceed waist-height in its austere natural haunts, it is likely to go berserk when sown into a bed of fluffy, rich garden soil and may billow into an airy, five-by-five-foot orangish cloud.

Coreopsis tinctoria seed sown in fall will germinate to form flat, winterproof rosettes of dark, much-segmented leaves. After summer's bloom the tattered, exhausted plant can be yanked out. Chances are plenty of seed should have already scattered about for next year's crop.

Of Houseplants, Slugs, and More

The houseplants go out the first of May, whether the weather has settled or not, simply because I'm sick of fooling with them inside. It's such a relief to have them out where they can be easily bathed and watered with the hose—even the African violets; it does them no harm that I can see. The big precaution to take is to set them all—even the succulents intended for arid environments—into the shade at first—never the sun, for they will scorch and bleach appallingly. They need a gradual introduction to sun, and some, of course, can never take full sun, particularly on an oven-like brick or concrete patio.

I do a bit of fertilizing in May and June: shrubs, ferns, bedding plants—almost everything. I slacked off the granular fertilizers several years ago when I heard there was concern that it was ingested by birds seeking gravel for grinding food in their gizzards. More recently I've been told by a veterinarian who works extensively with birds that this isn't likely. Nevertheless, I continue to use the powdery type that must be mixed with water, for, since I finally bought a fertilizer dispenser that attaches to the hose, I can kill two birds with one stone, so to speak.

I've never liked slug bait. The smell is sickening to me and I've always fretted that birds, cats, dogs, or kids would ingest it before the intended victims oozed onto the scene. Now I read that slugs fed granular metaldehyde bait get so sick so quickly that they're unable to consume a fatal dose of the poison. For a couple of days they lie around feeling blah. Then seventy percent of them get up and slide home.

Slugs, I've read, will not cross a copper barrier—they're shocked, so I understand, when their wet skin comes in contact with the metal. But as Rachel and I just proved, they will, after much investigation and deliberation, escape a ring of pennies or a circle of copper wire. Perhaps ambient temperature plays a role; it's warm tonight—a bit over 70 degrees Fahrenheit—and perhaps the metal is not uncomfortable to touch. But then it's hard to reach a solid conclusion when Bart, the cat from next door, keeps sprawling across our experiment, in hopes of being petted.

The old beer-in-a-saucer trick works pretty well, but it's messy and unsanitary unless you change your beer daily. But then around here someone or something (probably Bart) devours the bait, slugs and all, every night.

Slugs, of course, will congregate under any solid object you leave lying around, so you can handily dispatch them, if you're not too squeamish. This makes you feel you're accomplishing something, though the vast majority remain safely hidden under the mulch (or even under the ground) where you'll never find them.

There are, I believe, plants which slugs and snails won't eat. Impatiens may be one. Awhile back I ran out of lettuce to feed the old aquarium snails who were being housed in a jar until I could take them to a friend's fish pond. When I substituted a sprig of impatiens for their lettuce, the snails turned up their noses, and eventually, the impatiens struck roots, still unmolested by the snails. In the shade garden beneath the white dogwoods out front the volunteer impatiens seedlings go untouched by the bountiful mollusk population.

The bedding plants we haven't yet found time to set out are rapidly attaining the ultimate dimensions their cramped quarters will allow and will soon be permanently stunted if we dither around any longer.

And there are weeds. Oh, my, are there ever weeds!

June

G ardening at dawn in June is almost a religious experience. A cool mist dampens the air and hovers, visibly, over the creek. The grass is silvered, frostlike, with dew, through which our footsteps puncture a path of shadows. The sun gleams behind the purple-black mountain like an as-yet-unseen fire, casting a pink glow onto the underbellies of the clouds. Crickets trill sleepily from the dark side of the trees, and blue jays—as raucous as roosters—lecture the black cat from the yard across the creek as he slips down to the slow-moving water for a drink. As our hands work, the moist earth releases the weeds with magical ease, and we savor the sweet richness of its fragrance.

But by nine A.M. gardening in June is another matter. Sweat pours. Flies bite. The sun glares down, seemingly with personally directed anger. And so gardening becomes (for me, certainly) something one does but very early and very late in the day. I sympathize with Thomas Jefferson. Peter Hatch, Director of Ground and Gardens at Monticello, has written that one of his slaves recalled of Jefferson that, "For amusement he would work sometimes in the garden for half an hour at a time in right good earnest in the cool of the evening."

When the heat settles in, I, too, become primarily an after-dinner gardener. I slip supper back an hour and fantasize about moving to the Eastern Time Zone to give me yet a little more precious after-supper playtime.

VITEX

I wouldn't want a garden without a vitex. *Vitex agnus-castus*, or chaste tree, is a small (to twenty feet by a similar width), shrubby, highly aromatic tree belonging to the verbena family. The three to seven narrow leaflets of the pliant, palmately compound leaves taper to a point and are medium green on top, pale on the underside. Felted with minute hairs, both leaves and young stems are soft to stroke and leave a sharp, minty scent on the fingers. (The similarity of vitex leaves to those of marijuana has caused unnecessary alarm to the campus gendarmes at one local institution of higher learning on more than one occasion, I'm told. I should think, though, that this error would be likelier to occur with the related laciniated-leaved *V. negundo* 'Heterophylla', which bears toothier leaflets.)

But in June there can be no mistaking vitex for any other plant (well, butterfly bush, maybe), for the new stems are tipped with panicles composed of spiky racemes bearing opposite cymes of lavender flowers, which are stunningly set off by the yellow-banded bumblebees with which they are noisily weighted.

One of my sources notes that vitex is difficult to combine with other shrubs. True enough. It is best situated alone in open sun, where it can grow into a small, symmetrical tree (it shrinks from shade). Besides, vitex grows rapidly—it is simply not the shrub of choice for most situations.

On Ewing Street my vitex was within ten feet of the house and had to be cut back severely every winter—a chore I came to dread. (Above Zone 7 the above-ground growth is likely to be winter-killed, necessitating yearly removal.) When we moved here I brought cuttings, one of which—a widespread, shaggy little tree already—I granted an open sunny spot where it can go unpruned until the end of time and where it can be enjoyed from the kitchen and den. I position a biennial evening primrose (*Oenothera erythrosepala*) just outside the windows so that the oenothera's light yellow and the vitex's pale purple can visually mingle.

Our Ewing Street redbirds nested in the vitex, a few branches above the bird feeder, unconcerned that their bright scarlet and orange-tinged feathers and beaks clashed with the blossoms of their host tree.

Vitex is easy in most well-drained soils and needs no care. I've seen it used to magnificent effect in rather Mediterranean settings near the Gulf. Its winter aspect, however, is austere. The smooth yet faintly ridged gray-brown branches curve upward like the arms of a candelabra.

My vitex, I suspect, is the extra hardy and vigorous *V. agnus-castus* 'Latifolia', for it is coarse by comparison to the far daintier specimen in Inge Paul's yard. Other listed cultivars include 'Alba' and 'Silver Spire' (both white-flowering), 'Rosea' (pink), and 'Variegata' (variegated).

DAYLILY

As roses dominate May, so daylilies (*Hemerocallis*) take command in June. The daylily garden at the botanical garden becomes a sea of trumpets in every conceivable floral hue except lily white and blue (but the breeders are getting close with the white, and the geneticists may soon supply the blue).

There is no earthly reason for a daylily to ever die. One autumn many years ago we rented a house with a shrubby boundary against which a huge heap of the previous year's leaves had been dumped. When I finally removed the leaves, I discovered a bed of pale, spindly of daylilies. They just knew they'd eventually be rescued. And fellow gardener Mary Lou McNabb tells of a daylily bed that survived fifteen years as a parking area for trucks.

Some years back the great treat of high summer for my mother-in-law and me was to pay a call on Mrs. Myrtice Phillips, formerly of Oxford, Alabama. Mrs. Phillips was a gardener par excellence, and her yard contained a multitude of amazing plants. Her red hot poker (*Kniphofia*) must have soared to eight feet. But her great love was daylilies. She would accompany us, spade in hand, as we walked up and down the rows and rows of blooming daylilies, struggling to make our choices.

Mrs. Phillips knew the names of all her hundreds of daylilies on sight, never needing to consult the labels. And she dealt in daylilies for love, not money. According to my garden journal on June 26, 1979, I selected 'Ebony Prince', a red so dark as to be almost black; 'Bess Ross', a bright red; 'Saffron Beauty', a large, yellow-gold of great substance with evergreen foliage; 'Bama Maid', a pink; 'Milk Chocolate', a dainty brown; 'Annie Welch', an orange-throated pink; 'Little Emily', a small, many-flowered yellow; and a salmon-colored daylily with no known name—all for four dollars. (It's obvious I'm as hopeless at settling on a color scheme for my daylilies as I am at choosing a flat of pansies.)

'Ebony Prince' and 'Milk Chocolate' went on to become among my favorites for a number of years. I lost 'Saffron Beauty' to a hard winter (I don't think the evergreens are really as hardy as the deciduous daylilies). By the time we moved here my daylily bed had become a jumbled mess. Markers were long gone, and the aggressive 'Bright Spangles', a tall, slender, half-wild speckled gold, had overrun the bed, making it impossible to distinguish one cultivar from another unless they were in bloom.

I brought with me only my favorite at the time, 'Luke', a medium-high coral pink with good but uncomplicated substance. It has taken him three years to bloom again. At first I planted him in the heavily mulched bed by the garage, where the slugs (I suppose) repeatedly chewed him down to a nub. Now he's blissfully happy in the backyard in full sun with a less oppressive mulch, and this year he bloomed with gusto.

We often see the common orange, or tawny, daylily (*Hemerocallis fulva*), in both single and double forms, paired loudly with blue-flowering bigleaf hydrangea (*Hydrangea macrophylla*) or, more subtly, with creamy oakleaf hydrangea (*H. quercifolia*). This daylily was introduced to the gardens of Europe from Asia centuries ago and within the last 250 years or so has become thoroughly established throughout the eastern two thirds of the United States. Just how such rapid and wide naturalization could have occurred mystifies me, since *H. fulva* is suppposedly a self-sterile triploid which rarely sets viable seed.

They do spread rhizomatously, and in June the roadsides of northern Georgia (actually, we say *North* Georgia and *North* Alabama, but editors from the *North* don't think that's proper!) are lined with swaying orange trumpets for miles. (Don't tell me the Georgia Highway Department *planted* them all!)

The lemon lily, the yellow, lemon-scented *H. flava*, another sterile hybrid, is out there running around loose, too. (Well, like they say in the film *Jurassic Park*: "Life finds a way!")

The wealth of variety that's been bred into modern daylilies is just astounding. There are dinky miniatures and six-foot giants. Some have broad, ruffled petals; some have petals that are narrow and spidery. Some are boldly colored; some subtle. Some have contrasting stripes down the centers of the petals; some have prominent eye zones or halos. Some are fragrant; most are not. Some rebloom in late summer or fall. Many are tetraploid hybrids, whose extra chromosomes add size and vigor to every cell of the plant.

The majority of *Hemerocallis* cultivars listed in gardening catalogs are well under three feet in height, suited, I suppose, for deck planters and for the modern, scaled-down home environment. And the miniatures (those two feet and under, usually with proportionately smaller flowers) are long on charm. 'Mini Pearl', at sixteen inches high, is feverishly crammed with blushing apricot-pink three-inch blossoms with creped edges. 'Stella de Oro', which all the catalogs claim is the longest-blooming daylily on record, caps twenty-inch scapes with two-and-a-half-inch, brassy yellow trumpets. Stella follows her early-season flush with a respectable stream of follow-up blossoms all summer if she receives ample water.

'Happy Returns', Stella's hybrid offspring, is a perfect choice for a patio container. It is more compact than Stella, but the fluted, canary-yellow blossoms are an inch wider. The lightly fragrant trumpets open in early evening and remain open the following day. 'Happy Returns' gets a second wind in late summer for a decent but less prolific display than the first.

One of the most interesting of the miniatures is hybridizer Pauline Henry's 'Siloam Ethel Smith'. The interior of the ruffled, beige trumpet looks a bit like a Rorschach test done in delicate watercolor, as the eye zone consists of a red ring which bleeds into a luminous yellow halo that melts into the green throat.

I don't particularly relish the current fashion for big fat crinkly flowers on stubby stems about kneecap high. I'd rather see a big flower on a tall stem. I recently purchased (yes, I said purchased—daylilies are hard to steal) the classic, lemon-yellow 'Hyperion', introduced in 1925 and still going strong in the catalogs. The flowers are simple, scented, and lilylike, and, with its statuesque, four-foot grace, 'Hyperion' is the perfect companion for tall blue campanulas or the summer spiderwort. And it is a bit less raucous in the presence of the ubiquitous blue hydrangea than many other daylilies.

For sheer majesty in a daylily, though, you can't beat the giant, autumn-flowering Altissima strain derived from H. altissima, a six-foot, night-blooming

Chinese species. 'Challenger' sends aloft five-inch rusty-red trumpets with golden throats on six-foot scapes.

Another novelty which appeals to me is the twenty-six-inch 'King Alfred', whose double (usually), bright yellow blossoms represent an attempt to imitate a daffodil. The protruding inner petals do resemble a daffodil's corolla if you use your imagination.

There are thousands of fancy or just plain pretty daylilies, but, while I'm not really a novelty buff, I'm drawn to the mysterious, seemingly tropical 'Double Pom Pom', whose orangy-pink, sweet-smelling, five-inch blossoms appear to've been assaulted with an egg beater—twisted petals curve in all directions. This midseason rarity stands about thirty inches high.

If you like to photograph flowers, there is nothing like an intensely red daylily to jump out and say boo to a camera. 'Mallard', at twenty-six inches, shows crusty golden anthers against smooth petals that appear to've been cut from red velvet.

Daylilies are drought tolerant and accept any soil that drains at all. They accept shade but bloom best where they receive some sun. Each bloom lasts but a day, but weeks of successive blooms may be borne on a single scape. In sun colors fade as the day wears on. Some gardeners cut the grasslike foliage back to the ground after bloom to promote new, fresher-looking growth and to spark repeat blooming.

After a few years a clump may become so congested that flowering lessens and division will be necessary. Fall is ideal, but any time of year will do. When replanting divisions, spread the fleshy roots outward and set the crown about an inch deep. Fertilize sparingly in the spring. I remember asking Mrs. Phillips what kind of fertilizer she used to create such an explosion of bloom and she replied, "Whatever I can get."

L I L Y

Just as the daylilies are easy and reliable, the true lilies (*Lilium* species) are, with a few exceptions, difficult or, at least, fickle. Unfortunately, for most of us lilies fit Henry Beard and Roy McKie's apt definition of a perennial as "any plant which, had it lived, would have bloomed year after year."

One of the most successful lilies for me has been the Asiatic hybrid 'Enchantment', which, by the way, was introduced in 1949, making it almost as ancient as I am. It has upward-facing, spotted orange blossoms which are borne in massive profusion on three-foot stems. 'Enchantment' will increase if protected from severe competition with more aggressive neighbors.

Similar in form but strong red in flower is 'Red Night'. It, too, has freckles. It is a vigorous plant with dark green, lustrous foliage.

With lilies, by the way, three of the six "petals" that go into making up the flower are actually sepals. More learned texts than this refer to both collectively as "segments of the perianth." Or we could just call them "tepals." Oh, yes, and there are no true blue lilies, either, though there are many very fine white ones.

One of the whitest is 'Casa Blanca', a four-foot Oriental hybrid which blooms in midsummer. The large, curling, whiskery, ice-white blooms set off the bright orange-red anthers. The pink stigma tops a long green style. I mention this one because it's advertised to be a colonizer. I like that in a lily.

If you're desperate to astonish your friends and confound your enemies, you might take a chance on *Lilium auratum platyphyllum*, a variety of the Japanese gold-banded lily which, with flowers a foot or slightly more in diameter, is billed as the largest-flowering lily in the known universe. Each pimply white segment of the enormous, fragrant blossom bears a yellow stripe down the middle. In the Kimona strain, advertised as disease-resistant, the typical light carmine spotting is essentially lacking.

Elizabeth Lawrence tells us that gold-banded lily's culture requires coal ashes and poor soil, the notion being to duplicate its original home, presumably on volcanic Mount Fuji. Poor soil is no problem, but coal ashes are not easy to come by these days.

Lawrence's gold-banded lilies performed spectacularly the first year, each four-foot stalk producing ten lilies twelve inches across, but they soon fell prey to mosaic disease, to which *L. auratum* is among the most susceptible of lilies.

I like speckles on my lilies, otherwise they might as well be daylilies. Still, one can't disparage the unmarked, slick-as-silk perfection of the tawny gold 'Oreglow' or its ravishing deep scarlet tetraploid cousin 'Avignon', both early season, upward-facing Asiatic hybrids of medium height.

I have the same difficulty accepting short lilies that I do adjusting to stubby daylilies, though I admit they make sense for containers. Planted several to a twelve-inch or larger pot and skirted with a fluff of alyssum, the two-foot 'Sans Souci', with its white-edged, crimson-spotted blossoms, makes a cheerful splash for a lightly shaded deck or patio.

Likewise the crisp white, lightly dappled, upward-facing blossoms of the two-foot 'Apollo' fairly glow when set against a dark screen of shrubs.

Trumpet lilies impart an old-fashioned look to a garden, with their candelabras of enormous, downcast fragrant flowers. My favorite has long been the Black Dragon strain, though this lily sulked for me year after year and finally died. But we had gotten off to a rocky start. The bulb had arrived on an unseasonably hot autumn day and had evidently absorbed an excess of heat while the big brown delivery truck toodled around in the sun all day. The bulb was alarmingly warm to the touch when I opened the package, so I gave it a long soak before I planted it out. I'm going to try this lily again some day as I greatly admire its dark stems and ivory blossoms streaked in back with maroon.

Or perhaps I'll try the Chinese species lily *L. leucanthum* var. *centifolium*, which reminds me very much of Black Dragon, with its flaring, purple-backed white trumpets and its clapperlike cluster of enormous dark anthers.

One of the daintiest and sweetest of the species lilies is *L. callosum* 'Flaviflorum' from eastern Asia, which dangles two-inch, curled up, lemon-yellow blossoms from three-foot stems.

The showiest of the species lilies—and it does exceedingly well for us here in the South—is *L. speciosum* 'Rubrum', from southern Japan. The reflexed petals and sepals are streaked in white and shades of pink and the flower's face is darkly freckled and flocked. Put this one in partial shade where your friends can conveniently oo-and-ah over it. It blooms from July into August. *L. speciosum* 'Album' is the white version, the segments having a central green stripe.

If you love to grow lilies, then you won't want the common tiger lily (*L. tigrinum*, also listed as *L. lancifolium*) on the premises, for this towering (to six feet or more) turk's-cap, with its dramatic racemes of nodding, dark-spotted orange blossoms, is notorious for harboring mosaic virus. This lily suffers little or no obvious viral damage itself but transmits the disease to other lilies via aphids.

Lilium tigrinum is native to the Orient but has naturalized throughout the eastern two thirds of the United States. It is an exceedingly vigorous plant. It colonizes rapidly and stands up to wind and rain without staking.

The black, pealike bulbils, which form in the axils of the fleshy, spiky leaves, germinate rapidly after removal from the mother plant, even if they are stored in a plastic bag. They must be planted immediately or they'll dehydrate and be useless. Bulbil babies will winter nicely in a pot in the cold frame.

The mosaic problem aside, *L. tigrinum* is a perfect candidate for the wild garden.

I also grew the less statuesque (to four feet), upward-facing *L. tigrinum* 'Splendens' for a number of years and found it superb for cutting. In fact, the first time I saw a vase full of these elegant tiger lilies I thought they were artificial. They appeared to be made of wax and had a profound stillness about them.

Perhaps my voracious and infectious stand of *L. tigrinum* slew my more tempermental nearby *L. henryi*, for he failed to return this year, though he is supposed to have some resistance to mosaic virus. Frankly, I prefer the tiger lilies anyway. *Lilium henryi* is more interesting than pretty, I'd say. There is something almost repulsive about the flower as the extremely reflexed segments are studded with papilla like the surface of a very rude pale orange tongue. A rush of long green filaments and a narrow green style gush forth from a deep green throat.

With lilies good soil preparation greatly enhances performance and longevity. They like a light, fertile soil (either sand or loam) with added humus.

Except with a few species, good drainage is critical. Raised beds and slopes work especially well.

Lilies are never completely dormant and can be planted any time, but fall planting (October and November) allows a mature bulb to settle in and gather momentum for the following summer's bloom. Set the bulb into the ground so that its top is four inches below the soil surface. (I've read that lilies set down roots which literally draw the bulb down to the preferred depth.) Some lilies, such as *L. auratum*, *L. henryi*, and *L. regale*, are stem-rooters; that is, they produce fibrous roots above the bulb. The Madonna lily (*L. candidum*) and the Grecian scarlet turk's-cap (*L. chalcedonicum*) should be planted shallowly, no more than two inches down. Madonnas are exceptional, too, so I've read, in needing a bit of lime in their soil. They are among the longest-lived of lilies for the South, however, and increase freely.

Lilies are stronger-stemmed and more floriferous in sun, but they don't like baked soil and they suffer in a too-hot situation, such as a masonry planter in a sea of concrete. To have sun on their upper stems while the base of the plant is shaded by other vegetation seems a comfortable, fieldlike situation. They are especially fetching among ferns or woodland wildflowers with exceptional foliage, like false Solomon's seal (*Smilacina racemosa*).

When flowering is finished remove the developing seedpods and allow the foliage to decline naturally in order for the bulb to store up as much strength as possible for next year's bloom. (I have always wondered how much difference it really makes to remove the seedpods.) When cutting lilies for the house leave at least half the stem to replenish the bulb.

Mosaic virus is the most serious lily pathogen. The disease causes mottling, stunting, and distortion on every part of the plant; only the seeds are immune. There is no cure. Destroy affected plants promptly to prevent spread of the disease to healthy lilies. Species with a reputed measure of resistance include *L. henryi*, *L. martagon*, and the regal lily (*L. regale*).

Fertilize lilies in spring with any good complete fertilizer. Mulch to retain moisture, regulate soil temperature, and preserve soil quality.

HYDRANGEA

Southerners love hydrangeas, for no other shrubs make such an impression of billowy softness and welcome cool in the shady summer garden. The big blue (and sometimes pink) globular flower heads of the bigleaf hydrangea (*Hydrangea macrophylla*) are the most familiar of all. This form of *H. macrophylla* is called French hydrangea (though it hails from Japan) or hortensia. The enormous flower heads are made up almost entirely of male (sterile) flowers.

The characteristic blue, mauve, or pink flower color is an expression of the relationship between soil pH and the plant's ability to take up aluminum present in the soil. In acid soil the plant can take up more aluminum, and the flower is blue; in near neutral or alkaline soil aluminum becomes unavailable to the plant, and the flower is pink. To make a blue flower pink add lime to the soil; for a bluer flower add sulfur or aluminum sulfate. (A note of caution here: High soil pH also renders the iron in the soil unavailable to the plant and chlorosis may result.)

The cultivars 'Pia', a dwarf; 'Ami Pasquier'; and 'Bottstein' are supposedly genetically incapable of taking up aluminum and should truly be forever pink. The bigleaf hydrangea known as 'Forever Pink', however, is only pink-flowering in neutral or alkaline soil, so I'm given to understand.

'Nikko Blue', which has been around a long time, is a hardy six-footer with rich blue flowers when grown in acid soil. 'Otaksa' is a more compact but weaker-stemmed shrub whose big blue globes stack up on the ground like marbles in a jar after a rain. The prolifically produced blue blossoms of 'All Summer Beauty' are said to appear on the season's new growth, a swell idea, since folks who prune their bigleaf hydrangeas hard in winter prune away the buds for the following summer's flowers. 'Mme. E. Muillere' is a highly recommended white hortensia.

Bigleaf hydrangeas whose flower heads are borne in flat corymbs consisting of small fertile flowers surrounded by showier sterile flowers are called lacecaps. These are seen with far less frequency but have a delicacy and subtlety which commend them to situations calling for less spectacle than that provided by the hortensias.

There are many exquisite cultivars, including 'Lanarth White', whose pristine, blue-eyed white male flowers surround a center of tiny blue fertile flowers. The eyes and fertile flowers may be pink in neutral or alkaline soil. The blossoms of 'Blue Wave' are exceedingly blue in strongly acidic soil, shades of lilac in more neutral soil. 'Quadricolor' and 'Variegata' have variegated leaves that veritably glow in the shade.

The smooth hydrangea (*H. arborescens*), also known as hills-of-snow hydrangea, is a familiar native of the southeastern woodlands. The type is a bit dingy in flower, exhibiting flattish clusters of multitudinous, greenish fertile flowers ringed with just a light smattering of creamy sterile flowers. The cultivar 'Annabelle', however, has put this species on the map with her huge, globular clusters of snowy white sterile flowers. Michael Dirr recommends cutting 'Annabelle' to the ground in late winter and fertilizing her lightly for a stupendous display of bloom-bearing new growth in summer.

Another hydrangea that can be safely pruned hard in winter is the Peegee hydrangea (*H. paniculata* 'Grandiflora'), which tends to take on an arching, multistemmed tree form if allowed. It is noted for its great clusters of papery, white sterile flowers in midsummer, which age to shades of rose and rust by fall. The bark is flaky, and the shrub has a rather disheveled look. After autumn leaf drop, the flower heads persist.

I've noted a row of Peegees lining a stairway on the A&M campus, and I find them preferable to yet another train of institutional Chinese hollies. But the Peegee is a shrub that should be used in moderation.

I'm glad to see the oakleaf hydrangea (*H. quercifolia*) included in so many modern landscapes. Though it is coarse in appearance, it manages to look comfortable around some of the most elegant homes. It particularly suits a very large house, for the hydrangea's foot-long, sharply lobed leaves and long, conelike, creamy flower panicles are of an ambitious scale themselves. This hydrangea has by far the best and brightest fall color of the lot, and the peeling bark and dried flower heads give good winter interest.

The fertile flowers are fairly hidden by the sterile white outer flowers, but if you peek into the heart of the sweet-smelling inflorescence you may spy young lightning bugs frolicking in their pollen. The June blooms age to rose and finally brown by summer's end.

The *H. quercifolia* selection 'Snow Queen' is exceptional in that its snowy panicles bearing oversized sterile florets are held stiffly upright. 'Snowflake' is awesome, with pendant panicles well in excess of a foot long, whose sterile flowers are so stacked with sepals as to appear double. 'PeeWee' is a recommended compact form. 'Late Hand' has leaves described as "handlike" (sounds spooky) and blooms a few weeks after the rest.

All hydrangeas need copious amounts of water, particularly in sun (you can almost forget about using *H. macrophylla* in full sun, for it wilts forlornly). But I've found *H. quercifolia* to be easy to establish, whereas a newly planted *H. macrophylla* can never be watered enough. A deep mulch is most beneficial.

As with the bigleaf hydrangeas, there is no perfect time to prune an oakleaf hydrangea, for you are bound to lose either a portion of the current season's flower heads or those of the next year. The "proper" time is "immediately after bloom," but the drying flower clusters remain ornamental for months, so it's hard to find the nerve even if you recognize the moment.

Ideally these hydrangeas should be sited only where their mature size can be tolerated. You may, however, occasionally want to rejuvenate a spindly shrub by cutting out a third of the oldest canes at ground level.

One seldom sees the climbing hydrangea (*H. anomala* subsp. *petiolaris*) in the South; it can take winters down to −30 degrees Fahrenheit but languishes in summer heat, particularly if it bakes against a masonry wall in full, day-long sun. It is best given light shade or at least shade throughout the middle of the day.

Although it is a climbing vine, it is very hydrangealike, with exfoliating bark and broad, flat-topped corymbs consisting of sterile white outer flowers and dingier fertile inner flowers.

Climbing hydrangea grows slowly at the start, but can eventually reach sixty to eighty feet in height, clinging by aerial rootlets. Dirr is especially fond of this vine and makes much of its habit of extending branches outward from the tree or structure to which it is attached, thus providing a sense of form and depth and casting engaging winter shadows.

The ferns and hostas are lush and lovely in late spring. The lady fern (*Athyrium filix-femina*) is at her most fetching, her long, feathery fronds arching gracefully to their pointed tips. The minute pinnules (subleaflets) of the light green, bipinnately compound leaves are rather thin and therefore quick to scorch once the temperature soars into the high nineties and above, and they are ready snack food for the slugs and bugs, which tend to leave the thicker-leaved ferns alone. But for a few brief shining weeks this delicate, alluring fern is in her glory.

The Japanese painted fern (*Athyrium nipponicum*) offers considerably more resistance to wear and tear and, with its silvery-blue, red-stemmed fronds, will pick up the blue of such hostas as *Hosta* 'Hadspen Blue' or *H.* 'Love Pat'. This fern is typically smaller than the lady fern, though I've seen unusually large specimens that so mimicked the lady fern's vaselike, plumose habit that they appeared to be crosses between the two species.

In the South most ferns do best in full or partial shade. But, as the Birmingham Fern Society discovered a few years ago when a ferocious storm took down the canopy of large trees which had shaded the fern glade at their botanical garden, most ferns will make do with full sun if watered like crazy.

The majority of my ferns live in the little shade garden beneath the two white dogwoods in the front yard, where I struggle endlessly to transform rock-hard subsoil into fluffy black woods dirt. Ferns revel in loose, rich, constantly moist but well-drained acid (usually) soil, so I heap on the leaf mold (they *love* that yucky black stuff that comes out of the gutters). Wood chips, aged grass clippings, and an occasional light application of fertilizer are appreciated.

For all they love water, ferns are slower to register its absence than, say, impatiens or coleus, so it's a good idea to include such a ready indicator in the bed as a kind of early warning system for dry spells.

Ferns can be safely transplanted any time but summer. The fall or winter dormant season is easier because it isn't necessary to transfer as much real estate along with the roots. Planting a newly purchased dormant fern right out of the box presents a puzzle. Sometimes the rhizome has been so neatly shorn of accompanying roots and stems or they are so shriveled that I can't for the life of me figure out which is the top and which the bottom. Somewhere I think I heard that you can get by with planting them on their side, if you can figure out where that is. At any rate, plant them shallowly—not over an inch deep.

The maidenhair ferns are the most requested ferns at the botanical garden's annual plant sale, and yet they are among the more challenging choices for most gardens, needing high humidity and soil moisture and being, I find, difficult to move. When I lived on Ewing Street, Charlie Higgins gave me several young maidenhairs, both the northern maidenhair (*Adiantum pedatum*) and the southern (*A. capillus-veneris*). They survived but failed to thrive in the moistest, mulchiest bed I had to offer and they failed even to survive the move to our present home—at least for long. I believe one of the southern maidenhairs came up for a time the second year, but the tough, compacted soil and possibly the dry weather did it in.

Northern maidenhair, so I've read, likes acid soil, while southern maidenhair is found "on limestone softened by waterfall spray," according to one reference. I doubt that it's really that particular, but I'm sure having a waterfall on the premises doesn't hurt.

The northern maidenhair reminds me a bit of a circular TV antenna, as the wiry, near-black stalk splits into a pair of stems that curve around almost to the point of meeting. The dark, bluish-green pinnae (leaflets) fan out from the center of the circle. The southern maidenhair is the more delicate-looking. The semicircular pinnules are folded along the outer edge and have fanlike veining which gives them the appearance of tiny ginkgo leaves. The frond is airy and triangular. Both ferns spread slowly by creeping rhizomes (in Charlie's yard maybe).

The holly ferns are increasingly popular, for they cut a striking figure with their upswept fronds of large, almost leathery pinnae, and they endure the trials of summer with ease. *Cyrtomium falcatum* has very dark green, glossy fronds with coarse, wavy pinnae. *Cyrtomium fortunei* has a dull leaf. Both are at least semievergreen, which in the case of my *C. fortunei* means that by winter's end the part that is still standing is broken in the middle. Holly ferns make excellent houseplants, too, since they tolerate dry air.

Christmas fern (*Polystichum acrostichoides*) is less coarse than the holly fern and has the advantage of being evergreen, though, admittedly, the ample, dark green fronds with their characteristic boot-shaped pinnae are decidedly shopworn by winter's end. This husky, two-and-a-half-foot fern will make an extremely handsome clump in time, a fine accent for a shady border.

Wallich's wood fern (*Dryopteris wallichiana*), with its crisp, lacquered, three-foot fronds, is another excellent fern, which, though advertised as evergreen, certainly isn't with me. The yellow-green new fronds contrast sharply with the forest green of older fronds. It does, however, have slug appeal.

Almost as elegant as the lady fern, but with a broader, toothier, more durable frond, is the southern shield, or hammock, fern (*Thelypteris kunthii*). The color is a mild green, and the fern colonizes rapidly into a cool, waist-high wave.

The Japanese climbing fern (*Lygodium japonicum*) climbs by twining its spaghettilike frond tips around the nearest suitably thin object, be it a chain-link fence or another vine. This lacy, bright green fern can skitter ten or fifteen feet into a tree (even more near the Gulf, where it remains green all winter and is making a serious nuisance of itself). My favorite way to use this delicately airy fern is to train it into a Japanese maple, for the palmately lobed green pinnules mimic the maple's leaf and contrast vividly with the tree's flaming autumn colors. Japanese climbing fern lives forever under a variety of soil conditions and even takes full sun. But Zone 7, I believe, is its uppermost hardiness limit. It is late to come up in spring here, sometimes waiting till June.

The Japanese climbing fern is related to the Hartford fern (*L. palmatum*), native to the eastern United States. This is a difficult plant and very rare, so I am glad I've not seen it offered in catalogs in quite some time, for it was virtually always wild-dug. I confess I once purchased (and murdered) one myself.

Planted with sensitive fern and the osmundas, a constantly wet area can be transformed into a positively prehistoric landscape. The osmundas (cinnamon, interrupted, and royal ferns) reach from four to six feet in height in sun or shade, as long as the ground is wet (the wetter the taller).

Sensitive fern (*Onoclea sensibilis*) is more arching and creeping in habit. The widespread, wavy teeth give the light green sterile fronds the look of an old, well-used comb. The pinnules of the fertile fronds, which appear at the end of a stiff stalk in late summer, are rolled up so tightly they resemble clusters of brown beads. The stalk stands all winter, and the spores are released in spring.

Cinnamon fern (*Osmunda cinnamomea*) is an imposing beauty, first sending up fiddleheads that unreel to become wandlike fertile fronds bearing opposite cone-shaped clusters of balllike spore cases. These are at first green, later rusty brown. Around them emerge plumelike, light green sterile fronds whose long, toothy pinnae are tufted with stiff brown hair where they join the rachis.

Interrupted fern (*O. claytoniana*) is similar, but the fronds at the center of the plant are "interrupted" in the middle by a band consisting of conelike pairs of spore-bearing pinnae, which drop away in late spring, leaving the fronds curiously gapped.

Royal fern (*O. regalis*) is easily mistaken for something other than a fern. Its twice-divided leaves are frequently compared to those of the locust tree (*Gleditsia*). The fronds culminate in a panicle of tight spore clusters, which turn brown once the spores are shed.

Ferns, of course, need no pruning other than the occasional removal of dead fronds. Organic mulches often supply all the nutrients ferns need, but extra nitrogen can make them lusher, so you might elect to apply a well-diluted liquid fertilizer occasionally. Don't use insecticides or fungicides on ferns unless the label specifically states that the product is safe for ferns. Many ferns (notably the osmundas) send up a single major set of fronds each year, and, if these are damaged, the plant may never recover.

Certain ferns (here I'm thinking of the athyriums in particular) occasionally contract a white fungus at the base of the fronds. Ross Hunter, who grows some of the nicest athyriums I've seen in these parts, told me he treats this affliction by removing affected foliage and drenching the crown with terraclor (one tablespoon per gallon of water).

HOSTA

Hostas are a great investment. Except, perhaps, for the very tiniest of the dwarfs, which make no more than a snack for a hungry slug, a hosta will likely survive indefinitely, slowly expanding into a broader and broader clump. And while breeders are working to give hostas larger, showier flowers, it is primarily for the foliage that we grow this rich and varied genus. (I've read there's work afoot to cross the hosta with fellow lily family member *Hemerocallis*, the daylily. Imagine the possibilities!)

Most of the twenty or so distinct species of hosta are native to mountainous parts of Japan, where they are often cultivated for food. The Japanese also use hostas as pot plants and as ornamental garden perennials, and the showy leaves are incorporated into flower arrangements.

Few plants offer such a wealth of choices for size, texture, habit, and leaf shape and color. Certain hostas can be used as edgers, for they have a low, horizontal habit and yet do not creep stoloniferously. Leaves showing a great deal of white or yellow are reflective and can often take more sun than blue or solid green hostas. 'Gold Edger', for example, quickly forms neat mounds a foot across and not quite as high. The heart-shaped leaves are greenish-yellow and very tolerant of sun. They are topped by racemes of lavender flowers in midsummer. Hostas vary in their appeal to slugs, and this one is rated slug-resistant. 'Golden Tiara' is another perky little edger. It has heart-shaped green leaves that are softly edged with yellow and purple flowers. 'Golden Tiara' can take sun up to three quarters of the day.

Hosta tardiflora is a lance-leaved, dark green species hosta rated excellent for edging, even in full sun. It grows fast and blooms late, sending up its long-lasting lavender flowers in autumn.

Certain hostas are especially useful as groundcovers, stubbornly spreading to squeeze and shade out the weeds in their midst. 'Francee', for instance, makes rapidly expanding mounds of two-foot, dark green leaves, snappily edged in bright white. The lavender blooms come in midsummer. Up to three-quarters sun is acceptable.

'Shade Master' is exquisite to fill and illuminate a corner darkened by a mass of rhododendrons or hollies. The broad, deeply grooved, lime-gold leaves form a mound two feet high and wider than high. This hosta, too, takes a fair amount of (but not full) sun and has lavender midsummer blooms. 'Gold Standard' is another good yellow. The leaves are yellow brushed with green along the margins. Lavender flowers appear in midsummer.

One of the finest groundcover hostas is 'Ground Master', a fast-growing, stoloniferous, low mounding plant whose long green leaves are margined with

*Our southern native
azaleas bring a
cheerful airiness
to the spring scene.*

PHOTOGRAPH BY
PAT GARDNER

April

May

June

A frazzled puff of creamy bloom, fringe tree glows like a halo when suffused with sunlight.

PHOTOGRAPH BY
ELSABE HOLST-WEBSTER

Now, really, isn't this bellwort the saddest-looking plant you've ever seen in your life?

PHOTOGRAPH BY
CAROL B. HIPPS

*Shooting star
combines dramatic
beauty and grace
with rugged longevity.*

PHOTOGRAPH BY
PAT GARDNER

April

❧

May

❧

June

Even at the height of summer, 'Double Delight', a hybrid tea rose, bears luscious, two-toned blossoms.

PHOTOGRAPH BY
PAT GARDNER

Foxglove is an old-fashioned garden flower with an air of mystery.

PHOTOGRAPH BY
CAROL B. HIPPS

April
❧
May
❧
June

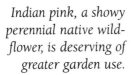

*Indian pink, a showy
perennial native wild-
flower, is deserving of
greater garden use.*

PHOTOGRAPH BY
ELSABE HOLST-WEBSTER

*A blue-flowering
clematis gussies up
a downspout.*

PHOTOGRAPH BY
DANIEL LITTLE

In June, the daylily reigns supreme.

PHOTOGRAPH BY
PAT GARDNER

A bank of cucumber-cool bigleaf hydrangeas makes a pool of shade all the more inviting.

PHOTOGRAPH BY
CAROL B. HIPPS

April

≈

May

≈

June

*Dwarf lady fern
(Athyrium filix-
femina var. minutis-
simum) mingles
charmingly with hosta
and ajuga in the shady
summer garden.*

PHOTOGRAPH BY
CAROL B. HIPPS

*Golden-rain tree—
an unbeatable shade
tree for a yard of any
size, large or small.*

PHOTOGRAPH BY
CAROL B. HIPPS

white. In late summer it erupts into lavender bloom. Planted in sufficient quantity, this hosta will control erosion. This is not to be confused with 'Grand Master', considered an improvement over 'Francee', with puckered, blue-green leaves edged in white, good pest resistance, and sun tolerance.

'Hadspen Blue' is one of the best blue groundcovers with heart-shaped, disease- and pest-resistant powdery blue leaves and lavender flowers in late summer. *Hosta tokudama*, a species hosta, makes spreading, foot-tall mounds of puckered blue leaves and produces eighteen-inch scapes of white flowers in early summer. The blues are best with considerable shade.

Hostas can be used in the composition of extraordinarily beautiful garden "pictures." For example, at the Birmingham Botanical Garden I was recently smitten by the cool, harmonious beauty of a shady scene in which a bank of oakleaf hydrangea was planted to the rear of a sea of the dainty variegated ivy 'Glacier', which flowed over the edge of a stone wall. And up through the ivy, just in front of the hydrangeas, came luxuriant specimens of Japanese painted fern and the enormous *Hosta* 'Sum and Substance', its huge, rubbery leaves glowing lime in the morning light, and the equally imposing, variegated *H.* 'Birchwood Elegance'.

Hostas are excellent to plant among bulbs and spring ephemerals, sending up their spears of furled leaves as the early bloomers decline. They work well in the shade garden in combination with epimedium, carex, helleborus, heuchera, liriope, ophiopogon, polygonatum, and pulmonaria, many of which are themselves available in assorted colors and variegated forms.

The small hostas are just as versatile and showy in their way as their larger counterparts. I, however, have not been lucky with the very small hostas. Twice, Mike Gibson has given me miniatures with narrow, pointed, four-inch leaves. As long as I kept them in a pot by the front steps (winter and summer) they lived. As soon as I decided they'd be cute in a pouch of soil tucked between a couple of rocks, I lost them. But some people do successfully grow the small hostas in rock gardens, in pockets of loose soil among tree roots, in masonry gaps, in planters on shaded patios, and among low-growing shade plants like wild ginger and partridge berry (*Mitchella repens*).

In full bloom *H. venusta* 'Shining Tot' would fit into a soup can. It is no more than a stack of shiny little green leaves topped by a few skinny stalks bearing white, tubular flowers. It will do with sun or shade.

The purple-flowering 'Sitting Pretty' has yellow-centered leaves streaked with green on the edges. It makes a cheerful little mound, six inches high by eight inches wide.

Hosta tokudama 'Little Aurora' is a puckered gold. *Hosta tardiana* 'Blue Moon' is a rich blue miniature.

I didn't realize until recently that one could grow hostas indoors over winter. The trick is to bring them inside before the temperature drops to 45 degrees Fahrenheit, otherwise they'll think they're entitled to a dormant period. Pot them in an equal mix of sand, loam, and leaf mold. Pay careful attention to watering, keeping them moist but never soggy. I suspect that watering the pot from the bottom might prevent soil compaction, which can suffocate the roots.

While we think of hostas as needing shade and ample water, in Japan various species are adapted to a widely varying range of ecological niches. For example, *H. longissima* is a bog-dweller with deep-green, straplike leaves. It has virtually no drought tolerance. *Hosta kikutii*, however, is an inhabitant of rocky outcroppings, and its shiny, wavy-edged leaves greet dry spells with indifference. Hostas derived from *H. sieboldiana* are often quite versatile in this regard, adapting to either wet or dry conditions. If a particular hosta fails to thrive in a particular site, try the plant in another location and try a different hosta at the first site.

Hostas are pH-tolerant, but, if you asked them, they'd probably tell you they like their soil at about pH 6. Any average garden soil suits hostas. They find the going rough in either pure sand or clay. I toss a layer of leaves over my hostas in late autumn, but this isn't necessary with established clumps. A slow-release fertilizer in spring or a squirt of liquid fertilizer from time to time during spring and summer may yield lusher growth.

Brown leaf margins suggest thirst. Hostas stand up to hose pipe brutality pretty well, I find, but some growers are reluctant to use an overhead spray of water on their blue hostas, insisting that this damages the waxy blue coating. I dunno. The wax on my 'Frances Williams' is pretty hard to scuff off with my thumbnail. She's used to the hose.

Early spring is the best time to divide and plant hostas. The more dirt you take with the division the more root hairs will be transported along to provide it nourishment. Established clumps can be moved any time. Water them well afterward.

PURPLE CONEFLOWER

The purple coneflower (*Echinacea purpurea*) is one of the great delights of the warm season garden, for it brings not just its own warm pink cheerfulness onto the scene, but the bold blossoms with their orange or auburn centers and bright pink ray flowers serve as feeding platforms for dancing butterflies, no-nonsense bumblebees, nasty-tempered crab spiders, and a host of other creatures.

Purple coneflower is an easy, forgiving, long-lived perennial, somewhere between two and four feet tall. The deep green leaves are elongate and scratchy, the flower stems stiff and thick.

The plant likes moist but not soggy soil, good ventilation, and some sun. It will grow and bloom in full shade, but the ray flowers are less colorful.

Though *E. purpurea* is the echinacea most often seen in gardens, there are several other North American species, including *E. pallida*, with very thin, drooping pink ray flowers ("petals," for all practical purposes); *E. tennesseensis*, the exceedingly rare Tennessee coneflower, with ray flowers that stand out stiffly around the sides of the central cone; and the practically mythical *yellow* purple coneflower, *E. paradoxa*. Though it is on the Federal Endangered Species List, Tennessee coneflower is available from a few nurseries licensed to propagate it.

With these coneflowers, as with the black-eyed Susans, individual flower heads last an incredibly long time, for the true, fertile flowers, found within the cone itself, bloom slowly over a period of many days or even weeks in ever-shrinking concentric circles. In any cut-flower arrangement the purple coneflowers are the last to go. The dark brown, uncomfortably prickly seed heads are not so bad in dried arrangements, either.

Many of the "cultivars" listed in catalogs are propagated by seed rather than vegetatively and some variation is to be expected. (Frankly, plants propagated vegetatively over the years incorporate accumulated mutations into their genetic recipe, so that changes creep into the stock. All things change; nothing stays the same. I think some rock 'n' roll singer said that.)

Echinacea purpurea 'Bright Star' is the purple coneflower most familiar to catalog browsers, and it is a beauty, with a bright orange cone further warmed by gradually descending, vivid pink rays. This strain was my introduction to the genus, and I fell in love.

In the backyard now I also have *E. purpurea* 'Bravado', given to me several years ago by Mary Lou McNabb. The cone is dark bronze, and the deep pink rays stand out stiffly. There are various white forms of *E. purpurea*. I regret I lost the 'White Swan' Mary Lou gave me. (I'm not hinting for a replacement.) Echinaceas don't always stand their ground when pressed by aggressors, particularly during dry spells.

Purple coneflower is also subject to the same fuzzy white fungal disorder that almost annually afflicts rudbeckias once the hot, dry weather begins, attacking at the soil line and causing entire stems to wilt. It seldom kills the plant outright, though.

An even more curious malady afflicts one of my favorite coneflowers. Instead of producing orange cones with long, extra-purple rays, the plant makes stubby little green ray flowers, and from the abnormally soft, green cones emerge long stalks bearing treelike bunches of more green flowers. Weird. The condition appears to return indefinitely. I suspect a virus.

QUEEN ANNE'S LACE

With its delicate, fernlike foliage and dancing umbels of crisp white flowers, Queen Anne's lace (*Daucus carota*) is America's (and possibly the world's) favorite roadside weed. In many ways it is the ideal garden flower, too. It is obviously beautiful and even enhances the colors of surrounding flowers. It is self-perpetuating and needs no care. And this Eurasian immigrant is not offered in catalogs because, having insinuated itself virtually everywhere, its seeds are everywhere free for the taking. Oh, and the root, its first year, is more or less edible, if you like carrots, for *D. carota* is the ancestor of *D. sativa*, the cultivated carrot.

Here I'd better mention, though, that Queen Anne's lace bears an uncanny resemblance to poison hemlock (*Conium maculatum*, an herb completely unrelated to the hemlock tree), a European weed now almost as wide-ranging in North America as *D. carota*, and, yes, the source of the poison used to silence Socrates. Queen Anne's lace has a tiny little dark reddish floret in the center of the umbel to distinguish it from hemlock. Who the heck eats Queen Anne's lace anyway?

This elegant runaway carrot, whose lovely common name supposedly commemorates Queen Anne's great fondness for flowers, creates a fire-and-ice effect when grown with red or orange lilies or daylilies or even with cannas. In rich garden soil where it may vault to five feet, Queen Anne's lace can be cut back before bloom to keep it in scale with the likes of butterfly weed or purple coneflower. It mingles beautifully with hollyhocks and larkspur and brings brightness and an airy fullness to cut-flower arrangements. Its pollen sheds like mad on the dining room table, though. (Some arrangers spray the flowers with a sticky sealant, but I doubt this works perfectly, since flowers are never still.)

In the beginning the inflorescence resembles an inverted bird cage, which gradually stretches open to form a broadly rounded umbel of minute, lacy flowers resembling a fancy parasol. Once the flowers are pollinated (by all manner of small critters, most of whom I can't identify), the umbel again contracts, clutching the developing seeds, which look like hairy little bugs (oops, some of them *are* bugs), in a kind of cage, or nest.

Once the plant starts to look ratty, I pull it up (it will die as soon as the seeds are set anyway), cut off the seed heads, and sprinkle the seed wherever I imagine I'll want the flowers next year. Well-prepared ground works best even with this supremely successful weed. A few of the new plants that get started this year will bloom in the fall, but most will bloom (and die) next year.

OENOTHERA

I grow two oenotheras, or evening primroses, which I think deserve a place in every garden, though they are frowned upon as weeds. The showy evening primrose, *Oenothera speciosa*, is an adorable little roadside-hugger that blooms in solid sheets of light-catching pale pink in late spring and early summer. It is far prettier along the poor dry side of a hot, sunny road than in rich garden soil, where it spreads for miles, lunges to three feet high, and bears but a few scant flowers, for it is too fat and well-fed to bother about reproducing itself. If it is to be pretty it must be cut back with a vengeance and otherwise neglected.

After bloom I yank up all the showy evening primroses I can find, confident I'll miss enough for the next year. Besides, all oenotheras seed themselves with great skill.

The other weedy oenothera I love is *O. erythrosepala*, which is almost identical to *O. biennis*, the common tall, yellow-flowering, lemon-scented biennial evening primrose, but with a larger, differently scented flower.

The first year this evening primrose makes a wheellike rosette of flat, paddlelike leaves. The following June a great branching bloom stalk rises up out of the rosette, somewhere between five and eight feet tall. The fun comes in when the blooms begin to open. As dusk settles over the hollow (or hill, depending on location), a fresh crop of buds begin visibly to swell and stir. Suddenly a sepal flicks back and a petal begins to unfurl. More sepals and petals spring into action and soon the plant is liberally decorated with four-inch yellow blossoms. These release a heady fragrance to summon the hawk moths, which hover before them like hummingbirds to withdraw their nectar. (Actually you may have to wait awhile for the hawk moths. It's a little like watching for meteors.)

Weeks go by and the show is repeated every night with flowers higher up the stem. But the blossoms grow steadily smaller, and the plant takes on a tired, run-down look. Though I sometimes remove them at this stage, I always leave a few, for the sparrows and finches find the ripe seed capsules most appealing. The candelabralike stems are sturdy and can be used as temporary trellises for summer vines like morning glory and hyacinth bean.

I particularly like to pair this oenothera with American bellflower (*Campanula americana*), whose true blue is musical with the oenothera's primrose yellow blossoms, which stay open to entertain the bumblebees until about noon. Biennial evening primrose works well with larkspur and hollyhock, too.

BUTTERFLY WEED

Butterfly weed (*Asclepias tuberosa*), with its clustered umbels of unique, burning orange flowers, is the showiest native member of the milkweed family.

Once established in the garden it is long-lived in most well-drained soils. In fields it blooms with Queen Anne's lace and common yarrow (*Achillea millefolium*); on our mountainsides it blooms in sunny spots with the prairie coneflower (*Ratibida pinnata*); and in the garden it amplifies the cheery brightness of *Coreopsis verticillata*.

Don't hesitate to cut the flowers for the house. The cut stem will fork and make two new flower clusters for every one cut off.

By summer's end the stocky, knee-high clumps of narrow-leaved, dark green foliage are tipped with fuzzy, tapered, okralike seedpods, which split to release silk-winged seeds.

Should you decide to liberate a butterfly weed from a construction site (the one I had on Ewing came from a field targeted for an interstate interchange, so I felt no guilt in removing it), you're going to need a serious digging tool, for the thick tubers are deeply and firmly entrenched. This, of course, gives the plant its imperviousness to drought and possibly accounts for its tardy appearance in spring.

Yes, butterfly weed is attractive to butterflies, particularly monarchs and swallowtails, and serves as the corner cafe to an assortment of vividly colorful beetles and to a milkweed-loving orange aphid which may become so numerous as to rival the flowers for attention. Wash these off with the hose.

GLADIOLUS

I always have a few gladiolus about the place, and they do me proud in June. All were acquired as freebies in orders of other plants, but, planted in a dinner-plate-sized clump and surrounded by a cheap hoop cage (if you paint it black or green it disappears), they erupt into rigid bouquets of multi-colored ruffled bloom, giving the neighbors (so I like to pretend) the impression that a *real* gardener lives here (or a florist, perhaps). Admittedly, they do look a bit formal for my disheveled garden. As the spikes of color wane, I plant morning glories and hyacinth beans around the cages to give us something more exciting to look at for the rest of the summer than a sheaf of four-foot swordlike leaves.

Glads behave pretty much like ordinary perennials in the South and should persist indefinitely, barring disease, so long as they're grown in full sun in moist, well-fed, well-drained acid soil. You will have to stake or corral them, though, or they'll fall on their fancy faces.

I think that for effect gladiolus are prettier planted in masses or crowded clumps than in neat rows. If you're growing them for cut flowers, however, you might prefer a practical arrangement. You can plant glads successively (from March through July, so I've read), spacing them six or eight inches apart (and four inches down). In fall dig the corms back up. Cut off the leaves, discard the flat, tired mother corm, and separate the new corms. Dust them with malathion (or seal them up with moth flakes for two weeks to kill thrips) and store them in a cool, dry place for the winter.

If thrips have been a problem, the following spring you can soak the corms in one-and-a-half teaspoons of Lysol to a gallon of water before setting them back out. I think thrips become more troublesome once the weather gets hot. In a desperate case you might try cutting off the foliage just before it yellows in late summer in hopes the thrips haven't yet migrated down to the corm for the winter.

I suppose the goldenrain tree (*Koelreuteria paniculata*) gets its name from the showers of golden, starlike blossoms with which it muffles the sidewalks in late June, as the bold, spiky panicles of radiant bloom give way to pendant clusters of pale green, balloonlike seedpods.

Goldenrain tree is an attractive, well-behaved tree, usually of modest proportions. The dark green, ragged-edged, pinnately compound leaves resemble those of trumpet creeper and form a dark, umbrellalike canopy that casts an inviting pool of shade.

The tree will grow anywhere the soil drains. My only complaint with goldenrain tree is that the papery seedpods, which pass from tender green to a pleasing yellow, turn a lifeless rusty brown by late summer and hang on for many weeks.

Powdery Mildew

By the end of June we're starting to see powdery mildew on phlox, crapemyrtle, and a host of other plants. Powdery mildew differs from most other fungal afflictions (including downy mildew) in that its spores do not germinate on a film of water but rather on a dry surface. Thus the warm, dry days of summer encourage its proliferation. I know we're told again and again that overhead watering encourages fungal disease, but powdery mildew is one disease I rarely see on a plant that's regularly bathed with the hose.

Some gardeners believe that a solution of dishwashing detergent affords protection from powdery mildew. And, of course, there are always fungicides, but these are best applied before the disease has permanently marred leaves.

Though the ground grows drier daily, still the weeds come to crowd the newly emerged seedlings of balsam and *Salvia coccinea*. "Weed 'em and reap," my husband says.

July

A kind of siege mentality settles on us in July. By day we scurry from house to car to office, library, or store to avoid as best we can the relentless heat. Through the window the midday garden appears as limp and miserable as we ourselves would be, were we out in it, and there's a feeling that both time and life have ground to a halt.

But mornings are still (briefly) pure and dewy, and a stroll around the garden surprises us with the revelation that some thirty different kinds of flowers are in bloom.

Water We Must

We have to water now, and only robins find cause for joy, as they feast on the worms that rise wherever the sprinkler whirls. Sprinkling is not the most efficient way to water, of course—so much is lost to runoff and evaporation. And dragging heavy hoses around and running back and forth from sprinkler to faucet to adjust the area of coverage gets tiresome.

The ideal is supposed to be an underground (or otherwise low-lying) irrigation system that snakes about the property, turning itself on and off with timers, while we're off jetting around to the great gardens of Europe for the summer. But no matter how carefully installed, these setups are likely to miss a spot here or there. And some of us little-old-lady types lack funds for such extravagance and are intimidated, besides, by the elaborate instructions that came with the timer we got for Mother's Day, and so we continue to hand-water with the hose—backyard beds in the early morning when we go out to feed the birds, front yard beds after supper when it gets too dark to pull weeds.

Hand-watering is very soothing, very Zen. In the evenings especially, we feel blessed as we sense the silent, shadowy outline of an owl glide past and come face to face with a hovering hawk moth among the ghostly evening primroses. (I used to make a wish on the evening star while I was at it, but the results have been disappointing.)

Hand-watering is said to be bad for the plants, that it encourages the development of shallow roots. Water well (an inch or more) once a week, we're told. But this doesn't keep the top inch or two of soil from baking to a crisp in the sun, and if seeds are to sprout and seedlings grow, the soil needs to stay damp on top. Besides, some of us contrary little old ladies get quite presentable results and keep our water bills down to boot.

I never water grass, though. It's against my religion.

RUDBECKIA

Our native rudbeckias ignite a warm glow within the hearts of their beholders. No other flower projects such an innocent insouciance and an uncomplicated joie de vivre. It is impossible to look at a pitcher of black-eyed Susans without smiling (particularly if it's on someone else's dining room table and there are ants crawling all over it).

The most common garden rudbeckia is *Rudbeckia hirta* in its sundry variations. The fancier concoctions with bands of red or mahogany encircling the cone and sometimes with doubling of the rays, as in the 'Nutmeg' strain, are often called gloriosa daisies, though originally 'Gloriosa Daisy' was the cultivar name for a tetraploid strain with six-inch daisies flushed with shades of brown and red.

Gloriosa daisies have not been long-lived with me, but Inge Paul has them every year. They mingle with her lavender phlox, and, though you'd expect such a combination to be harrowing, it's actually pleasantly stunning.

Rudbeckia hirta thrives in average, sunny garden conditions, spreading slowly into drifts of coarse, fuzzy leaves which for weeks in summer and often into fall are hidden by a solid sweep of relentlessly cheerful color. Individual plants are not necessarily long-lived, and, unless you grow this rudbeckia in great quantity, you might want to save a little seed each year for insurance. Usually, however, rudbeckias seed themselves with proficiency.

The popular cultivar (or perhaps, more appropriately, strain) 'Goldsturm' is a selection of the closely related *R. fulgida* var. *sullivantii*, which crowns three-foot stems with rich yellow black-eyed daisies.

The three-lobed coneflower (*R. triloba*) is a stiff, profusely branching annual liberally sprinkled with countless yellow, brown-eyed daisies less than two inches across. You can grow this supremely adaptable plant in almost every conceivable situation. It grows naturally in the woods and along roadsides. It blooms out of cracks in the sidewalk. It adores gardens, where, in rich, fluffy, moist dirt it billows into a golden cloud, some five feet high and nearly as wide, and proceeds to shade out its more mannerly neighbors. And it sets seed by the thousands, all of which apparently germinate, for the next year you'll be down on hands and knees from February until May, scratching at a haze of fuzzy little *R. triloba* seedlings.

This irresistibly winsome thug should be reserved for naturalized, woody settings, meadows, and along the back fence, where it can duke it out with other bullies. Mercifully, it dies after bloom.

The green-headed coneflower (*R. laciniata*) reminds me a great deal of the prairie coneflower (*Ratibida pinnata*), for the rays are reflexed and of a softer yellow than other rudbeckias; the cone, or eye, is green where the fertile flowers have not yet opened and the leaves are similarly pinnate. It gets far taller than *R. pinnata*, however, reaching eight feet in moist ground, though the stems are not weatherproof.

Rudbeckia maxima is even more gigantic, stretching its brown, thumblike cones skirted with reflexed, sunshine yellow rays to eight feet or more on stiff stems, the lower reaches of which are clasped by large cuplike, blue-green leaves.

Among the rudbeckias that fall into the not-so-much-pretty-as-interesting category is the six-foot *R. occidentalis* 'Green Wizard', which completely lacks ray flowers and just presents knobby dark brown cones against a collar of pointed green sepals.

Rudbeckia 'Sputnik', to three feet, is a bit of an oddball, too, with the chocolate brown of the cone bleeding onto the ray flowers so that the flower is more brown than golden and has a plush, teddy bear quality.

With their unassuming informality rudbeckias bring something of the freedom of the open prairie to a landscape when combined with ornamental grasses like *Miscanthus sinensis* 'Morning Light' or the dwarf pampas grass, *Cortaderia selloana* 'Pumila'. Their brilliant yellows mix charmingly with the blues of *Campanula americana* or *Lobelia siphilitica*.

Rudbeckias are touted as drought-resistant, but really they are healthier and prettier when watered well at least weekly. They are prone to a hot-weather fungus that attacks right at the soil line, causing the stem to wilt and die. At the botanical garden we see this condition most often in dry, crowded stands. I suspect it is southern blight (*Sclerotium rolfsii*). Pest damage on rudbeckias is minimal.

LIATRIS

We have half a dozen species of *Liatris* in Alabama, including, so I've read, the florist's beloved *Liatris spicata*, known as dense blazing star, or gay feather, though I've not stumbled upon it in the wild. This striking member of the aster family is said to inhabit low, moist ground throughout the eastern two thirds of the country.

Dense blazing star produces a dramatic spike of bloom, unusual in that the small, thistlelike, violet-purple flowers appear first at the top of the bloom spike and then proceed to bloom their way down the stalk. The foliage is narrow and grasslike, the leaves coming right off the bloom stalk.

Liatris spicata is a tall plant, to five feet, but is more often seen in the garden in lower-growing cultivars like 'Kobold'. It is a magnet for butterflies and, even after bloom, the statuesque stalks bearing clublike clusters of furry brown seeds retain a commanding presence.

Dense blazing star is easy from seed and grows well even in a large, well-watered container in full sun, where it coexists contentedly with tulips, annuals, and even ajuga for a long season of interest. It multiplies rapidly to make an imposing clump.

Occasionally one sees a white cultivar, such as 'Snow White' or the slightly taller (to three or four feet) 'Floristan White'.

SUMMER PHLOX

All sixty of the world's phlox species are native to North America (*Phlox sibirica* is found in both Alaska and Siberia). We have many phloxes in the Southeast, some of them summer-blooming, and I can't pretend to recognize them all on sight. Most of our perennial summer garden cultivars are selections of *P. paniculata*, native throughout much of the eastern half of the country. This tall, fragrant, clump-forming species features dense, somewhat triangular panicles of salver-form—that is to say, "tray-shaped," or flat-faced—five-lobed tubular flowers in colors ranging from white through assorted pinks and purples to crimson. There is no yellow, and I've not seen a blue that wasn't really lavender.

Summer phlox is not the easiest of garden flowers. It must have fertile, loose, constantly moist but well-drained soil in either full or part sun. A shot of fertilizer makes for more blooms and a longer flowering period. Cultivated varieties must be deadheaded (that is, the spent blossoms should be removed), for their seedlings will likely revert to the ancestral magenta form, a form so vigorous that it will soon crowd out the cultivar.

Some of these old magenta phloxes are astonishingly tough. I've seen them grow tall and strong and bloom even after being absorbed into the dry shade of a neglected hedge. Of course, many gardeners are content with this form, which requires far less maintenance than cultivated show-offs like the brilliant white 'Mt. Fuji' or the prissy dwarf 'Pinafore Pink'.

Not only must phlox be faithfully deadheaded, but every few years the clump must be rejuvenated by division in spring. Discard the older portion of the clump and replant (an inch or two deep) a few healthy young crowns, spacing them a foot or more apart. Crowding and poor ventilation contribute to mildew, the great curse of all summer phlox. Those grown in shade suffer most of all, it seems to me.

Phlox can also be propagated by stem and root cuttings. Roots can be snipped into one-inch sections and sprinkled over potting soil, covered lightly with sand, and kept moist in a cold frame over winter. (Not *my* cold frame, yours—mine's full of slugs.) Propagation by root cuttings and replanting in fresh soil can eliminate stem eelworms, a problem in some areas. Dusting with sulfur addresses both hot weather spider mite buildup and, to some extent, the mildew scourge.

For a number of years I grew 'Miss Lingard', a very old white form of *P. carolina*, which blooms early, in May and June. I grew it primarily for sentimental reasons, because it was a favorite of the late Jim Crockett, the much-loved original host of Public TV's *Victory Garden*. Although the catalogs brag that 'Miss Lingard' is mildew-resistant, most years the mildew on mine outshone the flowers. *Phlox carolina* is available in the rosy-pink 'Rosalinde' and the salmon-pink 'Gloriosa', as well.

CLEOME

If summer phlox proves to be more trouble than it's worth in your garden, and yet you still long for a tall plant with a bold, bright flower head to create a similar effect, you might try spider flower (*Cleome hasslerana*). This South American annual bears airy, rather globular racemes of white buds which turn dark pink before spreading into four-petaled pink flowers which then fade back to white as the day wears on. The flowers have exceedingly long stamens and an ovary on an extended stipe that continues to elongate after bloom, so that the slender seedpods, together with the spidery stamens, give the inflorescence the look of a Sputnik satellite or perhaps a mid-1950s living room light fixture.

The petals wilt during the middle of a hot day, but the filamentous flower heads are spectacular when backlit by the morning or late afternoon sun.

Though the flowers have a faintly pleasant scent, the foliage is malodorous and reminds me a bit of certain insecticides. The palmately divided leaves are sticky and spined near the base. The stiff, strong, four- to five-foot stems are leafless near the bottom, so the plant is best skirted with a cloud of *Artemisia ludoviciana* 'Silver King' or frothy blue caryopteris.

Cleome is as easy and trouble-free as any garden flower can be. It germinates and grows quickly in almost any soil. Indeed, it is said of this plant that "once you have it, you have it," for it seeds itself reliably every year. The seedlings, in fact, should be thinned or they'll be spindly and short compared to those given room to stretch their muscles. They may bloom as early as June.

Cutting back tall, tired cleome in late summer does not encourage a new flush of bloom, I find, but it's easy enough to start new seed in midsummer for a fresh supply of flowers in fall. Cleome is an exquisite cut flower, opening fresh whorls of bloom for several days.

Cleome is offered by seed in white ('Helen Campbell'), carmine, violet, and rose and in mixtures. I can't recall, but I believe that mine originated from the 'Queen' mixture many years ago, and I like it so well that I'm unwilling to introduce another strain to the yard, for I've never seen another display of cleome with such big, bright blossoms (the inflorescence can be six or more inches across).

Hawk moths—nocturnal hummingbirds without the hum—flutter around cleome by moonlight, but the plant attracts few pests save the odd green caterpillar and a rare invasion of harlequin bugs, whose black, orange, and white shields clash tastelessly with the pastel blossoms. These bugs are so colorfully patterned that I've been tempted to string them like beads for a necklace (a great gift idea for the budget-conscious, no doubt).

COSMOS

The only floral color combination that grates on my sensibilities is that of pink or lavender with hard orange. And yet when the cleome and the descendants of the Klondyke cosmos 'Bright Lights' bloom together with their marvelous self-sown fecundity, my garden seems almost a study in pink and orange, and I find myself helpless to counter their overpowering exuberance.

'Bright Lights' is a yellow, gold, orange, and scarlet strain of *Cosmos sulphureus*, which hails from Mexico, nowhere near the Klondike. Until it blooms, this tall, irrepressibly vigorous plant could easily be mistaken for a ragweed, given the bipinnate cut of the leaf. It is a rapid grower, sometimes going through several generations in a single summer. The needlelike brown seeds are profusely produced and can be sprinkled over prepared ground wherever fast color is wanted.

I am far less successful with the seemingly more delicate, disease-prone, fern-leaved *C. bipinnatus* strains like the white form of 'Sensation'. I grow this one for its sparkling, shell-like blossoms, which draw together in harmony otherwise dissonant color combinations. But I always lose a good portion of these seedlings to disease, whether I start them in the ground or in cell packs, and even as adults they are less vigorous and shorter-lived than *C. suphureus* varieties.

Cosmos enjoy full sun and almost any soil. They can be pinched back when young for extra fullness, less height, and more flowers. Tall specimens are stunning when viewed against a dark background of evergreen shrubs or in an elevated container against the blue sky. They are first-rate cut flowers, too.

FOUR O'CLOCK

The four-o'clock (*Mirabilis jalapa*) is a most serviceable perennial for the South. Planted thickly, it can make a flowing, three-foot hedge or a colorful cloud around a mailbox. The fragrant, funnel-form, two-inch flowers are clustered at the tips of branching stems and are somewhat dwarfed by the pliant, medium-green leaves.

The flowers, which typically open only for the afternoon (it's cute to pair four-o'clocks with morning glories along a fence to create a scene which switches on and off), are available only in seed mixtures featuring a full range of colors, including striped and mottled forms. If you want a particular color, I suggest you start the seed in a tub and transplant your choices once blooming begins, discarding the colors you disdain. Once in the ground, seedlings quickly make hard-to-dig tubers that I've read eventually grow to forty pounds. (How many of us would bother with tulips if the bulbs weighed forty pounds apiece!)

A good deal of crossing and self-seeding goes on among four-o'clocks, and, with me, no matter how grand a selection of colors and patterns I have the first year, the extra-vigorous magenta form ultimately takes over.

Four-o'clock is not particular as to soil and blooms in either sun or shade. It is remarkably persistent. I've seen it survive years of routine mowing.

One author recalls that as a child he liked to pull the flowers from the calyx and suck the nectar as if it were that of honeysuckle. But Thompson and Morgan's catalog notes that all parts of the plant are poisonous. If I were braver (or better insured) I'd let you know who's right.

CAMPANULA

One never sees seeds of American bellflower (*Campanula americana*) listed in catalogs, and this is a shame, for it is a wonderful, tall, spiky blue annual that comes into its own as the larkspur goes by in late June and July, when such a cool, statuesque accent is sorely needed to quell the tempest of yellows and pinks stirred up by the mallows, oenothera, and coneflowers.

American bellflower is common to moist woods throughout eastern North America. Yet it is little known, perhaps because the lovely blue, star-shaped flowers melt so inconspicuously into the woodland shadows that only bees are apt to notice them, or perhaps because this bellflower blooms in midsummer, when we are unlikely to brave the discomfort and perils of the hot, snaky, poison ivy–infested forests.

The hardy seedlings appear from fall into spring and form a low-lying rosette of bluish, spade-shaped leaves. They have an irritating habit of springing up everywhere but where you want them. They can, however, be moved. In summer the bloom stalk commences to rise, branching as it ascends, and the toothy leaves become more lancelike and graceful. Flowering takes a number of weeks, progressing bloom by bloom up the wandlike stem. Afterward the plant dies and can be uprooted and the seed scattered.

I'm not supposed to like *C. rapunculoides*, the common garden bellflower, but I do. All the books warn us that this Eurasian import, which blooms in sun or shade with tall spires of purple, bell-like flowers, has imperialistic designs on our gardens and will rapidly drive out everything else. Inge Paul gave me a start of this badly maligned plant several years ago, and I don't think it's been a pest for either of us, but then we both grow other aggressive plants along with it, so perhaps the rough competition keeps it in check.

BELAMCANDA

Blackberry lily (*Belamcanda chinensis*) is a widely naturalized Asian escapee and an excellent summer-blooming perennial. The fans of swordlike leaves betray its family ties with the iris clan, but the two-inch flower, with its six-part orange perianth liberally peppered with red spots, could easily be taken for that of a lily. In late summer the seed capsule splits to reveal a blackberrylike cluster of shiny black seeds.

This plant needs full sun and does best in loose, gritty soil. It has increased with wild abandon in a berm made of sand and sawdust in the wildflower area at the botanical garden. It must have full sun and protection from thugs like *Rudbeckia triloba*.

Some years ago I also started seed of what Park Seed Company calls its candy lily, ×*Pardancanda norrisii*, which they claim is a bigeneric cross between *Belamcanda* and *Pardanthopsis* (a genus not listed in *Hortus Third*). The resulting plants ranged from one to four feet in height, and the freckled flowers came in a broad assortment of colors. The taller specimens fell over. When we moved, I brought with me only a nice, short, sunny-faced yellow-flowering plant much like the belamcanda cultivar 'Hello Yellow'.

CROCOSMIA

Crocosmia (also known as montbretia and once included in the genus *Tritonia*) is a cormous iris family member whose fans of swordlike leaves very much resemble those of the gladiolus. Crocosmia seems a bit sturdier, though: The three-foot stems lean but seldom flop completely. The flaring, tubular flowers, alternately arrayed along the zigzag stem tips, are as scarlet as tongues of flame. The fiery red cultivar 'Lucifer', the crocosmia typically offered in most catalogs at present, is a bigeneric hybrid resulting from multiple crosses between *Crocosmia masoniorum* and *Curtonus paniculatus* (formerly *Antholyza paniculata*).

This crocosmia is a superb cut flower and is a fire-spitting accent for a bed of yellow daylilies in either full or partial sun. It multiplies prodigiously and may need occasional division. Yellow-flowering cultivars of crocosmia are occasionally offered and, rarely, *C. rosea* with fine, grassy foliage and small pink flowers.

Many years ago my Ewing Street neighbor Bea Hall gave me a division of her tall rose mallow (*Hibiscus coccineus*), perhaps the most gorgeous creature to ever lurk about the southeastern swamps. (I mean the plant, not, necessarily, Mrs. Hall.)

Rose mallow exemplifies a kind of Victorian excess. The smooth, green and red branching canes rise to six feet or more and are feathered with deeply cut palmate leaves. The rose-red, satiny, seven-inch flowers last but a single day and are borne one to a stem per day, maximum. In typical hibiscus fashion the stamens are fused into a long, protruding tube, which bristles with anthers bearing sticky, yellow, ball-like pollen grains and from which emerges the five-parted, red-tipped stigma. Ruby-throated hummingbirds pause prettily for a split second at the mallow before whizzing on to the preferred red salvia.

Rose mallow thrives in sun or partial shade in almost any soil as long as it's constantly moist. You can't overwater this plant.

The leaves, which offer so little surface area to begin with, are skeltonized repeatedly during the course of the summer (by slugs, as best I can tell). It surprises me that the plant bounces back so gamely.

Rose mallow dies to the ground in winter and takes its time about coming up in spring.

The more familiar garden hibiscus is *H. moscheutos*, also called swamp or rose mallow. It has creamy, off-white or pink, violet-centered blossoms much like those of okra and a broad, dull leaf. In the wild it spends its days standing around in sunny marshes. 'Disco Belle' is a currently popular version of this plant. It makes a showy summer hedge, waist-high or thereabouts, plastered with nine-inch, platelike blossoms in white and shades of red and pink.

If you go in for the extreme, you'll enjoy *H. moscheutos* 'Blue River II', which sports stark white blossoms in excess of a foot across on five-foot stems.

I have several big blowsy *H. moscheutos* specimens in the backyard, started from seed sent by a correspondent. They've an old-fashioned ambience with their rich pink flowers so large that they all but singlehandedly make the garden. They are much more satisfactory—to my mind—than hollyhocks. They need no staking, for one thing, their leaves suffer less disease, and they come back reliably every year.

Eventually I hope to try the tropical (i.e. annual) *H. acetosella*, a tall mallow grown for its burgundy foliage and deeply cut leaves.

Althea, or rose of Sharon (*H. syriacus*), is a weed in my yard. I pull up hundreds of taprooted seedlings in my flower beds and from around other shrubs where they're not wanted. Yet I have a few large specimens which I encourage, for, with proper pruning to eliminate the shrub's inherent scraggliness, it is a charming plant, with lavender, pink, or white mallow-style blossoms which appear in great quantity throughout the summer. I wouldn't place it by a sidewalk or driveway, though, for the spent blossoms it drops in equally great numbers make for slippery footing.

Rose of Sharon is a tough, drought-resistant plant. It has a naturally treelike, skinny-at-the-bottom, arching habit when left unpruned. If cut back at ground level it becomes a full bush. The flowers are borne in greatest profusion in full or partial sun, but the plant tolerates shade—even dry shade.

Cotton (*Gossypium* species) is a mallow, too, and I always try to grow a little just for fun. It's always nice to have on hand to use with red berries at Christmastime. The seeds in a single boll will usually be more than enough for this purpose. They germinate quickly, but the seedlings are prime slug food and can disappear over night. The little mallow blossoms are hidden by the sleek leaves. There are purple-leaved varieties which are highly ornamental while you're waiting for your crop to mature.

AMARANTHS

The amaranth clan, which includes the popular garden genera *Amaranthus*, *Celosia*, and *Gomphrena*, exults in the heat of midsummer. Until I tired of it, I used to grow the hulking, beet-red prince's feather (*Amaranthus hybridus* var. *erythrostachys*), which I had begged of Mrs. Hall. It is a difficult plant to place— unwieldy (to six feet), coarse, and strongly colored. Both the blood-red foliage and the countless infinitesimal seeds that form in the massive, matching, plumelike inflorescence are edible. I think I wrote somewhere once that on a dark night this monstrous shaggy weed could be mistaken for Bigfoot.

Prince's feather seeds itself with abandon (the birds are delighted to help), so you'll have it as long as you want it. I've even had it survive the occasional extra-mild winter.

Prince's feather can be pinched back to keep it at a reasonable height, or, better yet, you can grow the three-foot *A. tricolor* 'Illumination', with its chocolate-bronze lower leaves and newer, upper growth of luminescent rose, or the more familiar *A. tricolor* 'Joseph's Coat', whose two-foot bundles of lancelike leaves are splashed with yellow and scarlet.

Love-lies-bleeding (what a yucky name for *A. caudatus*!) is an old-fashioned novelty with long, ropy red inflorescences resembling dreadlocks. I've seen it used to excellent effect pouring from massive pedestaled concrete bowls on a formal terrace. *Amarantus caudatus* 'Viridis' is a green-flowering— and therefore less jarring—version.

I particularly dislike the cockscomb celosias (*Celosia cristata*), which look to me like dried brains on a stick. Arrangers of dried flowers, however, love their sturdiness and strong, long-lasting color. I'm willing to tolerate the plume-type celosias like the very dwarf bronze-leaved, red-plumed *C. plumosa* 'New Look'. And I actually admire the feathery soft, muted rose of the two-and-a-half-foot *C. p.* 'Flamingo Feather'.

For the most part the whole amaranthus family is a bit weedy for my taste, yet one of the most refined bedding-out displays I've seen lately was a pink and blue dream composed of a circle of soft blue caryopteris enclosed by a rosy cloud of globe amaranth—*Gomphrena globosa* 'Lavender Lady', to be exact.

Globe amaranth's flowers are bunched into cloverlike balls at the tips of branching stems. It is a bit more difficult from seed than the rest of the amaranth gang and is best started early indoors.

While the amaranths prosper under ordinary garden conditions, they are often chosen for their talent for providing fast, long-lasting bloom in even hot, dry spots in poor soil. Even the rattiest of the lot is not unsightly when grown in healthy masses. And all are excellent cut flowers, both fresh and dried.

MELAMPODIUM

Melampodium paludosum is too good to be true. A cinch from seed, this tidy little composite stays picture-pretty all summer, the clean, bright green, sand-papery leaves serving as a flawless backdrop to a host of clear yellow, inch-wide daisies, which drop away quickly and cleanly as they fade, leaving behind a calyx holding a ring of rough, brown seeds (achenes) like a shallow cup.

Malampodium grows exponentially. From the center of each pair of opposite leaves emerges a long peduncle bearing an inflorescence. At the base of each leaf a new pair of leaves and a new blossom emerge, so that the plant becomes an ever-expanding globe of new leaves and flowers, ballooning to some three feet in diameter by frost if grown in moderately rich, loose soil in full sun. In our climate, therefore, melampodium can be used at the front of the border only if it *is* the front of the border, for it will swallow ageratums and the like whole if they are planted closely together.

Still, it works well with the airy little spitfire blooms of tassel flower (*Emilia javanica*), and its bright yellow is sufficiently lacking in orange to allow its inclusion in a "cool" scheme with the blues of convolvulus, *Lobelia siphilitica*, or caryopteris and the pinks and lavenders of summer phlox or echinacea.

Melampodium seeds itself about with fair generosity, but I always save an envelope of seed and start seedlings in cell packs in spring so that I can place them where I judge a puff of sunny yellow and bright green will be welcome. Although they are taprooted, they transplant well. Melampodium is amenable to pot culture, too. The larger the pot the better.

EMILIA

I'm careful to save an envelope of fuzzy little *Emilia javanica* seeds as well, for though I'm learning to trust it to return from self-sown seed, I'm not taking any chances.

Emilia is a delightful plant, though more of a condiment than an entree with small (less than three quarters of an inch), shaggy, intensely orange composite flowers shaped like shaving brushes and borne in swarms at the tips of slender, two- to three-foot stems. One would not think such spaghettilike stems could support the weight of a swallowtail butterfly, but they do. The smooth leaves are large and clasping.

Individual plants are short-lived, but a continuous supply of new seedlings comes along all season to shower the border with sparks.

SUMMER AMARYLLIDS

Magic or resurrection lily (*Lycoris squamigera*) is the easiest plant in the world. Bury the bulb five or six inches down in any soil that drains, sun or shade, and forget it. It may take a couple of years to bloom, but should increase from year to year by multiplication of the bulb and by seed and should be around long after you've gone to the great compost bin in the sky. (The main problem with most concepts of Heaven is there's no dirt up there.)

The genus *Lycoris* is not filed among the lilies but belongs to the amaryllis family. In late winter *L. squamigera* sends up a bouquet of straplike, blue-green leaves which fade away by summer. Then suddenly in July tumescent green, two- to three-foot scapes rise from the now bare ground above the bulbs, bearing umbels of large, silken trumpets of pink or lilac swabbed with blue.

Sometimes we see them naturalized in mown lawns, looking just as surprised to be there as we are to see them, their naked, tubelike stems seeming indecently exposed. Elizabeth Lawrence liked to grow Hall's amaryllis, as this lycoris was formerly known, among bleeding-heart (*Dicentra eximia*), which hid the ungainly scapes with its feathery leaves and echoed the lilac and violet tints of its blooms.

Lycoris squamigera works well with liriope, blue hosta, and certain ferns as well. In full sun it is striking arising from a dark pool of purple *Setcreasea pallida* 'Purple Heart' with its small violet-pink spiderwort flowers.

I don't seem to have any rain lilies (*Zephyranthes* species) anymore, though I was quite sure I brought some with me when we moved. These little bulbous amaryllids come from warm regions of the New World but most are hardy at least through Zone 7.

Except for the fact that they're not lilies, rain lilies are aptly named, for, within a day or two after a summer dry spell is broken by a good shower, the clumps of grassy foliage send up bouquets of small, lilylike blossoms in shades of pink and white borne on slender pedicels. The little brown bulbs increase at a gratifying clip and have a tendency to erupt from the ground during droughts. I used to stick them back in. Who knows, perhaps they'd have replanted themselves eventually.

My pink rain lilies were either *Zephyranthes rosea*, from Cuba, or more likely, the larger *Z. grandiflora* from southern Mexico and Central America.

At the botanical garden we have the very similar spring-blooming white atamasco lily (*Z. atamasco*), found in shallow ditches along roadsides for miles in the southern part of the state.

Alabama is home to at least four other showy, white, moisture-loving amaryllids, including the exceedingly rare spring-blooming Cahaba lily (*Hymenocallis coronaria*), the preservation of which has become something of a cause célèbre around Birmingham. In our state it is found primarily along the Cahaba River, growing from bulbs snugly lodged between rocks in shallow water.

Cahaba lily closely resembles the more common and widespread (throughout much of the Southeast) *H. caroliniana* (also listed as *H. occidentalis*), a spider lily which, though it occurs naturally in moist woods and sunny marshes, willingly provides almost any garden with a dramatic spectacle. The blazing white fragrant flowers are borne in umbels of three to nine atop stout two-foot scapes. The straplike leaves may wither away before the flowers appear. Each flower consists of a central jagged, cuplike crown edged with six long, gold-tipped stamens, and, emerging from the flower's center, a starburst of six narrow petals and petallike sepals. The fleshy seeds, which soon emerge from the plump capsule atop the scape, are easily started in flats.

The white spider lily is rather like the so-called Peruvian daffodil (*H. narcissiflora*) from the Andes, the bulb of which must be dug and stored over winter for surest results. It, too, is summer-blooming.

The sea daffodil (*Pancratium maritimum*) of the Mediterranean region bears a strong family resemblance to *Hymenocallis* but is even more narcissuslike, with a more trumpet-shaped crown or corona. Its flower-bearing scapes rise less than a foot above the ground, thus it is good to plant among thrift (*Phlox subulata*), where its summer blooms won't be missed. The foliage is bluish.

This sunny seaside dweller needs light, dryish soil and sunshine.

Near the Gulf Coast the swamp lily (*Crinum americanum*) sends up thick scapes bearing umbels of spidery white, six-segmented flowers from early spring deep into fall. The leaves are sleek, grooved, and beltlike. This species will thrive—albeit less floriferously—in most gardens. Abundant moisture encourages abundant bloom.

Crinums are useful where a look of exaggerated tropical opulence is desired. Most of the crinums grown in southern gardens are of foreign origin. *Crinum kirkii*, one of the so-called milk-and-wine lilies, is from Zanzibar; another, *C. kunthianum*, is from tropical America; and *C. latifolium*, a third crinum whose white-lobed flowers are keeled with red, is from tropical Asia. Perhaps eventually we'll be seeing some of the five or six Australian species as well.

Because of their imposing size, one typically sees crinums treated as specimen plants, slumped all alone in the middle of a lawn, their great mops of long, crumpled leaves looking as unkempt as a belt rack that just fell from heaven. It is better, I believe, to set them into borders where the elegant scapes of white, pink, or red flowers can be contrasted against a dark-leaved shrub, perhaps, and the ungainly foliage is blended with that of its neighbors.

Crinums can be grown in tubs, too, and rolled (do put the tub on casters before you add dirt) into the garage for the winter.

Left undisturbed, a clump of crinums will expand yearly. Individual bulbs may be as large as a cantaloupe. Rich, loose soil, sunshine, and plenty of water are needed for summer-long flower production.

GLORIOSA LILY

The gloriosa lily (*Gloriosa rothschildiana*) is not a true lily but a closely related tuberous climber from tropical Africa with a bewitching lilylike flower whose backswept red and yellow segments resemble tongues of flame. But for the tendrils at the stem tips, the foliage could be taken for that of a weak-stemmed lily.

I'm sure this exotic vine is only marginally hardy here in Zone 7, for the specimen I grew for many years on Ewing Street seldom emerged before mid-June. The tendrils must be given wire or string on which to climb. Once I moved my gloriosa lily, deciding that the young ginkgo was starting to shade it too much, but the very next June the vine again appeared under the tree, a sure indication that the tubers had multiplied.

CANNA

With their bold, rubbery leaves clasping stalks topped by large, gaily-colored, flaglike blossoms, cannas (*Canna* species and hybrids) impart an ambience of tropical verdure to many a southern garden. Cannas are available in assorted sizes from eighteen-inch dwarfs to eight-foot giants and in a tempting array of flower colors—all hot. They are effective in masses of a single color or as accents in a cluster of perhaps three plants. Cannas are especially elegant by water, and smaller selections work nicely in containers (which can be stored in the garage or basement over winter).

Some cannas are grown more for their strong foliage than for their flowers. The towering 'Red King Humbert', a selection, I presume, of *Canna indica*, is just the ticket to shield your swimming pool from prying eyes, and the powerful, seven-foot, bronze-tinged foliage seems all the richer when paired with a contrasting yellow-leaved plant, like the variegated *Yucca filamentosa* 'Gold Sword'. There are even variegated cannas: The alternating yellow and light-green striations of *C.* 'Generalife Variegata' give this orange-flowering canna something of the bright, big-leaved look of a tobacco plant.

Cannas need loose, humusy soil and lots of water. They are supposed to need full or part sun, but I recall former neighbors having an absolutely thrilling stand of medium-height red cannas (perhaps the four-foot 'The President') against the north wall of their house. They far outpaced the 'Pfitzer's Salmon Pink' I was growing against our south-facing brick wall. The foliage soaked up the grueling summer heat with apparent enjoyment, but my flowers were history before they fully opened. Fertilizing and removing spent blossoms should prolong the span of bloom.

Cannas make little pealike black seeds which can be soaked overnight and started in a pot if you can't bear to see them go to waste.

Cannas can usually be left in the ground over winter in Zone 7, though occasionally we experience such severe cold that, if we excavate the spot where our cannas have been planted, we will find a number of dead, blackened rhizomes.

I doubt I'd bother with cannas—or dahlias either—if I had to dig and store them over winter the way northerners do. It would just be the situation with caladiums all over again: Stored too wet, they'll rot; stored dry, they'll shrink beyond redemption. I've read that Christopher Lloyd stores his cannas in old potting soil in boxes in the cellar and waters them once a week. I do well to water the houseplants in plain view once a week. And dahlia tubers, I know, will all but vanish from dehydration in a wink.

DAHLIA

Dahlias (*Dahlia hybrida*) are almost as easy from seed as zinnias and many kinds—both large and small—are sold in seed mixes rather than as tubers. I save a few seed heads from my favorite dahlias each year and shred them into a flat of potting soil the following spring. The resulting seedlings are usually as showy and satisfactory as the parent (though not necessarily identical, of course).

Tall dahlias, like the simmering, four-foot, red 'Envy', need to be staked or caged to prevent their sprawling over their neighbors, and dahlia fanatics disbranch and disbud relentlessly to assure that the remaining buds will produce exceptionally large flowers. (I'm afraid my own dahlias lounge around unstaked and with all their buds intact, though I do deadhead a bit for neatness.)

I don't grow show flowers and prefer my plants to be bushy. Even if they're split wide open by hard rain, that's okay, because each sprawling branch soon behaves like a separate plant, sending up new vertical blooming stems. And besides, who says horizontal dahlias aren't beautiful?

I grow many red dahlias, primarily because dahlias produce some of the purest, clearest reds to be found in a garden.

In a well-mulched bed dahlias typically survive winter here, though they may take their time about showing up in spring. Well-fed and watered, they should bloom until frost.

ZINNIAS

Most zinnias are a disappointment. The seeds germinate practically overnight. The seedlings race to blooming size, then, just as the first bright blooms open, the leaves develop a sudden solid coating of powdery mildew, and the plant makes out its will and bites the dust. Regular spraying with sulfur or a fungicide from the minute the first true leaves develop may help (or it may not), but the best plan is to stick with varieties advertised as mildew-resistant.

The Classic zinnia (*Zinnia angustifolia*, also listed as *Z. linearis*) is actually immune to mildew, as far as I can tell. This low-growing, drought-tolerant Mexican species has fine, narrow-leaved foliage and small, flat-faced, single daisies. It is most often seen in the hard-to-take-in-large-doses orange form of the 'Golden Orange' variety, but color mixtures are now available which include light yellow and white. The mildew-resistant 'Pinwheel' series zinnias appear to have this species in their ancestry, for the flowers are primarily single and the leaves more narrow than those of *Z. elegans*, the most commonly cultivated species.

The white form of *Z. angustifolia* is an invaluable garden plant. I'm particularly taken with the cultivar 'Star White', whose flowers are a little whiter and larger than others I've seen. This plant is a marvelous filler and a mediator between warring color factions. *Zinnia angustifolia* is slower to grow than other zinnias, but once blooming it covers itself with flowers till frost. And the individual flowers last for weeks. Last year I promised a friend seeds from my 'Star White' plants, and we waited literally for months for a few flowers to turn brown so that we could collect the seed. I had one plant in a pot, and once it came into full bloom I moved the pot into the shade and it held its flowers until frost. This year I plan to pot one up for the house as frost approaches.

If you're looking for disease-resistance in a pompon zinnia, you might investigate the 'Small World' hybrids, which are described as "disease tolerant." They are neat and compact, and we are told that faded blooms are promptly concealed by fresh new leaves and flowers. They come in both bright and very dark shades of pink. This year I've had quite acceptable results with 'Starlight Scarlet'. Though the foliage eventually sickened, the great, shaggy, glowing, red-orange blossoms have hummed along, first with the coreopsis, then with the black-eyed Susans, and finally with the *Silphium integrifolium* and the Maximilian sunflowers.

Zinnias are content with average garden soil and sunshine twenty-four hours a day, or as close to it as practicable.

PETUNIA

I'd forgotten how wonderful petunias can be. Until this spring I'd not planted any for a number of years (I'm not sure why) and I was amazed at their endless generosity, for they've given me delicious color all season, weaving among their bedmates, here flashing pink among the sultry *Verbena* 'Homestead Purple', there rubbing a velvet purple cheek against a lemon yellow marigold.

I don't go in for the picotees, pinwheels, and doubles—they lack the sincerity and unself-conscious simplicity of the accommodating solid singles. I do admire the contrasting veining of the 'Daddy' series, and I don't mind the cherry-sweet 'Fluffy Ruffles' mixture, whose silly frilliness, after all, conceals slug and bug damage.

And then, of course, there's fragrance, particularly evening fragrance. A mass planting of petunias near a sitting area is sufficiently intoxicating to save the host considerable expense on refreshments. (Those carnation-style doubles I was just grousing about are unequaled in this regard.)

Since hybrid petunias come in such an impressive assortment of floral colors and designs and overall habits (from squat mounds for edging, like the 'Celebrity' and 'Countdown' series, to trailing cascaders for hanging baskets, like the 'Supercascade' series), they are among the most versatile of garden flowers. They thrive in any well-drained soil, but they must have plenty of sun.

During the course of the summer new seedlings spring up and bloom about the originals (they all tend to be pink for me) and some will pop up from seed the following year.

A tired petunia can be rejuvenated by trimming it back and giving it a long drink of liquid fertilizer.

One of the most eye-popping and long-lasting displays of color I saw around town this past summer consisted of a fountain of tall red *Salvia splendens* (possibly 'Bonfire') arising from a frothy pool of emphatically white single petunias.

TITHONIA

The Mexican sunflower (*Tithonia rotundifolia*) is not easy to place in every garden, being tall (to six feet) and having broad, golden-centered daisies of an intense, near-scarlet orange that seems to pulsate against the large, coarse, green leaves. The flowers—usually sporting a butterfly or bumblebee—are borne singly on long hollow stems and are spectacular when viewed against the bright blue sky.

Tithonia's long brown seeds are quick to sprout in a flat, but the seedlings grow so rapidly indoors that holding them in check becomes a problem if they are started too early in the spring to set out. They love hot weather, so I wouldn't bother to start seed before May. True, you'll have to wait until July for the first bloom (the plant attains considerable size before it attempts to flower), but it won't hurt you to wait, and, anyway, you'll be sick of them by October, when most of the leaves will have yellowed and the plants will look thin and bedraggled. (But you won't dare take them down, for finches you've never seen before will be feasting on the seeds.) A few of the seeds that overwinter on the ground may germinate the following spring, but this is not a sure thing with this half-hardy native of Mexico and Central America, so collect a few seeds for yourself.

The current catalog offerings are of a more manageable size than the type, though, given our long, hot summers, we can safely add a foot to the estimated listed height. *Tithonia rotundifolia* 'Goldfinger' has three-inch flowers of the customary electrified red-orange and can be expected to reach at least three (let's say four) feet. *Tithonia rotundifolia* 'Yellow Torch' is a bit taller but the bright yellow daisies are a tad smaller. (Do we really *need* another yellow daisy?)

Full sun, of course.

BALSAM

Balsam (*Impatiens balsamina*) is lovely and old-fashioned, but I regret the way the narrow, saw-edged leaves conceal the blooms, which are double and hug the succulent, upright, two-and-a-half-foot stems. The color range is much like that of the more familiar (nowadays) shade-loving *I. wallerana* hybrids and some, like *I. b.* 'Double Strawberry and Blackberry Ice', have brightly colored blossoms splashed with white variegation. Balsam is most effective planted in masses in fertile, warm, moist soil. It is exquisite in pots, too, if the soil is kept moist, and will draw hummingbirds to a patio or porch. The twelve-inch 'Extra Dwarf Tom Thumb Mixed', sold by Thompson & Morgan, is advertised as drought tolerant and therefore recommended for containers.

The plant enjoys full sun (unlike impatiens) but container-grown plants may need afternoon shade.

Balsam reseeds itself from year to year. The bursting seed pods assure that every other pot on the porch will soon be growing balsam, too. Balsam is quick to sprout from seed and grow. With me plants come and go quickly in the garden (maybe that's why the genus is called *Impatiens*), but books claim they bloom until frost.

SUMMER GROUNDCOVERS

I inherited a couple of patches of variegated goutweed, or bishop's weed (*Aegopodium podagraria* 'Variegatum'), when we moved here. One patch, around a young rhododendron on the north side of the house, has reverted to the tallish, dark, solid green form. It is far more vigorous and aggressive than the neat, low-lying variegated form and, unlike the variegated sort, which seldom if ever blooms, sends up lacy umbels of tiny white (no doubt very fertile) flowers. It has all but wiped out the last vestiges of the variegated aegopodium and has swept across the adjacent strip along the chain-link fence where I was trying to start four-o'clocks.

I didn't have to let this catastrophe happen; I could have yanked up every solid green leaf as it appeared, and the situation would never have gotten out of hand. So let this be a lesson to you.

I've every intention, however, of protecting the integrity of the variegated aegopodium by the back porch, where the little bed of yellow-green leaves harmonizes with the mossy brown bricks of the porch wall and both together provide a smashing backdrop for the golden starburst blossoms of the shrubby native St.-John's-wort (*Hypericum frondosum*).

Aegopodium's compound leaves are composed of three leaflets and are really quite lovely in the variegated form that I have, which is not silver-edged as that described in the catalogs, but rather the feathered edges of the light, yellow-green leaves are stroked with soft cream.

Aegopodium ramps about by tangled, spaghettilike roots and stems. It is not really heat- and drought-proof. The variegated leaves are especially fragile and will sun scorch once the temperature hits the high nineties.

One of the best summer groundcovers for sunny, sometimes dry expanses in most soils is Aaron's beard (*Hypericum calycinum*), a low-growing Old World St.-John's-wort. It spreads rapidly to cover a difficult dry or stony bank with a flurry of shrubby stems crisscrossed with opposite pairs of smooth, oblong leaves and bearing at their tips two-and-a-half-inch starry, five-petaled yellow blossoms with an astonishing profusion of stamens. The individual flowers come and go quickly and, though the plant has a long period of bloom, the blossoms are rationed. How I wish there were more of them in evidence at a time. What a show that would be. Michael Dirr observes that *H. calycinum* does bloom with greater zeal in the Pacific Northwest and in Europe. Aaron's beard is a very fast worker. Set out in spring, a single rooted cutting will make a three-foot-wide mat by summer's close. Although catalogs describe it as evergreen, mine turns a hideous rusty doornail brown in winter. It is actually beneficial to the health of the planting to mow it down in winter and allow it to start afresh in spring.

Something else to cover a dryish sunny or even partially shaded spot is the low-growing leadwort, or plumbago (*Ceratostigma plumbaginoides*), which liberally sprinkles its bronzy-green leaves with small, flat-faced, sky blue flowers for many weeks in late summer and fall. We've a sizeable planting of this at the botanical garden's administration building, and I've admired its beauty and ruggedness again and again.

Fairly new on the summer groundcover scene is *Houttuynia cordata* 'Chameleon'. This is indeed a gorgeous plant when grown well, that is to say, in rich, loose, unfailingly moist soil with enough sun to sharpen the bold colors which give the plant the exuberant individuality of a preschool art project.

Houttuynia is a rhizomatous creeper whose wavy-edged, heart-shaped leaves are dribbled with shades of red, green, and yellow. In heavy shade the leaves of my houttuynia are disappointingly subdued and prone to unsightly fungal assault besides. Spider mites take a toll in hot dry weather. But it is a super little plant for a well-watered hanging basket or to grow beside a pond or in a marshy spot.

To Do in July

Seeds of pansies, most perennials, and quick-blooming annuals can be started now. Seedlings of zinnias, marigolds, and other heat lovers may be fine in flats in strong sun if care is taken to see that the container never goes dry—a real challenge in July. With few exceptions, I move my seedlings into the shade now. I've found I must carefully inspect containers and soil mixes before use, otherwise seedlings vanish overnight even on my supposedly slug-free "elevated cold frame."

Watering, feeding, deadheading, and spaying or dusting as needed are July's prime garden activities. The chrysanthemums should have been pinched back one last time by midmonth. And, of course, there's mowing. Thank God for healthy teenage daughters (even if they do charge ten dollars).

August

No, I certainly don't see why, if we must have an Income Tax Day, that it can't come in August (not in April, the busiest and most enthralling time of the gardener's year). The only good thing about August is that at last we can assure ourselves that "a month from now this wretched heat will have let up—maybe."

The incessant scream of the cicadas drowns out the tired chuffing of the air conditioner's compressor. The stench of euonymus blossoms hangs heavy in the still air. The brown grass crunches painfully at our step, and in the shade even the weedy ground ivy (*Glechoma hederacea*) and the common blue violets lie prostrate, all awaiting instant revival by the passage of a hit-or-miss shower or perhaps even a long drenching from the remains of a run-aground hurricane.

Kudzu (*Pueraria lobata*) is in bloom, the racemes of lovely violet pea flowers all but hidden by a solid sheet of massive, trifoliolate leaves. We may detect the deliciously sweet, grapelike fragrance of the blossoms even before a kudzu patch looms into view, and we're apt to hear the machinelike hum of the countless attending bees even before we catch the scent.

On the porch Aunt Mary Lee's climbing onion has enshrouded the poor ponytail palm (*Beaucarnea recurvata*) with a wispy veil of spaghetti-thin foliage now festooned with tiny green six-pointed stars dotted with yellow anthers. The *Pentas lanceolata* (I suppose it is) bears stiff stems tipped with rigid, mounded clusters of small crimson trumpets. This tender tropical African shrub is magnetic to hummingbirds, so much so that they venture to hover and dart about it even when Rachel and I are breakfasting at the table only inches away.

Pentas could easily rival lantana as a bedding-out plant. It is a bit more upright but softened in effect by largish, fuzzy leaves. My potted pentas is three feet tall now at summer's end, but it was started from a cutting last fall that took months to strike roots and grow. (*Hortus Third* says I should have used bottom heat.)

At what passes for the cool of the morning, Inge's garden is at its pinnacle of beauty in August. A frothy train of sweetautumn clematis binds together sturdy stands of hot purple ironweed, cool, chrome yellow rosinweed, and deep pink phlox. In the shadows cardinal flower smolders amid rosy pockets of impatiens, while in the sunny foreground fiery red spires of *Salvia coccinea* mingle with sun-catching tickseeds (*Bidens* species), and the redbirds feast from the cleome's first dry seedpods. Grown fat on the garden's largesse, the black and yellow garden spider (*Argiope aurantia*) hangs headdown in her ornate web, the zigzag pattern down the middle prompting us to call her "the writing spider" when we were children.

The Late Summer Shade Garden

My little front yard shade garden offers visual (if not literal) relief from August's searing heat. Strong-willed ferns like the southern shield (*Thelypteris kunthii*), the holly ferns (*Cyrtomium* species), sensitive fern (*Onoclea sensibilis*), and the Japanese climbing fern (*Lygodium japonicum*) still look as fresh and inviting as they did in early June, though the lady fern (*Athyrium filix-femina*) and certain of her thin-leaved companions have as much as excused themselves from the scene.

The hostas still are stout and handsome (if you don't mind overlooking a few holes in the leaves), and in the sunken black plastic livestock-watering pan that serves as this tiny garden's pool, the water hyacinth (*Eichhornia crassipes*) Wade Wharton gave me sends up a great, compressed spike of extraordinarily beautiful segmented lavender flowers, exclamatorily marked with blue and yellow on the upper lobe. Each blooming stalk lasts but a day.

This invasive, floating South American species with its balloonlike petioles and smooth, rounded leaves has become a waterway-gagging nuisance in warm parts of the Southeast. Since I no longer fool with fish, I must change the water in the pan every few days to interrupt its use as a nursery for mosquito hatchlings. The water hyacinth's furry roots must be strongly hosed off to flush out the larvae.

I've not been able to overwinter water hyacinth indoors. I don't know why. Wade keeps his in a shady spot in his greenhouse. They need no supplementary feeding, he tells me.

By late August the caladiums, whose large, vividly painted, arrowhead-shaped leaves overhang the make-believe pool, are starting to pale, signaling that it's time to mark the tubers for digging next month. The garden will seem greatly diminished without them. On Ewing Street I loved the way caladiums mixed so soothingly with blue ageratum along our rock-rimmed front walkway.

In fact, the garden on Ewing Street seems more and more gorgeous the more I compare it to this one. There I had clouds of impatiens which grew knee-high and stayed covered with bright bloom until frost. Here I've almost given up. My poor impatiens, which do, at least, reseed a bit, are so stunted, so *meager*. If you listen carefully, you imagine you hear them gasp for breath as their roots struggle to penetrate the spade-bending soil to which I've faithfully—and apparently uselessly—added so many amendments. Both gypsum and organic matter seem to help only temporarily, and suddenly the soil is hard and compacted again.

Possibly I should just have a load of gravel dumped on the bed. At the little house on Cypress Avenue which we rented when we first came to Huntsville, I was amazed to find I could grow impatiens in a bed of pure driveway gravel, as long as I kept it watered. In Inge's leaf-mold paradise impatiens self-sow and blossom so prolifically that she must weed many of them out. How I long for such weeds!

Coleus (*Coleus* ×*hybridus*) seems to cope somewhat better with the heavy soil as long as it's watered daily. Certainly no other shade-loving plant can touch coleus for diversity. And it's so easy to grow, indoors or out. Come to think of it, I first took an interest in plants some twenty-odd years ago when a neighbor lady in Atlanta gave me a few coleus cuttings, which I rooted in water and admired winter-long on a shelf that my husband built for them in our apartment.

My hardy begonia (*Begonia grandis*) is a perfectly elegant plant, readily hardy in Zone 7 and, with protection, further north. It grows from a tuber and in organically rich, loose soil can reach over two feet in height. The large, lopsided, heart-shaped leaves are mild green on top, rosy-red on the back and sparingly scattered on both sides with hornlike projections (trichomes, I suppose), which give the leaf a faint, unpleasant scratchiness. The prominently jointed stems are succulent and hairy. The satiny pink blossoms are borne in gracefully cascading cymes, which give way to stiff sprays of triangular red seed capsules that are showy in dried arrangements. In light soils hardy begonia increases appreciably both by seed and by bulblets that form in the leaf axils.

Torenia (*Torenia fournieri*), too, self-sows a bit in humusy soil. This personable little shade-loving Vietnamese annual looks like a cross between a pansy and a snapdragon (it is kin to the latter). It is sometimes called wishbone flower, for the two stamens within the yellow-splashed throat are shaped like a wishbone.

Torenia fournieri is a much-branched plant of some twelve inches in height and width with abundant glossy, saw-edged leaves. All summer it is liberally sprinkled with quarter-sized, two-tone blue tubular blossoms whose widely flaring lips give them a sour-faced expression. The larger-flowered 'Clown' strain is more compact and lacks the admirable daintiness of the original, but it introduces a broader color range. 'Panda' is downright tiny with jewellike blossoms trimmed with purple or hot pink.

Not everyone realizes that scarlet sage (*Salvia splendens*), the Brazilian species from which most of the bedding-out salvias are drawn, is prosperous and content in light to moderate shade, particularly in very moist, humusy soil.

For years I scoured garden centers every spring for 'Bonfire', an aptly named variety with sufficient height (three or four feet) to play backup to the river of impatiens which flowed across the bed curving from the front steps to the northeast corner of the Ewing Street house. 'Bonfire' had been an old standard, but it got harder and harder to find as the new dwarfs like 'Red Hot Sally' began to crowd it off the shelf.

When I could find it, I liked to mix a tall, dark purple variety with the red. They tell us that purple appears to the eye to be retreating and thereby increases the apparent distance between the viewer and the purple object, while red seems to be advancing. I suppose that when both purple and red salvia are grown in the same bed one can't tell whether the bed is coming or going.

It is tempting to grow red *Salvia splendens* on a porch or deck as a hummingbird lure (which it surely is), but I've found to my dismay that, if the hummers glimpse the salvia's reflection in a window or door, they will dart at the mirage and dash their little brains out against the glass.

It's certainly not impossible to grow this salvia from seed, but it's slow and awkward and ever so much easier to purchase a season's supply at a garden center. *Salvia splendens* is really a tender perennial rather than an annual and, if you have room and don't mind the bother, you can winter cuttings indoors.

Probably because I mulch so heavily, I've seldom had *S. spendens* self-sow, but the most glorious bed of red salvia I've ever seen came up year after year of its own accord on the north side of a dazzlingly white clapboard house. The owner merely weeded, watered, and fertilized.

I don't think there's a white *S. splendens* that doesn't look grungy once the flowers start to brown (some salvias shed spent flowers more promptly than others), but there are some very presentable pinks, purples, and lavenders. (There are some discouragingly muddy purples, too, unfortunately.) Mary Lou McNabb considers the rich-toned 'Top Burgundy' to be the best annual she's ever grown. When it sags into the August doldrums, she cuts it back, fertilizes it, and it roars back to make a strong sweep of color to accompany her chrysanthemums in September and October.

The apricot sorts mix well with blue ageratum or convolvulus, but they strike me as unnaturally anemic. Of course more sophisticated gardeners than

*The fire-breathing
crocosmia heats up
the summer border.*

PHOTOGRAPH BY
PAT GARDNER

July
❧
August
❧
September

*Melampodium makes
a cheery backdrop for
cool blue convolvulus.*

PHOTOGRAPH BY
CAROL B. HIPPS

*Magic, or resurrection,
lily (Lycoris squam-
igera), surprises us in
midsummer when
silken trumpets unfurl
atop naked scapes
which seem to arise
as if at random
from bare ground.*

PHOTOGRAPH BY
DANIEL LITTLE

The native spider lily
(Hymenocallis car-
oliniana) *is hard to
match for drama
and excitement.*

PHOTOGRAPH BY
PAT GARDNER

*Sweetautumn clematis
sweeps across Inge's
garden in August.*

PHOTOGRAPH BY
CAROL B. HIPPS

July

❧

August

❧

September

*Impatiens lends gaiety
to a dark, shady
corner.*

PHOTOGRAPH BY
PAT GARDNER

The stately cardinal flower is one of very few tall, brightly colored perennials for shade.

PHOTOGRAPH BY
CAROL B. HIPPS

July

ও

August

ও

September

*Annual asters are easy
to grow from seed
and make excellent
cut flowers.*

PHOTOGRAPH BY
CAROL B. HIPPS

Physostegia virgini-
ana *takes a bit of
maintenance to keep
it in bounds but puts
on a fine show in
late summer.*

PHOTOGRAPH BY
CAROL B. HIPPS

*Like the cool breath
of autumn, mistflower,
or hardy ageratum*
(Eupatorium
coelestinum)*, drifts
among the black-eyed
susans.*

PHOTOGRAPH BY
CAROL B. HIPPS

July

🐚

August

🐚

September

Swamp, or narrow-leaved sunflower (Helianthus angustifolius), dazzles passersby with its golden, dark-eyed daisies.

Soft as kitten paws, the furry purple blossoms of Mexican bush sage are worth the summer-long wait.

I shudder at the brazen gaudiness of the scarlet salvias. I do feel they clash with pink flamingos. (Ah, but an old tire painted white would be another matter!)

LOBELIA

Viewed at a short distance, *Salvia splendens* resembles cardinal flower (*Lobelia cardinalis*) in habit and sultry coloration. No doubt if it played as hard to get (and keep) as cardinal flower and were as stingy with its bloom, then even the most discriminating gardeners would court and pamper it. As it is, the appearance of cardinal flower's four-foot, torchlike spires is one of the most eagerly anticipated events of late summer.

Cardinal flower's intensely red flowers are borne on racemes and feature stamens fused around the upward curving style so as to form a straw from which hummingbirds are wont to sip the flower's nectar.

In Inge Paul's woodsy garden cardinal flower skips about from year to year with prodigal abandon; in mine it gives me one good year and vanishes. The seed, however, is easy enough to start in containers, so all is not necessarily lost forever.

Cardinal flower is distributed (all too sparingly, alas) throughout eastern North America, where it grows in damp meadows and ditches and along streams. It accepts full sun to full shade and is adaptable to a wide assortment of soils—even heavy clay—as long as it is moist (better yet, wet). It is considered a short-lived perennial, but at the botanical garden we've concluded that its rosette of lancelike, rough-edged leaves is more likely to survive the winter if it's kept clear of leaf litter. Cardinal flower has naturalized nicely along (and even within) the garden's shaded creek and has surprisingly survived for several years even in a sunny berm which is allowed at times to go appallingly dry in summer.

Catalogs usually offer only the type or the 'Queen Victoria' variety, with dark stems and maroon leaves. I've read of a purple-flowering cross between this and the great blue lobelia (*Lobelia siphilitica*). Occasionally pink or white versions of *L. cardinalis* are offered. (I should think the red- and white-flowering lobelias would be smashing together.) At the botanical garden this year we had red lobelia blooming with a white spider lily (*Hymenocallis caroliniana*) and bouncing bet (*Saponaria officinalis*)—a real fire and ice combination.

The great blue lobelia (sounds humongous but is actually about a foot shorter than *L. cardinalis*) is a far easier garden subject. It is not a blue replica of cardinal flower but has a shorter stamen tube, and the lobes of the lower lip are shorter and parallel, giving the flower a pleated look. The lower leaves are a bit broader and never dark.

This lobelia increases with the least encouragement. I now have quite an impressive self-sown colony in a mossy spot down the hill from a bed in which I planted three blue lobelias a couple of years ago. Sometimes a seedling will bloom in its first year.

Blue lobelia dearly loves moisture but gamely adapts to routine garden culture. The lovely, cool blue racemes mix charmingly with yellow melampodium, purple coneflower, or black-eyed Susan. We have a crisply handsome stand at the garden consisting of both blue and white ('Alba') *L. siphilitica*.

SPIDER LILY

In August spider lilies (*Lycoris radiata*) start popping up like toadstools. When I was a child, in fact, I thought this bizarre, leafless creature was indeed a flamboyant fungus of some sort.

Erupting from the earth as a tight, fistlike cluster of nubby pinkish buds atop a naked green tube, *L. radiata* bursts into an umbel of scarlet or crimson segmented flowers with crinkled, reflexed tepals and extraordinarily long, upcurved stamens. The complete inflorescence resembles a brilliantly hued spider, suspended upside down in its web.

The foliage—narrow, dark green leaves much like those of liriope— emerges shortly after bloom and persists through winter.

This flashy amaryllid has long been confused with the Guernsey lily (*Nerine sarniensis*), which shares the trait of presenting flowers in autumn and foliage in winter. I once read a very logical explanation for this cockeyed behavior on the Guernsey lily's part. Since it hails from South Africa, the reasoning goes, it simply has its seasons switched and still thinks that the Northern Hemisphere's autumn is spring and its winter is summer. But this hardly accounts for the spider lily's contrariness, since *L. radiata* is native to China and Japan. (Let's chalk it up to plate tectonics and go on.)

Spider lilies live forever and eagerly naturalize in lawns. They have bumper years in which one sees them in masses all over town, and then there are years when the few that do bloom serve to remind us of the many which don't. Some years they seem to come and go quickly, others they bloom into October.

The bulbs can be dug and moved any time, but they may take two years or more to bloom again after disturbance. When we moved to this house, I stuck spider lilies all over my front yard shade garden, and now, four years later, only a handful have bloomed.

Lycoris radiata 'Alba' is a white form of this lycoris. *Lycoris albiflora* is a rare Japanese species with smaller, cream-colored flowers and wider leaves than those of *L. radiata*. The golden hurricane lily (*Lycoris africana* but, being of East Asian rather than African descent, is often sold as *L. aurea*) has exotic, bright golden flowers that are larger than those of *L. radiata*, though the plant, at about twelve inches, is half a foot shorter.

Yes, every southerner needs a shade garden—a quiet place where one may sit on one's bird-dropping-dappled bench and gaze into one's pan of water and Think Great Thoughts.

LANTANA

Meanwhile, on the sunny side of the yard, the yellow lantana is languorously stretching about, weaving itself into a cozy if contorted embrace with a great, sprawling red dahlia, so that the two together have become one great patchwork of yellow, red, and green. Bumblebees pass back and forth between the two plants, as content to gather pollen from one as from the other.

The prickly, highly aromatic lantana is a member of the verbena family and thus is sometimes called shrub verbena. Garden lantanas are primarily derived from the shrubby tropical American *Lantana camara* and the trailing *L. montevidensis* from South America. Both are naturalized along the Gulf Coast. The harsh orange flower clusters and dark green, scalloped leaves of *L. camara* are among the most familiar sights along roadsides near Orlando. In fact, I've read that this species is a serious pest in Hawaii, too. (I'd like to find out for myself some day.) But lantana is a superb garden flower, blooming to beat the band from May until frost outdoors and all winter in a pot on a sunny windowsill indoors.

Lantana bears rounded heads of tiny tubular flowers with a flaring, four-lobed corolla. The flowers on many cultivars are exceptional in that they change color as they age, so that, on the *L. camara* cultivar 'Radiation', for instance, a single flower head may bear concentric bands of hot pink, scarlet, and yellow.

Lantana seeds are BB-like drupes about a quarter of an inch in diameter. (Unfortunately, a BB is .18 inch in diameter, so there goes my dream of getting rich peddling organically grown air rifle shot.)

Though lantanas love heat and tolerate poor, dry soil (how else would they be taking over Florida?), they appreciate the good life—rich, humusy, well-drained soil and frequent water, occasionally laced with fertilizer. They are unexcelled for use around hot pavement and for sunny window boxes, patio containers, and hanging baskets.

Lantanas grow fast but are easily controlled with pruning. Compact cultivars like the yellow-flowering 'Samantha', with its variegated leaves of mingled pale and dark green, are more refined and need little upkeep.

In autumn lantana can be cut back and potted up for indoor bloom or cuttings can be carried over winter in water.

If you haven't grown the annual, or China, asters (*Callistephus chinensis*), you ought to give them a try, for they are easy from seed and come in an array of heights and floral colors and styles for either bedding out or cutting. A few mixtures include yellow, but the standard color range runs from white to pink, lavender, purple, and violet. Floral forms are very much like those of chrysanthemums and include single daisies, double pompons (some with contrasting centers), and forms with quills or mops of incurved rays.

Annual asters bloom in mid to late summer and, though they are marvelous cut flowers, they do not respond to cutting with a flush of fresh blooms. I would not depend on them for long-lasting color as I would marigolds or impatiens, but successive plantings can be made two or three weeks apart to prolong bloom.

China asters enjoy rich, gritty soil that is never allowed to go dry. Jim Crockett's Time-Life book on annuals mentions that annual asters may need lime added to their soil. I've never given them lime, but I do know that they veritably frolic in a mulched bed heavily amended with used cat litter. They make do nicely with as little as two or three hours of direct sunshine a day.

Annual asters are susceptible to aster yellows (*Chlorogenus callistephi*), a viral disease transmitted by leaf hoppers, and to fungal diseases that flourish where susceptible plants are grown in successive years. Controlling insects, tidying up in fall, and practicing a bit of crop rotation are helpful. It is recommended that one plant wilt-resistant varieties like the two-foot 'Prinette Pink', an explosion of toothpick-thin rays of an unusual watered-down scarlet tipped with white, or the fifteen-inch 'Gusford Supreme', a crochetted red pompon with a white center.

Don't plant annual asters if your heart is set on something with the willowy grace of the fall-blooming perennial asters. *Callistephus chinensis* is stiff and upright with coarse, husky leaves.

MARIGOLD

I'm not sure life would be worth living without marigolds. Sure, they're common, but I can't think of another flower that so selflessly and successfully devotes itself to filling our days with sunshine from early summer until frost. (Gee, I hope I didn't just say the same thing about something else. If I did, I was probably lying. This time I really mean it.)

Even wee toddlers find marigolds endearingly cooperative, which is why so many marigold seedlings come home from nursery school in paper cups. They are quick as a wink from seed, and the dwarf types are often in bloom even before we can get them out of their cell packs and into the ground.

Marigolds (*Tagetes* species and hybrids) are native to warm parts of the Americas, even the so-called African marigold (*Tagetes erecta*), the species which has given rise to such imposing inventions as the thirty-inch 'Toreador' F1 hybrid, with its great spongy blossoms like bright orange Nerf balls. I've never been overly fond of the large-flowering marigolds, not even the far more compact 'Discovery' series, whose tennis ball–sized blooms are piled atop foot-high hummocks of dark, aromatic, fernlike foliage.

But I am hopelessly enamored of the French and signet marigolds (*T. patula* and *T. tenuifolia*, respectively), whose small, intensely warm blossoms of yellow, orange, and mahogany are produced in such magnanimous abundance that they make their larger-flowering cousins look stingy.

Among the many objects I've misplaced over the years (maybe it's in one of the boxes in the attic that we never got around to unpacking after we found the coffeepot the last time we moved) was a black iron soup bowl which was a replica of an old three-legged cook pot. I used to fill it with water and venture out into the garden and cut dozens of dwarf French marigolds, strip off the leaves, and slip the flowers into the bowl until it was such a solid mound of bloom that it would not hold another blossom.

Then I'd sit and look at it for hours, for I simply couldn't tear my eyes away from the flamelike color and fascinating patterns of the tightly packed blossoms. (No, I was not on drugs at the time. I obviously didn't need them.) If you, too, would like to try this in the privacy of your own home and haven't an iron soup bowl, an old brown coffee mug works almost as well. In fact, a mug brimming with pungent, pretty marigolds and crawling with ants, yellow crab spiders, and a snail or two is just the item (short of a box of all-nut chocolates) to cheer an ailing friend.

French marigolds (yes, they're really American, too) are available in both single and double forms. I'm partial to mixtures which include both clear yellows and two-toned red and yellow doubles, like the Sophia and Hero series. The single French marigolds retain the innocent appeal of wildflowers. 'Naughty Marietta' is especially sweet with her bright yellow petallike ray flowers broadly dabbed at the base with maroon. The 'Disco' mixture is a rich blend of pinwheellike gold, orange, and mahogany single blooms, many of them bicolored.

French marigolds crackle with color when paired with red *Salvia splendens*. And the bright yellows, like the parasol-flowered 'Susie Wong', are electric with purple petunias.

Tagetes tenuifolia (often listed as *T. signata pumila*), the signet marigold, is sharply aromatic, low-growing and bushy, with fine, feathery foliage and multitudes of tiny single flowers, making it a popular edger for herb gardens. It is most commonly represented by the Gem series ('Lemon Gem' and 'Golden Gem'), but Thompson & Morgan's current catalog also offers 'Paprika', a deep scarlet, and 'Starfire', which ranges from scarlet to yellow, with most blossoms offering at least a hint of each.

I don't know why, but for many years W. Atlee Burpee and Company diligently sought a white marigold and offered a substantial reward for the first acceptable specimen received. The current catalog offers three, all large-flowered (three inches or so across) carnation-types, twenty to twenty-four inches high. The creamy, full flowers of their 'French Vanilla' hybrid are advertised as lacking a typical marigold's pungent perfume (a pity in my view, but then, if it isn't going to look like a real marigold, it may as well not smell like one either). 'Snowdrift' has slightly shaggier flower heads with narrower petals and is said to need afternoon shade. The 'Sugar and Spice' mixture includes a white.

Contrary to what books often tell us, marigolds are not drought-resistant. In fact, if grown in compacted soil, they will never develop an adequate root system and will always be stunted and prone to hot-weather wilting. If grown in any poor, dry soil they'll likely bloom out and die as early as July.

But given loose, moisture-retentive soil, full sun, and abundant water and fertilizer, the same marigold that sizzles with the butterfly weed in July may be around to rival the chrysanthemum in October.

Marigolds, whether young seedlings or rooted cuttings, are easily transplanted even during the height of summer if care is taken to keep them watered. Thus they are an apt replacement for pansies or nemophila, which play out in early summer, and can be started in July or August for fall display. A sweep of the Aurora series' 'Yellow Fire', in fact, equals the showiest chrysanthemum for autumnal impact, and it blooms far longer.

Marigolds are rarely debilitated by pests and diseases. An abundance of lush green foliage accompanied by paucity of bloom suggests that the plants are receiving either too much shade or fertilizer. Let up on the fertilizer and flowering should pick up. The cool days of autumn excite many annuals—marigolds included—into a fresh frenzy of bloom.

If you like, you may save marigold seed from year to year, but the results may disappoint, since the offspring of a hybrid will differ markedly from its parent. A pack of marigold seed is relatively inexpensive and goes a long, long way if you transplant the seedlings that you thin out rather than discarding them. And named hybrids and strains give satisfyingly predictable and uniform results.

CATHARANTHUS

One of the best flowers for strong sun is *Catharanthus roseus*, or Madagascar periwinkle, often listed as *Vinca rosea*. A tender perennial native from Madagascar to tropical Asia, it is often confused (at least in conversation) with its hardier evergreen groundcover cousins, *Vinca major* and *V. minor*, both of which are also known as periwinkle.

While it may appear as delicate as an impatiens, catharanthus is among the most heat- and drought-resistant of garden plants. This hardiness, along with its sparkling color and dark green, glossy leaves, accounts for its popularity as a bedding-out plant for fast-food restaurants and other commercial ventures surrounded by a sea of concrete.

Catharanthus blossoms, which do resemble those of impatiens somewhat, come in rose, pink, a truly dazzling white, and white with a red eye. The cultivar 'Parasol' is especially showy, having extra large (two-and-a-half-inch) white flowers punctuated with a bright red eye. The 'Pretty In ...' series offers large, plush flowers with overlapping petals in white, pink, and deep rose. 'Magic Carpet' is a low-growing spreader useful in hanging baskets and as a temporary groundcover.

Catharanthus reseeds just enough to account for its spotty but highly visible presence among next season's bed of marigolds or geraniums. It is not a good cut flower.

The Vines of Summer

Vines have a degree of freedom denied other plants and a wanderlust that, if indulged, presents the gardener with delicious surprises and allows him or her to garden in creative new ways. Children love tepee houses made from bean plants allowed to twine over a cone of tall, thin stakes or along strings stretched from the top of a clothesline pole and anchored to the ground. A chain-link fence is not an object of great beauty, even if we paint it black and pretend that it's made of wrought iron. But shingled with morning glory or rendered three-dimensional by the exclamatory, oversized yellow flowers and broad, protruding leaves of a pumpkin vine, it ceases to be a nondescript necessity and becomes as much a part of the garden itself as a shock of hollyhocks or an edging of marigolds.

Morning Glory

It came as a surprise to me to learn a few years back that *Ipomoea purpurea*, the common purple- and pink-flowering morning glory with the flaccid, heart-shaped leaves, is not native to our region but was introduced from tropical America. The same can be said for the fetching ivy-leaved morning glory (*I. hederacea*), with its sky blue flowers and attractively lobed leaves (a species, however, which, like *I. purpurea*, has justifiably drawn the farmer's ire) and for the showy red-flowered *I. coccinea* and the closely related cypress vine (*I. quamoclit*), whose feathery, fernily cut leaves are as bewitching as its dainty scarlet blossoms.

The familiar wild potato vine, or man of the earth (*I. pandurata*), however, with its lovely white, violet-throated funnel-shaped flowers and almost arrow-shaped leaves like narrowed hearts, is a resident of ancient standing, considered native to the eastern two thirds of the country. It is a perennial, growing out of an edible tuber that can be several feet long and weigh twenty pounds, according to the late revered chronicler of Alabama's flora, Blanche Dean.

The garden sweet potato, so delicious baked with brown sugar, butter, and pecans, is *I. batatas*, a tropical tuber. Suspended in a jar of water, it is also an amazing house plant, with a talent for turning an ordinary kitchen into a luxuriant jungle within a few short weeks.

Seeds of certain of the morning glories are said to possess hallucinogenic properties and some are considered purgative. I don't advise experimentation to find out which is which. Besides, some morning glories may combine both properties, which could really be interesting.

The popular 'Heavenly Blue' morning glory, which possesses one of the clearest, brightest blue blossoms one can find for the summer garden, is a variety of *I. tricolor*, a species the Aztecs incorporated into religious rituals and medicine. I like to let it twine up the night-flowering biennial evening primrose (*Oenothera erythrosepala* or *O. biennis*), for the oenothera's primrose-yellow blossoms stay open until noon and mingle deliciously with the morning-flowering ipomoea's flaring blue trumpets.

The blazing crimson 'Scarlett O'Hara' is a cultivar of *I. nil*, the globe-girdling tropical species from which the imperial Japanese morning glories were developed.

The one ipomoea I find indispensable is the moonflower (*I. alba*), often listed as *Calonyction aculeatum*. Shortly before dark the great tapering flower buds, the folds of which are swirled to the tip like a freshly made vanilla ice-cream cone, unfurl into saucer-sized, silken blossoms of whitest white, which release a subtle perfume to lure moths.

The oversized, beaconlike flowers remain open for a time in the morning (and even most of the day in autumn), so they can be viewed to effect in concert with the diminutive, tubular, starlike scarlet blossoms of cypress vine or with searing red *Salvia coccinea* or *S. splendens*.

Moonflower is a strong, husky vine with very large dark green heart-shaped leaves and purplish-tinged stems. It requires a sturdy support. (It will slide right back down a mere string, preferring the substantial grip afforded by a chain-link fence or wrought-iron railing.) It is unmolested by pests and is even unaffected by the summer rusts that encrust the foliage of other ipomoeas.

Moonflower is perennial in the extreme lower South, but I must collect a supply of the bulbous purple seed capsules after frost.

Morning glories do fine in containers as long as they're watered. They need full sun, but shading the pot itself may enhance vigor in a specimen grown on a sunny patio. I keep a bit of water in the pans beneath my pots so that the roots won't cook to a crisp on our sunny back porch.

Morning glories make do with any well-drained soil. Fertilizer adds luster to the leaves. They can be grown indoors in a "cool, sunny window," whatever that is. Collect seed of favorite varieties after frost. Soak seed overnight before planting out in spring. It isn't necessary to start seed in containers.

MADEIRA VINE

The hefty, heart-shaped leaves of *Ipomoea alba* remind one of those of Madeira vine (*Anredera cordifolia*), though Madeira vine's leaves are lighter and glossier and more obviously veined. This is a vigorous climber for a mailbox or porch railing, but the flowers are insignificant. It is called potato or simply tater vine, for small, potatolike tubers form in the leaf axils. These should be removed before frost and stored over winter. I've read that Madeira vine's underground tuber survives winter, but it hasn't with me. I've always started fresh plants from the "taters" in spring.

LEGUMINOUS VINES

If you entertain a secret fondness for kudzu, chances are you'll love hyacinth bean (*Dipogon lablab*, formerly *Dolichos lablab*), a far showier and, mercifully, less rambunctious climbing legume. Like kudzu (*Pueraria lobata*), hyacinth bean has broad floppy leaves, consisting of three wide leaflets with pointed tips, and racemes of purple pea-flowers, which, in the hyacinth bean, are longer and more upright but less fragrant than kudzu's.

In very warm climates (Zones 9 and 10) hyacinth bean is a woody perennial; elsewhere it is grown as an annual. The seed should be started after the soil is warm (mid-May will do). The seedlings are temperamental about being transplanted, so you may as well start the seed in the ground. You may lose a few seedlings right at first, but, once they're off and running, there's no stopping them as they rapidly vault up the nearest support to fifteen feet or more. If you don't give them something to climb, the violet-stemmed vines will streak about the garden and find something on their own. They remind me of cobras, all stretched about, raising their headlike flower spikes here and there as if to look around.

I love to let this vine ramp through my Japanese maple. The violet-tinged leaves are inconspicuous among the maple's own deep-tinted foliage, but the protruding, candlelike stalks of bright purple blossoms cause passersby to do a double take.

In time the flowers give way to brilliant violet seedpods. I found a lavender caterpillar on one pod this summer. I like to imagine that it turned into a lavender butterfly or moth.

You can grow hyacinth bean indoors in winter if you've room for an all-vegetable great dane.

Scarlet runner bean (*Phaseolus coccineus*) is a bit more restrained than hyacinth bean but still manages to come across as a flamboyant fence-swallower when fed and watered regularly and given some sun. It, too, is a tropical perennial grown as an annual.

The trifoliolate leaves provide a rich green, contrasting backdrop for the loose racemes of showy red sweet pealike flowers. The edible beans are near-black and mottled with red. There is a comparatively boring white-flowering form (cv. 'Albus').

BLACK-EYED SUSAN VINE

Black-eyed Susan vine (*Thunbergia alata*) is seldom voluminous enough to suffice as a screen but is a superb little vine for a basket or pot even in a hot, sunny spot, as long as it's watered daily.

This tropical African perennial (grown as an annual in temperate regions) is quick and easy from seed. The scratchy, crudely heart-shaped leaves are opposite and held at a short distance from the wiry stem on winged petioles. The flowers, which may be white, yellow, or orange, emerge on stalks from between the leaves. The corolla is sliced into five broad petals and laid open about the black (really a striated purple) "eye," a hole down which the anthers and stigma can barely be viewed.

The leaves may acquire a bit of stippling and rust, but the charming flowers should appear from midsummer well into fall.

The fuzzy seed capsules are globular at the fertile end and have a prominent, pointed beak at the other. As the capsule dries, the beak acts as a trigger, splitting the capsule open with a resounding *SNAP!* and hurling the brown seeds, which look like curled-up porcupines, for vast distances. The sound can be unnerving if you're drying seed indoors, for you at first assume that you're hearing a major electrical short in progress. I dry thunbergia seed in sealed envelopes. The sound effects still make me jump, but the seeds stay where I want them.

PASSIONFLOWER

Our native passionflower, or maypop (*Passiflora incarnata*), has evidently been judged by the company it keeps for if it weren't a common habitué of roadsides and weedy vacant lots, no doubt this unusual flowering vine would be as respected and sought-after as a hybrid clematis.

The passionflowers were first described and named for Europe's benefit by priests who accompanied the Spanish conquistadors to the New World. They detected in the flower's unique and complicated structure symbolism related to the passion of Christ: three knobby stigmas representing the nails that held Christ's hands and feet, five stamens signifying his wounds, a frizzled corona for a crown of thorns, and the ten petallike parts representing the disciples—not counting Peter and Judas. (Perhaps these priests had been sampling the morning glory seeds.)

Most *Passiflora* species are tropical and include some beauties that'll knock your socks off—like the stark raving red-flowered *P. coccinea*—if you have a greenhouse or other indoor situation in which to grow them. But our hardy native maypop is stunning in its own right, with its three-inch flowers like a fringed, lavender wheel backing a complex arrangement of sexual apparatus. A white-flowering form is available as well.

Passionflower is a challenge to photograph at close range, for the height and intricacy of the flower structure make it necessary to shoot for all of the depth of field you can get. *Passiflora incarnata's* smooth leaves are edged with fine teeth and are artfully cut into three curving, sharply pointed lobes. From each leaf node spurts a corkscrew tendril that enwraps all it encounters and works to lift the vine above ground level. (This is not the vine to use for screening; it prefers to writhe away at the top of the fence. It is, however, a first-rate mailbox or lamppost vine.)

Passionflower is slow to emerge in spring, but, once moving, will bloom all summer long. It doesn't care about soil, but it must have sun. Cuttings, I'm told, can be rooted in damp sand or water. This sounds quicker than starting a new plant from seed.

Passionflower produces large, egglike, seedy fruits called maypops, which are yellow and edible at maturity.

The yellow passionflower (*P. lutea*) is less common and is encountered in the woods. Though its small, greenish-yellow flowers are not showy, *P. lutea* is a neat vine with flat, shallowly lobed leaves that remind me of little waving hands.

CUCURBITS

Almost any of the cucurbits, or gourd family members like squashes, melons, cucumbers, and pumpkins, come on like gangbusters and, with their broad, palmately veined leaves and big, bright, buttery flowers, are as ornamental as they are functional. A big-leaved cucurbit, like a pumpkin, can do amazing things with a chain-link fence, as it sweeps along, snapping itself into place with its ever-ready tendrils. Even if the vine becomes plastered with mildew, well, that's sort of ornamental, too. The bees don't mind flowers large enough to get lost in, and kids delight in watching a watermelon or pumpkin swell into eating or carving size.

Cucurbits magically appear around compost heaps and wherever vegetable scraps are thrown. Last year a mighty cucurbit rose up and swallowed our back porch railing. The leaves were almost a foot across. The orange flowers were as broad as salad plates, but I saw no fruit. It was not until I was pulling the vine off the railing after frost and found a single perfect orange pumpkin dangling inside a porchside nandina that I concluded that the vine had resulted from our chucking the remains of the previous Halloween's jack-o'-lantern over the rail (for I'm often too lazy to walk all the way across the yard to the compost heap, which is how our great pink-flowering rosebush has come to have a banana peel mulch).

CUP-AND-SAUCER VINE

One exceedingly handsome vine I must try again some day is *Cobaea scandens*, better known as cup-and-saucer vine or cathedral bells, a fast-growing perennial from the Mexican tropics that is grown as an annual above Zone 9. Malodorous while still young and green, the deep, bell-like flowers, which are nestled into a saucerlike calyx, turn purple or white when mature. They are thought to be pollinated primarily by vegetarian bats in Mexico. I suspect bumblebees will attempt the trick here, since purple is one of their favorite colors.

The vine climbs by means of twirly, branching tendrils at the tips of its dark green, pinnate leaves. It is said to prefer light, rich soil and as much sun and moisture as you can give it (but it will take some shade).

I grew this very beautiful, rapid climber one year along the front porch railing on Ewing Street and was shocked when it suddenly screeched to a halt and died for no obvious reason. Were I not such a low-budget operator, I'd have tried cup-and-saucer vine again by now, but in the catalog before me the price is $2.95 for nine measly seeds.

NASTURTIUM

Now, I can get forty seeds of climbing nasturtium for $1.99. Of course, I'll spend a small fortune in insecticides keeping my nasturtiums (*Tropaeolum majus*) free of aphids, but that's literally all I'll likely have to do for them, for, with nasturtiums, the more you pretend you don't see them and withhold water and fertilizer, the harder they'll bloom.

Nasturtiums come in mixtures of garish, sunny colors to spice up a dreary fence or interweave with other sun-lovers in patio containers. And, if you tire of their insistent cheeriness or if it looks like the aphids are winning the war, you can always eat them (aphids and all, I guess), for nasturtium's round leaves add tang to salads.

Plant seed of nasturtium in warm, average to poor soil (they resent transplanting). 'Parks' Fragrant Giants' is a good choice. Seedlings will climb by coiling leaf stalks. Water sparingly and, if you fertilize at all, use a low-nitrogen product. Deadheading may prolong bloom.

Things to Do after Supper

We can fertilize most trees and shrubs one last time now. Any new growth this encourages should have plenty of time to harden off before the cold hits. If shrubs need shearing, don't wait any longer or the tender regrowth triggered will likely be killed back over winter. So many boxwood hedges go through the winter singed brown when delicate young stems and leaves are subjected to the sudden arctic plunge we typically experience around Christmas or early January.

If we poke around our Japanese climbing fern, we might locate a few baby ferns to pot up or move elsewhere. This is one of the few ferns that will successfully come up from spores in the garden (in the *lawn*, actually).

There still should be tomatoes and okra to pick. There is about the okra plant (*Abelmoschus esculentus*) an air of mystery, an aura of sacredness. The flower is almost identical to that of the marsh mallow (*Hibiscus moscheutos*), but is hidden by the foliage. When we lived in Jacksonville, Alabama, I grew okra so tall I had to stand on a chair to pick it, but the itch I acquired from contact with the foliage and the fuzzy, sticky pods—even when I wore long sleeves and gloves—was maddening. I love okra, but now, in my lazy middle age, I buy it on the frozen food aisle at the grocery store—cut, breaded,and ready to toss into the pan.

Real gardeners should be preparing the fall vegetable garden now, by month's end setting out transplants of broccoli, cabbage, and kale and sowing seeds of peas, spinach, turnips, and lettuce. Count me out.

Signs of the Times

Along our nature trail at the botanical garden the black gums (*Nyssa sylvatica*) are flashing a smattering of red leaves, and the goldenrod, whose mile-long, ropy roots we pulled back in the spring as if we were hauling in an anchor, has outsmarted us again and lifts spires of gritty yellow from every sunlit bed. Here and there we spot an aster—yellow here, purple there.

I refuse to believe my eyes, but at home, in every backyard bed, I see dead nettle infants (*Lamium maculatum*) coming up by the thousands.

September

Seeptember sees the grip of summer broken. There are whole days when we can work outdoors in relative comfort—which is good, for our after-supper playtime is limited by the shortening days. By midmonth nights are cold, and early mornings are too chilly for breakfasting on the porch.

Yellow jackets turn nastier than ever, and bumblebees, in some strange seasonal confusion, alight on our blue jeans. (They're merely mistaking us for a blue flower, or course, and intend no harm, but the experience is always invigorating.)

The liriope lining the front walk is purpled with spiky bloom. The goldfinches feast on the prickly brown seed heads of purple coneflowers, even as all the coneflowers (*Echinacea*, *Ratibida pinnata*, *Rudbeckia*) revive with a fresh flurry of bloom (many of them this year's seedlings just now hitting their stride).

The green is draining from the dogwood leaves, leaving them yellowish-pale and here and there flushed with orange or red, made all the more evident by the now-scarlet berry clusters.

The airy canopy of the hackberries, underpinned by incongruously massive, warty, gray trunks, fades from weak green to washed-out yellow. No two of the jagged, pointed leaves are alike, of course, as each is dappled with its own unique arrangement of nipple galls, bug holes, and brown fungal stippling. (Not long ago I discovered the same stippling brushed onto the wings of a still, yellow moth suspended, leaflike, beneath a hackberry stem, so that only the smoothness of its wing margins gave away its clever secret.)

Fields sway with goldenrod, ironweed, and starry white aster, and, at the edge of the woods, the flame and garnet leaves of the early-to-color sourwood set off the tree's faded flower tassels.

Along woodland paths poison ivy briefly flickers yellow and orange then quickly drops its leaflets, as if in haste to render itself invisible. Meanwhile, veils of Virginia creeper glow in every hue known to autumn—crimson, scarlet, yellow, even pink.

PARTHENOCISSUS

Virginia creeper, or woodbine (*Parthenocissus quinquefolia*) frightens some people by its resemblance to poison ivy (though its palmately arranged, compound leaves have five leaflets, and, as every child knows, poison ivy has "leaves of three"). It is a fast-growing native member of the grape family (Vitaceae) with an ungrapelike talent for clinging to even the slickest surface with branching tendrils having stick-on tips like tiny tree frog toes.

I used to let this vine ramp over my greenhouse in summer when I wanted to shade it. Then in winter, when I was ready for the sun to stream in, I peeled away the Virginia creeper in great sheets. The vine leaves a bit of residue, but nothing like that left by English ivy, and Virginia creeper is a million times easier to remove from a structure.

It is equally fond of racing up trees, but I think in most cases it does them little or no harm.

Civilized folks are perhaps more familiar with Virginia creeper's oriental cousin, best known as Boston ivy (*P. tricuspidata*), the "ivy" enshrouding many an institution of higher learning. It is used to great effect, as a matter of fact, at the University of the South, just up the road at Sewanee, Tennessee, where in autumn this clinging creeper with its ivylike three-lobed leaves glows like rubies against the gray stone walls.

There are a number of named varieties of *P. tricuspidata*, most with larger or waxier foliage than the type and excellent fall color. *Parthenocissus tricuspidata* 'Purpurea' is purplish-red summer long.

SOURWOOD

Grown in full sun, sourwood (*Oxydendrum arboreum*) celebrates fall early and spectacularly with a blaze of rich color. This heath family member is also known as sorrel tree or lily of the valley tree, the latter name owing to the down-splayed panicles of creamy, bell-shaped flowers, which appear in summer. It is a small (usually), exceedingly slow-growing tree with a columnar, drooping outline. The branches hang down to the ground, at least when the plant is young (which is for a long, long time).

Sourwood tolerates shade and most well-drained soils, but it is often found in gritty, acid soil along roadbanks and in precipitously exposed locations. Sourwood makes a presentable solitary specimen in the garden but is more effective, I think, when massed in groups of three or more. It can be tricky to transplant. Please don't attempt it in summer.

I once collected seeds of a sourwood jutting from what appeared to be bald rock at the very tip of one of the state's highest peaks. I risked my life dangling over the guardrail, and then I couldn't get the seeds to germinate. Perhaps they have to pass through the digestive system of a Concorde. Actually, Dirr writes that an acquaintance of his germinated oodles of sourwood seeds in flats of peat kept under mist.

My "English" Garden

Oddly enough, in August and September I have one of those misty, pastel beds so drilled into our consciousness by the English garden books as the ideal for which we all should strive. It harbors frilly lavender physostegia; great pink and white spidery globes of cleome; a silvery cloud of silver king (*Artemisia ludoviciana albula*); a silver and lavender-blue shaft of Russian sage (*Perovskia atriplicifolia*); an unidentified white-flowering tickseed (*Bidens* species, we think), which Willodene Mathews found in south Alabama; a puff of lemon-yellow melampodium; a 'Pink Radiance' rose emerging from a gentle haze of caryopteris; a few spires of *Lobelia siphilitica*; a burly, rose-flowering mallow; a few stray pink and purple petunias; assorted snapdragons; a not too stridently yellow marigold; and a harsh orange cosmos, which ruins the whole thing and should be pulled at once.

Earlier on the cosmos fit right in, for this bed was pepper hot with scarlet canna and crocosmia and the sunny yellows of coreopsis and *Hypericum calycinum*.

Physostegia virginiana, commonly called obedient plant or false dragonhead, is a fine native perennial requiring just a bit of management but unfailingly loyal—once you have it, it will likely remain with you till the bitter end.

The pink, lavender, or white flowers are so puffy and tightly packed onto bulky spikes that one is apt to mistake physostegia for a member of the snapdragon family, like foxglove or penstemon. The flowers have a faint, fresh scent and the foliage is virtually odorless, so only the square stem hints at the plant's kinship with the normally aromatic mint clan.

Physostegia passes the winter as a stoloniferously creeping colony of rosettes of slender, toothy, dark green, almost rubbery leaves. In organically rich, moist soil a single plant may expand into a colony four feet across in as many years, but the roots are shallow and any growth deemed excessive is easily removed.

In summer it sends up tall stems to four feet or so which are eventually crowned with multiple spikes of flowers. Certain of the white-flowering forms may bloom as early as June, while the more common lavender form and the ultra-pink *P. v.* 'Vivid' bloom from August into October.

I cut my physostegia back almost to the ground in early summer, which forces it to branch and ultimately to produce more flowers. This also prevents its rather weak stems from flopping over for four feet in all directions. Some stems still lean, but a goodly portion remain standing at two and a half to three feet by season's end. Physostegia will tolerate some shade, but is stronger and more floriferous in sun. It requires a lot of moisture and can take quite heavy soil as long as it's moist.

Physostegia is remarkably free of pests and diseases. The only thing that's ever threatened the survival of my physostegia was an invasion of the annual Asiatic dayflower (*Commelina communis*). The physostegia declined alarmingly until two seasons of diligent plucking of dayflower seedlings eradicated the pretty, blue-flowering pest.

Some gardeners deadhead early-flowering forms of physostegia to induce a second (smaller) flush of bloom. Mine blooms late (in part because of my having cut it back), and I simply rip out the flowering stalks once bloom is done, which prevents massive self-seeding and neatens up the place. Plenty of healthy young rosettes are always left behind for next year.

Recently we added a lovely lavender-flowering variegated form to the nature trail at the botanical garden. I suspect it'll take watching to prevent its reverting to normal.

I can't think of a plant I love more dearly than the soft-as-mist, silvery gray silver king artemisia (*A. ludoviciana albula*). Native to the arid Southwest, silver king is a frothy blur of wispy stems and tiny, narrow leaves, both coated with a close mat of fine white hair. Though borne by the thousands, the minute composite flowers are thoroughly inconspicuous. For garden effect, the artemisias are strictly foliage plants.

An aromatic perennial reaching three or four feet in height and spreading by rhizomes, silver king hides the skinny legs of cleome and works to both separate and reconcile conflicting colors like lavender and orange, pink and scarlet, and hard and soft yellows.

I used to grow this luminous artemisia beside a 'Tropicana' rose and was quite taken with the way the rose's coral petals seemed more beautiful once they'd shattered and spilled onto the artemisia.

The electric purple of *Verbena canadensis* 'Homestead Purple' is all the more dynamic when fronting silver king, while the delicate pink blossoms of the Asiatic hybrid lily 'Zephyr' have a tender, etheral quality when suspended above a cloud of silver king. Association with this elegant plant improves almost anything.

One highly respected source proclaims *Artemisia* 'Powis Castle', a cross between *A. arborescens* and *A. absinthium*, to be the "best artemisia for the South." This somewhat lower-growing, almost aqua-gray, frilly leaved plant can be used to excellent effect in beds and borders when it is kept in bounds. My own *A.* 'Powis Castle' lapsed into a yards-wide sprawl, making an attractive groundcover of itself beneath a raging scarlet canopy of *Salvia coccinea*. Alas, when the long wet winter arrived, the artemisia passed away.

Unfortunately the artemisias' adaptation to dry climates makes their survival in the muggy and sometimes mushy South an iffy proposition, for they are quick to rot. I lost my Ewing Street silver king one exceptionally wet summer. When I set out my current plant, I prepared the soil well, mixing in copious quantities of sand and elevating the plant atop its own little hill in the bed. Good air circulation is important; it mustn't be crowded or shaded by its neighbors.

For some lucky people silver king artemisia spreads about alarmingly in spring. Any unwanted surplus can be dug up and shared with friends. Silver king can be air-dryed upside down for long-lasting enjoyment in dried arrangements.

Russian sage (*Perovskia atriplicifolia*) is similarly silver-leaved and rot-prone. It is a strongly aromatic sage (mint family) about four feet high with tightly opposed cymes of small purple flowers arranged in spirelike panicles. Its health and vigor depend in part on its being given plenty of elbow room.

Caryopteris, or bluebeard (*Caryopteris ×clandonensis*), is a more durable blue-gray ingredient of my "English" bed. Caryopteris is a pleasantly aromatic verbena family member with soft, faintly downy opposite leaves, the axils of which give rise to dense, fat-topped cymes of very small blue flowers. Plants bloom for perhaps a month—not as long as I'd like.

To me this particular blue is far more exquisite in combination with pink than with yellow—better with Gomphrena 'Lavender Lady' (which looks pink to me) than with melampodium.

Another good blue fall-flowering perennial, which I plan to establish in this bed, is mistflower, or wild ageratum (*Eupatorium coelestinum*). It is much like a large version of *Ageratum houstonianum*, the familiar little bedding-out ageratum. It bears serious watching, for in moist ground hardy ageratum's rhizomes burrow along with great haste in all directions (an attribute that makes it great for covering large, poorly drained areas in sun or shade). Hardy ageratum must be thinned ruthlessly in spring and kept cut back until midsummer to control its unwelcome height (to three feet) or it will likely conceal earlier-blooming neighbors.

In my front yard flower beds on Ewing Street I let this rambunctious native wildflower weave between the impatiens and the tall red and purple *Salvia splendens*, for I delighted in the way it brought a refreshing end-of-season change to the color scheme. In out-of-the-way areas it combines deliciously with goldenrod or the lemon-yellow, starlike blooms of rosinweed (*Silphium integrifolium*). It even mixes entertainingly with the annual ageratum and provides a loose, cool, contrasting background for the tightly packed dwarf chrysanthemum 'Yellow Jacket'.

Something very different we might try either at the edge of a bed such as this or in the shade garden is the ultra-neat, compact *Exacum affine*.

The plant is impeccably neat and rather waxy in appearance, with dainty, half-inch, open-faced blue (or sometimes white or rose) flowers with shockingly yellow anthers peering out from a ball of small oval leaves. It is known as either German or Persian violet, though it's no more a violet than you or I but rather a member of the gentian family, and it hails, not from Germany or ancient Persia, but from Socotra (an island somewhere in the Indian Ocean, if you must know).

Sometimes sold as a houseplant in supermarket floral departments, *Exacum affine* is nonetheless easily started from dustlike seed on a windowsill in February or from cuttings in March and planted out in late April. It is pretty with something equally small and prissy like *Alyssum* 'Carpet of Snow', *Torenia* 'Pink Panda', or a dwarf yellow hosta like the lance-leaved 'Kabitan'.

One last possible addition to this fall-blooming bed would be patrinia. *Patrinia scabiosifolia nagoya* sends up sprays consisting of umbels of tiny bright yellow flowers, while *P. villosa* provides a similarly frothy veil of white. Both are from eastern Asia. These perennials are sometimes compared to *Verbena bonariensis* for, though they may attain considerable height (from two to eight feet), they can be left wherever they seed themselves unless they become too numerous (which they may), for they have a gauzy airiness which lets us see right through them to the garden beyond.

Patrinia is a weed at heart and enjoys eternal life in sun or part shade in any well-drained soil.

Fall Flowers for Moist, Partial Shade

I've a very different bed at the northwest corner of the house where the driveway connects with the garage. The upper end of the bed bakes a bit due to the sun-on-brick-and-concrete effect, but as it slopes down the north side of the house it is fed by a downspout which, along with its heavy mulch layer, keeps the bed moist. In September the main attractions here are *Lobelia siphilitica*, ironweed (*Veronia altissima*), and rosinweed (*Silphium integrifolium*).

We have several native silphiums, the differences between some of them being fairly subtle. Even within a given species considerable variation occurs. In *S. integrifolium*, for example, the sandpapery leaves may be lancelike or ovate with either smooth or serrate margins.

Rosinweed may not seem immediately endearing and yet, year by year this tough, reliable plant works its way into one's affections. True, it is coarse and exhibits all the grace of a refrigerator, gradually expanding into imposingly tall (to five feet), dense clumps of rigid foliage. But its cool, lemon-drop yellow daisies with their six petallike ray flowers (drat, he loves me not!) are borne in gratifying profusion for two solid months, starting in mid-August. As a background for *Lobelia siphilitica*, they enhance the lobelia's subtle blue spires of bloom, but they are particularly complementary of the ironweed's flattened cymes of small, bushy, intensely violet flower heads.

Both rosinweed and ironweed can be cut back repeatedly to prevent their presenting a blank wall of boring green from May until mid-August. (I like to keep the view of the distant backyard beds clear.) Of course, ironweed zooms to ten feet without really trying, so you might prefer to exploit its talent for making a sentinel of itself in your garden design.

My only complaint with this majestic, showy field weed is that the flowers seem to flare up and fade so quickly. From start to finish I doubt the event lasts more than two weeks, though the tall, straight stems and the brushy brown seed heads remain ornamental in a fallish sort of way for weeks. The stems, though herbaceous, may stand all winter—a reason, I'm told, for the plant's common name. Or, as sometimes happens, a storm may flatten them at the height of bloom.

S U N F L O W E R

I think we're all familiar with the cultivated annual sunflower (*Helianthus annuus* and its hybrids), whose seeds find their way from our bird feeders to our flower beds. But America offers dozens of *Helianthus* species, many of them reliable, easy, garden-worthy perennials.

One of the best of the local natives is the swamp, or narrow-leaved, sunflower (*H. angustifolius*), a dark-eyed daisy to seven feet with stringbean narrow, inrolled leaves. You see it tumbling about in brilliant profusion in damp fields and along roadsides in late summer and autumn. Another is the Jerusalem artichoke (*H. tuberosus*), a hairy giant (to twelve feet, weather permitting) with gorgeous, golden, four-inch flower heads from August until October. Jerusalem artichoke, of course, is known for its edible (but not particularly digestible, so I understand) potatolike tubers. The plant spreads by leaps and bounds and thus should be relegated to the back fence (that's where mine is) or some other neglected spot where its jubilant determination to be fruitful and multiply won't be resented. If Scarlet O'Hara had stuck a few of these babies into the vegetable patch, she and her people would never have gone hungry in the first place.

For a couple of years I've grown Maximilian sunflower (*H. maximiliani*), another towering perennial which raises coaster-sized golden disks against the clear blue sky. The grayish, lancelike leaves can easily be mistaken for those of goldenrod. My plants bloom beautifully in September, but the stems are so easily toppled by wind and rain that I surround the plants with three-ring wire cages in spring. Since the leaves along the lower half of the stem always curl up and die, it's a good idea to plant cosmos or a tall salvia in front to hide the naked stems.

A PAIR OF SALVIAS

Salvia coccinea, variously known as Texas, tropical, or scarlet sage, begins to germinate once the weather is good and warm. I usually start noticing the pairs of little blue-gray, spade- or heart-shaped cotyledons (seedling leaves) in June, and, within a few weeks, butterfly- and bumblebee-laden spires of scarlet, split-lipped blossoms rise, flamelike, here and there all about the garden. Of all the flowers I grow *S. coccinea* is the hummingbird's number-one favorite.

At a glance this not particularly aromatic salvia could be taken for the deliciously scented pineapple sage (*S. elegans*), but the upper stems and whorled calyxes of *S. coccinea* are streaked with a near-black purple.

There is an airiness to this salvia that is lacking in the chunkier *S. splendens*, so that *S. coccinea* is seen to best advantage when combined with flowers or foliage of a different color—yellow *Rudbeckia triloba*, wild white aster, silver king artemisia, or even smoldering purple *Perilla frutescens* 'Atropurpurea'.

Salvia coccinea's blooms seem to come in great wavelike surges, and new seedlings appear and burst into bloom until frost. *Salvia coccinea* returns reliably year after year unless the beds where the seeds are dropped are so heavily mulched afterward that any seedlings that may issue forth haven't a prayer of making their way to the light.

Cultivated versions of *S. coccinea* include the dwarfer-than-type 'Lady in Red' (under two feet) and the endearingly sweet, two-toned pink and white 'Cherry Blossom', which has bloomed its heart out at the entrance to the herb garden at the botanical garden this year. I've seen this one faring reasonably well in light shade, too.

Velvet sage, better known as Mexican bush sage (*Salvia leucantha*) is such a sought-after plant at our botanical garden's spring plant sale that some years the supply has been exhausted at the members-only preview party the night before the sale opens to the public.

This is a large plant, four feet or so high and easily as wide by summer's end. The narrow, aromatic leaves have an olive or grayish cast, depending on the light, I suppose. It is for the eighteen-inch spires of fuzzy, soft-as-kitten-paws flowers that one willingly waits all summer. The downy white corollas, protruding from velvety purple calyxes, resemble Easter bunnies peeking out of a basket.

This beautiful sage can be preserved by air-drying stems upside down in a warm, dark, well-ventilated area. (Unfortunately for my photography, my photographic darkroom is made to order for this.)

Velvet sage is a tender perennial. One year I potted up a huge plant and took it indoors for the winter, but it pined away, though Mary Lou McNabb has no trouble preserving hers over winter in her greenhouse. I probably should have just started a cutting. I think cuttings of Mexican bush sage are quicker to rot than those of less desert-oriented salvias, though. You can, of course, save seed. Or you can keep your *S. leucantha* in a pot year-round so that its roots aren't traumatized when it's time to move back indoors. It will have to be a large, heavy pot, however. In milder climates than mine I'm told it will pull through winter if it's grown in a protected spot and/or thickly mulched. (Then again it may rot away.)

You can make many beautiful plant combinations with velvet sage. At the botanical garden it grows in the "butterfly garden" with buddleia and 'Lavender Lady' gomphrena. Mary Lou uses it as a tasteful foil for the towering, yellow-flowering forsythia sage (*Salvia madrensis*). Or you can do like I do and allow it to associate with orange cosmos and then wait for the neighbors to present you with a petition.

Work, Work, Work

Shorter, cooler days allow us to cut back on our watering, and, for most established trees and shrubs, this may even be an aid to braking their surge of tender summer growth and preparing them for winter. But azaleas and camellias should not be allowed to dry out completely, and young dogwoods, still plumping out their few flower buds for next spring, should be given extra water, particularly if the leaf margins show the browning and shriveling characteristic of drought.

Caladiums should be dug and the tubers cured and stored now before they become hard to locate. Pines will be shedding their dead needles now. Be sure to lay in a supply of pine straw for mulching azaleas, rhododendrons, dogwoods, and so forth.

Rooted cuttings of perennials and shrubs begun since spring can be set out if they are growing vigorously. Mulch well and mark them to prevent their being trampled or mowed and make sure they don't go dry over winter.

Bulbs purchased now can be stored in the refrigerator until circumstances permit setting them out. Check them often to see that they neither shrivel nor rot.

Before the month is out the first taste of winter will drive nighttime temperatures into the forties or even the thirties, and tropical houseplants will have to be brought in. Smart plant lovers plan ahead, repotting or dividing the potbound or overgrown in advance, washing foliage or spraying for pests and getting their charges acclimated to the drearier indoor light before the furnace is turned on to compound their distress with bone dry air.

I, of course, am stumbling around with a flashlight the evening of the "Great Plunge," rounding up the bromeliads from under the dogwoods; the pineapple from under the juniper; the palms, ferns, and arums from off the front porch; the succulents from the back porch; et cetera. Then, slugs, ants, and all, the motley jungle is deposited in the den. Over the next few days the syngonium, sansevieria, and palms will find their way to the poorly lighted living room; the ferns and African violets will venture back onto the porch for awhile once the temperature moderates; but most will wind up with their noses pressed against the den's sliding glass door, later to be joined by cuttings of impatiens, coleus, and lantana, which serve to brighten up the place all winter.

Much of September gardening consists of removing bloomed-out annuals. As *Rudbeckia triloba* sets seed and turns brown, it can be pulled up. New plants will be coming into bloom right up until frost anyway. Much the same can be said for cosmos, melampodium, emilia, and many others.

If you've not had enough of mowing, now's the time to repair or replant fescue lawns with dwarf varieties like 'Bonsai', 'Rebel, Jr.', or 'Taurus' or, as many of my neighbors do, overseed a dormant Zoysia or Bermuda lawn with ryegrass for a winter-long carpet of velvety emerald green. Remember, though, ryegrass needs ample water to look its best, so one could conceivably be dragging hoses around on New Year's Eve if we have an unusually dry winter. (None of this information applies to those of us who don't know which end of a blade of grass is up and are just grateful to park the mower for a few months and concentrate on digging violets and pulling dead nettle out of the flower beds.)

October

Bittersweet October. The mellow, messy, leaf-kicking, perfect pause between the opposing miseries of summer and winter. Mornings (some of them) start off foggy, the cold, soaked bumblebees buried, immobile, in the flower faces or maybe bumbling around in the mulch, dirty and barely able to crawl, like drowsy drunks. Along the creek hordes of just-back-from-somewhere starlings converse squeakily and incessantly as they breakfast among the hackberries.

The wind comes up with the sun, batting away the fog and driving the ash leaves down, shower after golden shower, onto the lawn and into the street, where they hiss along the pavement.

In the bed surrounding the Japanese maple the reinvigorated sweet alyssum and ageratum foam like waves breaking around a warm-toned island of golden marigold, lantana, and melampodium, piping-hot orange emilia, waxen red dahlia, and antique white, orange-centered 'Star White' zinnia.

The Japanese anemone, 'Honorine Jobert', which looked so frail and hopeless when I planted her in March, has a few holes in her leaves, but she proudly waves a half-dozen pearllike flower buds and at least as many ivory-skinned blossoms. Shows how much *I* know.

Roses revive, blooming as if they're convinced May has come again.

A wild, anarchistic beauty seizes the neighborhood. The dry leaves blow where they will, even onto the neatest lawns; an army of leaf-blowing landscape technicians couldn't deter them. The crapemyrtles (surely they must be tired from all that blooming) turn russet-orange, and, Cinderella at the ball, the common mulberry, so drab and unappreciated the remainder of the year, suddenly (briefly) glows brilliant yellow, a beacon of splendor.

In the late afternoon sun the mountain above us is a rusty amalgam of old-gold hickory, ruby-red dogwood, firelit sugar maple, pink and orange persimmon, and the fruit basket hues of sassafras. The smoketrees along the winding roadsides are all fire and no smoke now, while, nearer ground level, *Salvia azurea*, as intensely blue as the October sky, mixes with the reblooming butterfly weed and prairie coneflower.

In the fields Queen Anne's lace blooms anew with the golden aster. The velvet-stemmed staghorn sumac discards its red and purple leaves but holds the cones of furry, blood-red fruit, to be meted out to the birds once winter settles in.

MAPLE

I love thick-waisted old maples in autumn, especially when their saturated red, orange, or yellow leaves stand out against a rain-blackened trunk.

The sugar maple (*Acer saccharum*) is a slow-growing native of the eastern half of the country. Northern portions of Alabama, Georgia, and Mississippi are the southernmost limits of the typical subspecies, *A. saccharum* subsp. *saccharum*, which normally has a five-lobed leaf. This tree is plentiful on our local mountainsides. Further south one is apt to be more successful with the less massive and more tender southern sugar maple (*A. barbatum*, also listed as *A. floridanum* or *A. saccharum* subsp. *floridanum*) or the similar chalk maple (*A. leucoderme*, also viewed as a subspecies of *A. saccharum*). Fall color among maples is highly variable, but that of southern sugar maple is said to tend toward yellow, while chalk maple shows orange as well.

The comparatively fast-growing red maple (*A. rubrum*), which typically displays a three-lobed leaf, is widely distributed from Canada to Florida and west to Texas. In the landscape it is adaptable as to soil but is one of the most plentiful species in low, wet ground in our area.

To be assured of the brilliant red fall coloring for which this species is noted one should purchase a named cultivar like 'Red Sunset', which is rated one of the best all around, according to Dirr.

Unlike the wispy, no-fall-color, water-line-invading silver maple (*A. saccharinum*), sugar and red maples cast a dense shade which, together with a network of tough, superficial roots, makes growing anything other than vinca or liriope under them a challenge.

GINKGO TALES

When we lived in Atlanta in the early 1970s, I made annual fall pilgrimages to all four of the known (to me) ginkgo trees within walking distance of the Ponce de Leon and Argonne Avenue intersection, where we lived, for I don't believe I've ever seen anything before or since to rival the stark, unadulterated beauty of a ginkgo at the all-too-brief peak of fall splendor, when every leaf is a single shade of pure, unblemished yellow. Then suddenly a squirrel sneezes and every gorgeous leaf drops, seemingly at once. (I've never actually witnessed this phenomenon; all I know is that one day the tree is a vertical splotch of pure, unsullied yellow, and the next day the ground beneath the bare branches is a huge horizontal splotch of pure, unsullied yellow.) Of course, there is the occasional early freeze which browns the leaves before the anticipated spectacle gets underway, but this is rare.

Near or beyond the point of extinction in the wild, *Ginkgo biloba* was introduced to western horticulture in 1730 from China, where it was discovered growing in temple gardens. It is the sole survivor of an ancient order of gymnosperms which, fernlike, requires the presence of water for its motile sperm to swim to the egg. (No, I don't know how the sperm gets from a boy tree to a girl tree, but I would love to see the pictures.) As with other gymnosperms, the seed is considered "naked," that is, not borne in a protective ovary, or seed case, though in this case it does have a fleshy outer wall.

Sometimes called maidenhair tree because the fan-shaped leaves resemble those of the maidenhair fern, ginkgo is a slow-growing tree (unless prodded with fertilizer and water) with massive potential and a lifespan measured in centuries. It casts a filtered shade under which grass will grow, particularly if lower limbs are removed.

I don't know why the ginkgo is rare-to-nonexistent in the wild, for it is easy to grow, tolerating temperature extremes and almost any well-drained soil, and is essentially pest- and disease-free. (Perhaps its former enemies are now extinct.) It has an easily transplanted fibrous root system.

Unless you move a lot, you'll be living with your ginkgo for a long time, so purchase only a male clone that exhibits the growth habit your landscape can accommodate. 'Mayfield', for example, is a narrow, columnar male, reminiscent of Lombardy poplar, which might be grouped for a vertical accent or lined up to define a boundary, if such soldierly formality seems called for. I've seen this or a similar columnar form used with the nearly as rare (in the wild, that is) and ancient dawn redwood (*Metasequoia glyptostroboides*). 'Autumn Gold' and 'Saratoga' are among the more spreading male selections of ginkgo known for outstanding fall color.

Female trees are equally lovely and desirable in every way except that the grape-sized, persimmonlike, overripe seeds with which they litter the ground in autumn raise a stench that can best be compared to that of a fraternity house bathroom the morning after homecoming. Stick to male clones or prepare to issue clothespins to your neighbors for their noses a few decades hence, when your female ginkgo reaches sexual maturity. (Actually, the meat of the stony inner seed coat is used as food in the Orient, an acquired taste, I'm sure.)

My husband and I learned the hard way that there's another good reason to treat yourself to a tried and true named selection. When we bought the Ewing Street house, I wasted no time in ordering a ginkgo. Our nameless, bargain, bare root tree arrived at sundown some days later. Flashlight in hand, we eagerly trudged out into the dark to insert this curious little wooden skeleton into the ground. Somehow we ran out of back fill and finished covering the stubby, triple-pronged roots with virgin cat litter.

Soon our ginkgo stick sprouted branches, which grew akimbo, as if they had no idea which way to go. When fall came, we waited, alas, in vain, for the colorful spectacle. We had evidently purchased the only ginkgo tree in catalog history with absolutely *no fall color*. I couldn't believe it, but year after year this weird little tree turned from light green directly to brown. So consider yourself warned.

ONE LAST EUONYMUS

I suppose *Euonymus alatus*, winged euonymus, is overdone elsewhere, but, really, I don't see that much of it here in Huntsville, which surprises me, because it is an excellent hedge or border plant, every leaf of which turns stop-sign red in fall.

There is quite a bit of winged euonymus around Carter Hall on the A&M campus, where it blazes away in late autumn despite its siting on the shady north side of the building. The only thing that bugs me about its appearance is the bareness about its bottom. I think more compact forms like *E. a.* 'Compacta' or the particularly slow-growing 'Rudy Haag' are more spreading and fuller at the bottom. Certainly they are more suitable as foundation plants, because the typical *E. alatus* slowly but steadily takes on ten to twenty feet of height and girth. Fortunately, the stiff, corky, winged stems take pruning well (and provide cuttings for starting new plants).

In early autumn the seed capsules split to reveal orange-red seed coats which are too hidden by the normally dark green leaves to be showy.

Winged euonymus is happy in any moist but well-drained soil. It dislikes dry soil and benefits from mulch and extra water. It isn't supposed to attract scale as readily as most other *Euonymus* species.

VINES FOR FALL

All of the grapes, both domesticated and wild, take on wondrous fall coloring. The native muscadine, or scuppernong (*Vitis rotundifolia*), conceals a rusty chainlink fence as well as any vine alive, provides luscious red-purple fruit for man and beast alike (another acquired taste), and gives radiant yellow fall color. The grapes are rampant woody vines, ultimately as big around at the base as a person's arm and so will likely need pruning in all but the wildest settings, particularly if ample fruit production is a consideration. They grow more vigorously in sun than shade but do well enough in either and in most soils that aren't actually under water.

My favorite vine for October color is virtually never seen in catalogs, though it hangs like a curtain from many a southern roadside tree. Carolina moonseed vine, or coralbeads (*Cocculus carolinus*), is a twining vine whose faintly fuzzy yet glossy leaves vary from heart- to ivy-leaf-shaped, even on a given stem.

The vine is dioecious, that is, the elongate panicles of insignificant male and female flowers appear on separate plants. In October, just as the leaves begin to yellow, the clustered berrylike drupes on female plants turn a brilliant, lacquered red, presenting a very rich, triple-tone effect. The fruit is savored by birds, which is how I've come to have several of these handsome and (I think) mannerly vines along our back fence.

PEPPER

Peppers (*Capsicum* species) are ornamental, tasty, high in vitamins A and C when ripe, and easy to grow. The bright fruits often retain their color for a time after frost, making them particularly valuable in the fall garden. Peppers are perennials from tropical America. Most are tender, but a few manage to survive winters here in Zone 7.

There is a weedy wild pepper that we pull from our sunny wildflower beds at the botanical garden. It gets about knee-high, has a loose, rangy habit and fiery, pea-sized fruit. Some people call it bird pepper, so I suppose that makes it *C. annuum* var. *aviculare*, which can actually be pretty if well grown.

Most of the peppers we cultivate for food and ornament are classified as *C. annuum* var. *annuum* (Tabasco sauce is made from *C. frutescens*), but the variety is further divided into five groups. Pimento and bell pepper, for instance, belong to the mild-flavored Grossum group, whose fruits have ribbed sides and are apple- or bell-shaped. Cayenne and chili peppers are members of the Longum group, whose long, tapering fruits are exceedingly pungent. (The ground pepper that sits in a shaker beside the salt on our kitchen table is not a capsicum at all but the fruit of *Piper nigrum*, a vine from the southern Asian tropics.)

With their polished fruits, crisply tidy foliage, and shrublike stance, peppers work well in even the most formal of settings. The very dwarf and bushy 'Midnight Special', with deep purple leaves crowned by small, upward-pointing, brilliant red peppers, makes a superb edging for a sunny walkway. On Ewing Street I grew this little show-off for many years along our south-facing wall, where its fruit often held color until Christmas.

Of course, you can always pot up dwarf peppers before frost and use them for holiday color indoors. 'Treasure Red', 'Holiday Cheer', and 'Holiday Flame' are made-to-order Christmas decorations, with fruits of various shades on the way to red contrasting with the dark green foliage.

Peppers take up to two months to reach setting-out size from seed. They love warm soil, so there's not much to be gained by starting seed indoors before March. For a fall display they can be set out as late as July.

In the garden peppers do best with full or part sun, plenty of water (but drainage is critical), and at least a monthly application of a balanced fertilizer like 8-8-8 or 10-10-10.

In warm, humid weather peppers are prone to a bacterial leaf spot, which may also damage fruit but which I understand can be controlled with a copper sulfate spray. They share with other members of the nightshade family a susceptibility to tobacco mosaic virus, which, unless I'm mistaken, is more likely to present a problem among the sweet-flavored bell-type peppers than among more pungent kinds.

If you enjoy Oriental cooking and sincerely feel that your dinner guests are being denied the full experience they deserve unless you see smoke curling from their ears and tears streaming down their cheeks, then surely you'll want to grow 'Park's Thai Hot' pepper, a deceptively cute puff of lancelike leaves topped with scores of upward-pointing, small red fruits—the most painfully hot little peppers used in cooking.

And if you're an aficionado of Mexican fare, you'll need a jalapeño or two on the property.

Peppers can be dried, pickled, or frozen for posterity. I usually wash, chop, and freeze them, since frozen peppers can be used in salads as well as cooked.

TOMATO OR NOT TOMATO

Most of the tomatoes offered us at garden centers and through catalogs are good varieties, bearing large quantities of tasty fruit if fertilized, watered like crazy and occasionally limed and sprayed. 'Big Boy', 'Better Boy', 'Early Girl' (notice there's no 'Big Girl'), and 'Homestead' have been standards ever since I've been gardening. Success with tomatoes depends so much on culture— full sun, water, and fertilizer—that variety is something of a secondary consideration. I've failed utterly with varieties advertised as resistant to wilts and nematodes and succeeded beyond reasonable expectation with freebie packets of unheard-of varieties with no letters after their names to denote disease resistance.

Some years back, for instance, I had a marvelous crop of 'Royal Ace' tomatoes. The plants bore countless tasty, easy-to-peel fruits over a long period of time. I think I obtained the seeds from a basket of year-old, marked-down seed packets at a dime store. I've never found that variety again. But almost any homegrown, vine-ripened tomato beats anything the supermarket can offer.

Before the month is out, we'll likely have one of those false freeze warnings that sends us scurrying out to gather the remaining green tomatoes. Some we'll wrap in newspaper and attempt to ripen in a box under the bed. A few will join the nearly ripe enough red tomatoes on the windowsill over the sink, and a few will go into the vegetable bin in the refrigerator in hopes they'll stay just as they are awhile longer. But some will be sliced, dredged in cornmeal, fried in a thin pool of oil, salted, peppered, and eaten for supper with a little mashed potato, corn, and hot buttered cornbread to take the edge off their tanginess.

MUM'S THE WORD

October doorsteps sprout pumpkins and potted chrysanthemums like damp logs sprout toadstools. Since chrysanthemums are troublesome little buggers to grow properly, many of us just pick up a pot or two at a garden center in September, when they start to come into bloom. (I suppose one could save money by simply removing them from someone else's front steps, but this is tacky and, besides, the selection is limited.) Such fall-purchased mums are often root-bound and, if set into the garden, seldom become established before freezing weather and are thus lost over winter.

Irritatingly, the taxonomists, who came to this planet strictly to wreak turmoil among garden writers and make our $135 copies of *Hortus Third* obsolete even before we've torn up the dust jacket, have raked up nearly all of the herbaceous perennials we've come to know and love as members of the genus *Chrysanthemum* and dumped them instead into a new genus, *Dendranthema*. (Our old hybrid friend the Shasta daisy now resides in the genus *Leucanthemum*.)

Perhaps I lack sensitivity, but to me the chrysanthemum—er, dendranthema—as fine and rich in variety as it is, is just another excellent fall garden flower. But in some gardeners mums inspire a kind of lunacy which crowds out all thoughts of spouse, kids, cats, dogs, and dinner at 6:00 P.M. sharp.

This foolishness (which, I warn you, is contagious) started centuries ago, probably in China, and has swept, plaguelike, across many cultures clear around the world. The result has been the development of an unprepossessing daisy into a panorama of elaborate floral forms (spiders, spoons, pompons, quills, etc.) and downright acrobatic habits (cushiony mounds, spheres, treeform standards, and the topiarian Japanese cascades, fans, fountains, and umbrellas). The color range now spans the spectrum save for true blue.

Chrysanthemums are easily moved, even in bud or bloom, so that a cool-colored summer bedding scheme might suddenly be converted into a warm-toned autumnal display by the removal of spent annuals and their replacement with bright-hued mums. Just be sure to water the chrysanthemums well before and after the operation.

Cushion mums can be grown from cuttings three to a pot in an out-of-the-way sunny spot and plopped onto the porch or into the garden in

September, where they'll bring down-to-earth solidity to an airy mix of salvias and wild asters. A minimum of six hours of full sun daily is needed for good flower production, but, once the buds have been set, they'll go on and bloom just fine even in shade.

Chrysanthemums set their flower buds in response to decreasing day length and, to some extent, night temperature. Exposure to artificial light sources, such as streetlights or even car headlights, may prevent or delay bloom.

There are two things that make chrysanthemums more bothersome to grow than most other garden flowers, the first being that, for best results, the clumps must be dug up every spring and new plants started from cuttings or outside shoots. And, secondly, all but the low-growing, self-branching cultivars require repetitive pinching back to achieve the desired fullness and/or staking to keep the eventual blooms from wallowing in the dirt.

The moundlike cushion mums, which require little pinching or staking, are best for landscape use and pot culture. Mary Lou McNabb, who grows the finest chrysanthemums in these parts, recommends several particularly effective combinations of cushion mums. The triple-toned yellow 'Jessica' shares the same height and an early October bloom period with 'Tracy', a frosty white. The bronze 'Denise' blooms with the lavender 'Lynn' in late month, while the brilliant yellow 'Sunny Morning' blooms for six full weeks, and is attractive with the bronzy-red 'Bravo'.

Mary Lou is convinced that chrysanthemums are more likely to survive winter if they are not cut back until spring. She never mulches her mums but dresses them generously with rich, coffee-dark homemade compost in April or May. The only other fertilizer she uses is muriate of potash (potassium chloride). One teaspoon per plant applied around the first of August helps, she says, to develop vibrant color and strong stems.

Many gardeners, of course, do fertilize mums, preferably with a low-nitrogen product and then not too close to season's end, when new, tender growth may prove frost-susceptible. Certain soils, particularly sandy, acid soils, are deficient in magnesium, a constituent of chlorophyll. Yellowing of the lower leaves is a symptom. One quarter pound of Epsom salt dissolved in a gallon of water is the remedy, according to Roderick Cumming in *The Chrysanthemum Book*.

Mums are shallow-rooted and fairly thirsty but must have porous, well-drained soil, since they are prone to winter rot. A pH around 6.0 or 6.5 is about right.

In April Mary Lou takes four-inch cuttings which she roots in Pro-Mix or sand and perlite. These go out into the garden on eighteen-inch centers in May. Chicken wire stretched across the beds a few inches above the ground discourages her dogs from digging up or trampling plants and provides the mums with support, preventing them from flopping open in the center after a heavy rain.

*Carolina moonseed
vine makes a brief but
flamboyant exit.*

Photograph by
Carol B. Hipps

October

❧

November

❧

December

*'Midnight special'—
a saucy little pepper
custom-made for
edging or potting up.*

PHOTOGRAPH BY
CAROL B. HIPPS

*No, it's not Oscar the
Grouch and his date;
it's a pair of curious
cleomes peeking over
a choice aster.
Gomphrena and
Salvia 'Firebrand'
to the right.*

PHOTOGRAPH BY
CAROL B. HIPPS

*'Yellow Knight', one of
Mary Lou McMabb's
spectacular show
mums.*

PHOTOGRAPH BY
CAROL B. HIPPS

October

&

November

&

December

*American beautyberry
is a coarse but
colorful shrub for
the fall landscape.*

*Thorns and berries,
berries and thorns—
that's pyracantha
all over.*

PHOTOGRAPH BY
CAROL B. HIPPS

*The rare Alabama
snow wreath and its
spring display of misty
white flowers.*

PHOTOGRAPH BY
CAROL B. HIPPS

October

❧

November

❧

December

*Zebra grass
(Miscanthus sinensis
'Zebrinus'), one of
many ornamental
grasses which strike
a dramatic pose in
the fall and winter
landscape.*

PHOTOGRAPH BY
CAROL B. HIPPS

*The faithful nandina,
seen here struggling
beneath the rare
blanket of snow,
provides ready-
made Christmas
decorations.*

PHOTOGRAPH BY
ELSABE HOLST-WEBSTER

*Dawn redwood makes
an exclamatory
statement in the
winter landscape.*

PHOTOGRAPH BY
CAROL B. HIPPS

October

❧

November

❧

December

The wondrous cinnamon and pearl bark of the crapemyrtle cultivar 'Natchez'.

I wish this was Christmas cactus, but I fear it is really the so-called Thanksgiving cactus (Schlumbergera truncata)*.*

All but the most compact cultivars benefit from pinching or shearing back. Shearing plants to six inches also temporarily eliminates the black aphids, which congregate near the stem tips.

Local lore dictates that one should pinch mums back until the Fourth of July and prune no more after that so that plants will have time to form buds and bloom before frost. Cumming allows the upper South to pinch until August 1, the middle South (that includes Zone 7, I presume) until August 15, and the lower South until September 1. Actually, I believe one may safely pinch back some varieties later than others. My most enduring mum, 'Yellow Jacket', a dwarf, bushy mop of shaggy yellow flower heads, often blooms well into November, resisting frost and the first few freezes. 'Sunny Morning' does the same, according to Mary Lou. Mum beds can be covered with Remay (spun-bonded polyester) for added frost protection.

ASTER

In October the wildflower of the hour is the aster. Reminiscent of the spring haze of *Phlox divaricata*, the woods once again stir with sprays of misty lavender, this time those of *Aster grandiflorus* and a host of other confusingly similar blue or white native aster species.

Almost any wildling aster may be introduced to the garden, enhancing the effectiveness of flowers around it and adding a touch of grace and refinement to the autumn scene. Most wild asters send up a few tall, wispy stems, which, while they're not unsightly, do lack ornamental value and conceal that of their immediate neighbors. Cutting or pinching these stems back in late spring and the first half of summer forces the plants to branch and become bushy, so that, when they finally come into bloom, they are veritable clouds of delicate color.

Aster is the Greek word for star. To me the aster's composite flower head is not particularly starlike in itself but, when these are borne in collective profusion, they are like the myriad stars of the sky.

Along our shady creek bank we have a lovely lavender aster (we'll pretend that it's *A. grandiflorus*, since it has a rather large flower head, but it's probably something else). Even with the intermittent torture of being whacked back several times a season to prevent its overcrowding its neighbors, it dearly loves garden life, producing at the called-upon time a sweetly scented, honeybee-covered mist of pale purple, yellow-centered blooms. (The centers of asters typically turn violet after fertilization.)

I've another wild aster in the backyard, a white one that serves as a silvery, veillike backdrop to the slim, weightless spires of scarlet *Salvia coccinea*.

Both of these pastel asters are sweetly enchanting in a vase with the lemon-yellow-flowered, asterlike silk grass (*Pityopsis nervosa*). Silk grass spends the summer disguised as a low, thick clump of grass, with long pubescent leaves. In autumn it sends up scores of silvery, felted stems bearing branchlets tipped with yellow daisies of a vivid yet not harsh yellow, a color that vibrates joyfully when touched by the glossy violet of a cluster of hyacinth bean seedpods or which blends soothingly with the softer purple of velvet sage (*Salvia leucanthema*).

This near-aster is found on gritty, acidic roadbanks in combination with yellow star grass and bird-foot violet. It is long-lived in well-drained garden soil and easily started from seed.

The various golden asters (*Chrysopsis* species) are typically coarser, almost undesirably vigorous, and rampant self-seeders, but they are brilliant meadow flowers and, with attention (i.e., cutting back to prevent legginess) they make bouquets of jubilant color for the fall garden.

Among the store-bought asters *A.* ×*frikartii* 'Mönch', a selected hybrid of a cross between the Italian aster (*A. amellus*) and the Himalayan *A. thomsonii*, is one of the biggest, bluest, and longest-blooming. 'Mönch' needs well-drained soil and sunshine, and it, too, makes lots more flowers if pinched back. Above Zone 7 this splendid would-be perennial needs winter protection.

Not long ago I planted along our nature trail a few small seedlings labeled asteromoea, which I assumed at the time was a semidouble version of some native American aster. But when I went home and started reading up on the plant, I discovered that its pedigree is debated.

There is no *Asteromoea* listed in *Hortus Third*. Allen Bush, writing in his Holbrook Farm catalog, labels the plant double Japanese aster, or orphanage plant, and lists several latinized monikers for it, among them *Boltonia indica* (also not listed in *Hortus Third*, though *B. incisa*, whose description sounds a bit like this plant, is). Bush's asteromoea was given him by Elizabeth Lawrence, reason enough to cherish this misleadingly dainty-looking aster even if it didn't produce an airy explosion of shaggy little white to pale purple daisies much of the summer and fall.

FALL TICKSEEDS

The closely related *Bidens* and *Coreopsis* are known as tickseeds. The white-flowering *Bidens* species that Willodene Mathews brought back from south Alabama contributes great sparkle to the backyard garden in autumn.

The one-and-a-half-inch composite flowers consist of a ring of broad white ray flowers surrounding a center of orange disk flowers. The seeds, which are manufactured by the thousands, are needlelike sticktights with an exasperating proclivity for working their way through clothing and into bare skin.

Make no mistake about it, this is a weed, but a *worthwhile* weed when well-managed. It reaches five feet in height with an equal spread, so it is best to force compact growth by cutting back its segmented foliage a time or two during the season.

Inge Paul grows *Bidens polylepsis,* a larger-flowering golden tickseed which, like the white species, is a perfect companion for *Salvia coccinea* and other late-flowering salvias.

October Chores

It's tempting to let the garden go now, since all the world is a bit of a mess at this time of year, but then, of course, we realize that our asters, for instance, will show to better effect if they're not overshadowed by a twiggy forest of dead and dying *Rudbeckia triloba*, and so a bit of housekeeping is in order.

If we look carefully, we'll see seedlings of next spring's larkspur and nemophila coming up, so it is imperative that we get down on all fours and scratch out the germinating violets and dead nettle that will surely shade them out if they're not dealt with quickly. (I have few such weeds in the front yard beds, where a resident from the distant past evidently had a real lawn and no doubt eradicated the competition with broad-leaf weed killers. The backyard beds, however, are a different story.)

If seed of butterfly weed (*Asclepias tuberosa*) is to be collected, now is the time, for soon the okralike pods will split and the seeds will be transported on gossamer wings to parts unknown.

The twin seedpods of *Amsonia tabernaemontana*, too, will soon spill their cargo. Amsonia seems to seed itself rather inefficiently in the wild, but you or I can peel open the pods and the cigarlike seeds, which are lined up single file like the cars on a train, will stream out into an envelope, which we can refrigerate until spring. Better yet, we can go ahead and shallowly plant the seeds where we hope one day to see more cool blue amsonias.

October is the perfect time to set out pansies, for they'll have a chance to become established and start to grow before the really cold weather stops them in their tracks, and they'll be more likely to put on a welcome show during winter warm spells. If I could bear to rip out my fall marigolds and the melampodium, I would certainly set my pansies out in October. As it is (as I am), I set out my pansies as I clear my beds after frost, in November, usually. I mix in a handful of organic matter (usually the ground-up leaves, grass clippings, and pine straw I've just collected from the neighbors' curbs), fertilize, water, and mulch them well. Be sure to keep your pansies watered, both while they're in the flat and during winter dry spells. Even though they're mulched, pansies grown in raised beds are quick to dry out in sunny, windy winter weather.

I mulch all the shrubs heavily in fall and mulch each mixed bed as I clean it off. The pine straw I heap around the azaleas, rhododendrons, and dogwoods.

If you've ordered bulbs of tulip, daffodil, anemone, lilies, or the like, set them out as they arrive or store them in the vegetable bin, checking on them frequently to make sure they don't dry out.

Gather materials for winter arrangements and hang them upside down to air-dry in a warm, dark room. Salvia, silver king artemisia, purple coneflower, dusty miller, goldenrod, hydrangea, lamb's ears, Queen Anne's lace, zinnia, and ornamental grasses are relatively easy candidates for air-drying.

November

November commences with such brazen flare that it is hard to believe that at its close the world will have faded to gray and brown, and we'll be wishing for a full-berried pyracantha or even another nandina to brighten the grim view along the back fence.

Ironically, the marigolds and dahlias bloom with newfound vigor just before frost. Salvias, ageratum, and even impatiens seem suddenly to grow brighter, fuller, more alert. Purple coneflower, spring phloxes, *Silene armeria*, and bird-foot violet rebloom, and the Carolina jessamine pops open a few yellow trumpets it might have saved for spring.

Yet inevitably one morning in November we'll step out to the bird feeder and feel the crunch of ice underfoot, for it is an exceedingly rare year when we still have our flowers at Thanksgiving.

But many flowers have a measure of resistance to cold, and we can expect them to be with us, at least for a time, after the velvet sage has become but a lavender skeleton. Certain chrysanthemums, *Verbena canadensis*, dianthus, snapdragons, the reblooming spring phloxes, a few (but certainly not all) *Rudbeckia trilobas*, and alyssum may choose to ignore the first few freezes. And then there are the indomitable pansies. Who has truly seen autumn who hasn't witnessed a crotchety crowd of deep purple pansies glaring indignantly at the world through a golden drift of ginkgo leaves?

Now the rowdy maples, still gold-on-blue against the autumn sky, are gentled somewhat by the subdued burgundies and mellow golds of the patient oaks. And autumn's last hurrah, the ornamental pears, are purpling, at last on their way to the candy-apple red and taxi-cab yellow that constitute fall's strident finale.

The bird feeder still draws migratory customers along with the regulars—all easy pickings for the hawk who, after all, figures that, being a bird himself, he has at least as much right to dine at the feeder as Bart the cat.

Temporarily, in autumn, the dogwoods become bird feeders, too. Though they glow like garnets now, soon the leaves will be stripped away by wind and rain to reveal a bare gray frame studded with hundreds of clustered crimson fruits. Once on Ewing Street I heard a commotion outside and rushed to the door to behold a flock of starlings vociferously banqueting in our newly denuded dogwood. In less than a minute they were gone—and so was every fruit on that tree.

So-called evergreen azaleas are burnished scarlet and yellow now, yet they, too, may be gray and near-leafless by spring (all the better to see the flowers with, my dear). A landscape that depends heavily on azaleas can be a dismal sight in winter.

BEAUTYBERRY

I'm grateful that Wade Wharton recently gave me a seedling of American beautyberry (*Callicarpa americana*), for in a year or two (if I remember to keep it watered until it becomes self-sufficient) it should give us an eyeful of violet-purple berry clusters to enliven our view of the backyard in fall and early winter. This native shrub has something of the coloring and coarseness of pokeweed, but the berries (drupes, actually) are tightly crowded into clusters about the stem nodes. 'Russell Montgomery' is a recommended white-berried selection.

Callicarpa dichotoma is a lower-growing (to four feet), daintier, more arching species from China and Japan that is becoming increasingly naturalized here (frankly, I suspect it has nuisance potential, but the birds appreciate the colorful fruit). It appears to me that this shrub strikes roots wherever the stems dip to the ground and so might be used as a deciduous cover for a bank.

PYRACANTHA

The thorns on a pyracantha, or firethorn (*Pyracantha coccinea* and near relations), could give even Br'er Rabbit nightmares. On Ewing Street I foolishly installed a pyracantha right at the corner of the house by the driveway where this fast-growing, decidedly free-form member of the rose family needed constant whacking back to prevent its impaling passersby. (Placed under a window, pyracantha will definitely hold would-be burglars until police arrive.) I loved its trusses of orange winter berries and so did the robin who set up housekeeping in that shrub every winter. But I hated to prune it, hated to handle the vicious trimmings, even with gloves, and felt sorry for the trash collectors who had to haul them off. I'm told that the armor-piercing thorns can be rendered harmless by a chipper/shredder. If this is so, it's great news.

If I ever plant another pyracantha, I'll put it where I don't have to touch it, ever, where it can sprawl to its heart's content and be admired from a safe distance.

Of course, there are macho gardeners who insist on espaliering pyracanthas to walls or fences and, while the effect of the orange or scarlet berries marching in formal or fanciful configurations across rough gray or blazing white masonry is stunning, I'd sooner take up bungee jumping. Besides, a subzero plunge occasionally kills pyracantha to the ground, and who wants to have to repeat such an elaborate and hazardous project?

Another reason to site pyracantha off the beaten path is that the evergreen foliage is prone to unsightly disease and insect damage, particularly to scab and fireblight. According to Dirr, certain hybrid cultivars have inbred disease resistance. 'Fiery Cascade', for instance, is one, with multitudes of long-lasting small red fruits. (Incidentally, a pyracantha's fruit is neither a berry nor a drupe but—hold onto your hat—a pome; that is, a fleshy fruit with a core containing five—give or take a few—seeds, like an apple.) 'Golden Charmer' is a disease-resistant yellow-berried form, while 'Navaho' is a mounding, densely branched, resistant form whose clusters of small, creamy, midspring flowers produce showy, scarlet, winter fruit.

Deserved or not (I'm suspicious), pyracantha has a reputation for being hard to transplant. Dirr recommends setting out container-grown plants in spring. Once established in well-drained soil, pyracantha tolerates drought.

RED CHOKEBERRY

I've only recently become acquainted with the red chokeberry (*Aronia arbutifolia*). We have the cultivar 'Brilliantissima' at the botanical garden, hard by the creek (though I've read it can stand dryish and even poor soils), and I am smitten with this shrub's proud, upright carriage, silvery smooth bark, rubyesque fall color, and cherrylike clusters of plump, lustrous crimson fruit (another pome). If its legginess bothers you, you can grow it in masses, or perhaps front it with the twiggy Japanese barberry (*Berberis thunbergii*, particularly var. *atropurpurea*), which sports a compatible reddish leaf color followed by red berries of its own.

SNOW WREATH

Another rose family member which gives late-season color of a different kind is the snow wreath (*Neviusia alabamensis*), a rare shrub naturally occurring in only four sites of which I am aware, three in Alabama and one along the Arkansas-Missouri border. Recently another species of *Neviusia*, the Shasta snow wreath (*N. cliftonii*), was discovered near Redding, California.

I don't know why our snow wreath is rare—perhaps there's some problem with seed germination or dispersal—for it is easy to grow, and, in cultivation, at least, the suckers are easily dug up and transplanted.

Snow wreath resembles its cousin the kerria just a bit, with supple, arching canes and medium-green serrate (though shorter) leaves. It's on the scraggly side on the moist, wooded hillsides and river bluffs where it is found in the wild but develops a pleasing spirealike roundness and fullness when cultivated in good light.

My snow wreath, donated as a wee sucker by Charlie Higgins, is situated on an easy slope at the northeast corner of the house, where rainy runoff rushes through it. It is now about five feet high and equally wide. I seldom water it, but Dirr notes that, while a snow wreath's soil should be well-drained, it can't stay dry for long without stressing the plant.

In April the whiplike branches burst into a mist of petalless, greenish-white flowers rendered showy by their profusion of spidery stamens. The eventual fruit (not a berry, drupe, or even a pome, but a miserable, dried-up brown achene) is all but invisible. In late autumn and winter, snow wreath turns leaf by leaf into such a strong, clear yellow that from a distance it could be taken for a forsythia in premature bloom.

VIRGINIA SWEETSPIRE

Virginia sweetspire (*Itea virginica*) is another shrub that has strong fall coloring. The finely toothed leaves take on rich red or purple autumnal hues in either sun or shade. The leaves may or may not remain on the plant, depending upon the severity of the winter. Those on the Virginia sweetspires at the botanical garden remained dark burgundy nearly all last winter. In late spring this very desirable native shrub bears fuzzy, upright spires of pleasantly fragrant, creamy white flowers.

Virginia sweetspire is adaptable but is especially fond of wet soil, where it suckers happily about. 'Henry's Garnet' is a cultivar with both flowers and fall coloring considered superior to the type.

BLUEBERRY

The genus *Vaccinium* gives us blueberries, cranberries, huckleberries, and, among others, farkleberries (the fruit of the latter is inedible, but the name alone makes the plant worth growing, and it has beautiful fall color and exfoliating bark, besides).

Both highbush blueberry (*V. corymbosum*) and rabbit-eye blueberry (*V. ashei*) are multipurpose native shrubs (the rabbit-eye's natural range takes in only Georgia, northern Florida, and southern Alabama) with beautiful bark and blue-green foliage, which ignites in late autumn into assorted savory fallish hues. The dangling white or pink urceolate (urn- or pitcher-shaped) flowers are borne on chainlike racemes in late spring. The flowers are usually self-infertile, so, if fruit production is a consideration, plant at least two and preferably three or more cultivars to assure good cross-pollination and fruit set.

Most blueberries actually enjoy poorly drained soil (the compact, self-fertile southern highbush variety 'Sharpblue' is an exception), but it must be acid: pH 4.5 to 5.5, so you may need to add sulfur or aluminum sulfate. A thick mulch will help preserve the ample water essential for summer fruit set.

There are numerous blueberry cultivars, many developed to meet the specialized needs of pick-your-own or mechanically harvested operations. Mary Lou and Bob McNabb, for example, whose Marymac Farm is perhaps our area's largest pick-your-own blueberry enterprise, heartily endorse the *V. ashei* cultivar 'Tifblue', both for fall color and lavish fruitfulness. Dirr wisely suggests asking your county agent about varieties recommended for your area. A locally owned nursery is more likely to carry suitable cultivars than the discount store chain's garden center. Wayside Gardens offers a three-piece set for both North and South.

For the landscape I would grow blueberries along a fence or in groups tucked among other shrubs.

FOTHERGILLA AND PARROTIA

I almost forgot to mention the fothergillas, which are among the best native shrubs for fall color, with broad, ridged and puckered, bluish-green leaves that flame into bright mixtures of yellow, orange, scarlet, and near-rose.

Fothergilla gardenii is a shrub of modest proportions (typically to four feet or less), native to the southern coastal plain, where it congregates in low-lying areas, while the larger *F. major* (to ten feet) hails from southern mountainous regions.

In the home landscape these witch hazel relatives make do with either sun or shade but must have moist, acid soil. Stubby spikes of off-white, honey-scented flowers appear in spring.

There are a few named varieties of fothergilla, *F. g.* 'Blue Mist' being the cultivar most often encountered in catalogs at the moment. Dirr cautions that, while its soft, bluish summer coloring and delicate habit are appealing, its fall coloring may not equal that of 'Mount Airy', a selection of his own that he suspects may be a hybrid of the two species.

Now to offset a grouping of fothergillas we really need a *Parrotia persica*, a small, slow-growing tree native to Iran but nonetheless related to the witch hazels and fothergillas and bearing similar leaves that take on varied and extravagant coloration in autumn. Small, frizzly red flowers occur in early spring, and the tree features multicolored, exfoliating bark year-round. It is less fussy about soil conditions than the fothergillas.

POPCORN TREE

The coastal regions of the Southeast are coming to rival New England for fall color due to the proliferation of *Sapium sebiferum*, the chinese tallow, or popcorn, tree. Though its leaf is a dead ringer for that of a poplar, this Asian interloper is a fast-growing, short-lived, but sizeable (to forty feet or so) member of the spurge (Euphorbiaceae) family.

On a mid-November trip to Gulf Shores State Park my friend Elsabe Webster and I were astonished at the vividness and variety of colors this tree displayed. Just across the highway from the beach we saw popcorn trees that were solid yellow, scarlet, crimson, or purple and trees that, like the sweet gum, carried leaves of a multitude of brilliant hues.

Hortus Third lists the tree as hardy to Zone 4. Dirr reports that the color is disappointing in his Zone 7b Georgia stomping ground and that the plant is highly adaptable as to soil conditions but requires full sun.

The tree is called tallow tree because the fatty seed covering is supposedly used by the Chinese to make soap and candles. The reason for the name popcorn tree is more obvious: in autumn the seed capsules split to reveal popcornlike clusters of bright white, pea-sized seeds, a few of which came home with me, so we'll see how popcorn tree does in Huntsville.

ORNAMENTAL GRASSES

Once autumn has died down to but a few dull embers, we view our ornamental grasses with fresh appreciation. Their interesting and varied architectural forms and textures take on new significance in the landscape, and we relish their rhythmic motion and the raspy sigh of the wind in their ribbonlike leaves.

Ornamental grasses (including, for convenience, the sedges and rushes with which they are commonly lumped) have been slow in catching on in the South apart from the Gulf Coast, where elegantly plumed clumps of the windproof pampas grass (*Cortaderia selloana*) outnumber sunburned vacationers. Grasses, I suppose, conflict with the ingrained tidiness with which so many gardeners are afflicted. Grass was put on earth to be cut, after all, and if it's higher than your ankle it's a personal disgrace. Except for controlling its lateral spread (or preventing its seeding itself about) there's not much the fussy gardener can do with ornamental grass. You can't very well shear it into a ball or square it off like a footlocker. You simply have to accept it as it is.

There are several magnificent displays of grasses at Huntsville's botanical garden, and they're so neatly arranged and maintained they're anything but messy. For starters, running down into the water on the north side of the pond is a towering stand of giant reed grass (*Arundo donax*), whose fifteen- to eighteen-foot canes are intersected by long, narrow, horizontal leaves like the rungs on a ladder and are topped by two-foot, greenish purple inflorescent panicles. This sun- and moisture-loving southern European behemoth spreads by rhizomes to form a visually impenetrable barrier. Giant reed grass has become widely naturalized in Zone 7 and below, from Maryland to southern California. Above Zone 7 it reportedly doesn't bloom.

The garden's second tallest grass (to fifteen feet)—housed in a well-prepared bed on considerably higher ground—is ravenna grass (*Erianthus ravennae*). Now naturalized in the South, this southern European import produces fountains of coarse, ribbony leaves from which shoot arrow-straight stems bearing upright plumes. The leaves are tinged brown and purple in fall. Ravenna grass is hardy to Zone 6, making it a good substitute for the more tender pampas grass.

Switchgrass (*Panicum virgatum*) is disdained in some quarters as a hard-to-conquer native weed. At the botanical garden, however, it cuts a handsome and graceful figure in late summer and fall when five- to ten-foot stems bearing airy, reddish panicles emerge from a shock of ribbonlike foliage, which itself takes on tones of blue, red, and purple. As with many perennials, the center of a clump of ornamental grass may die out after a few years, necessitating division and replanting. The comparatively dwarfish *P. v.* 'Rotstrahlbusch', which has three- to four-foot flower spikes, is reported to resist this problem.

Feather reed grass (*Calamagrostis ×acutiflora* 'Stricta') has thin, rigidly upright flowering stems that tower (at five feet) above clumps of wispy foliage. Its slender, feathery panicles glisten when backlit by the sun. At the botanical garden, it contrasts sharply with the loose, haystacklike habit of the assorted nearby miscanthus. *Calamagrostis arundinacea* 'Karl Foerster', which grows to four-and-a-half feet, is an equally desirable selection. Both forms need full sun and average soil.

If I were selecting a miscanthus for my yard and had room for only one, I'd have a world of trouble making up my mind. At the botanical garden we have the popular *Miscanthus sinensis* 'Gracillimus', with its interminably long, arching, silver-streaked leaves and silken flower heads. But nearby we have *M. s.* 'Sara Bandi', with very fine, curling leaves and even fluffier inflorescences. Across the road we have a new clump of *M. s.* 'Purpurascens', whose flaming, red-purple autumn leaves are topped by stems bearing frizzly inflorescences like well-worn pastry brushes.

I would also be tempted by *M. s.* 'Morning Light', which has silvery pale, white-edged foliage that turns auburn in fall. But I suspect I would wind up with something gaudy such as zebra grass (*M. s.* 'Zebrinus'), whose lofty (to six feet), spiky leaves are horizontally banded with creamy stripes and are especially dramatic by water. Or, I might get porcupine grass (*M. s.* 'Strictus'), an improved form of zebra grass with foliage that curves into almost ludicrous kinks as it dries in autumn.

Miscanthus is effective either massed or used singly as an accent or specimen. It does well in either full or partial sun. A light annual feeding with a timed-release, preferably low-nitrogen fertilizer keeps the center of the plant from succumbing to malnutrition while preventing an explosion of weak, floppy growth. One shouldn't encourage grasses to grow too fast, for dividing a massive, overgrown clump of any ornamental grass is no chore for mere weaklings.

We also have a strip of dwarf variegated ribbon grass (*Phalaris arundinacea* 'Picta') at the garden. This grass grows to two feet and spreads rampantly. You can unleash it around ponds and other wet areas, but in more confined situations it is best restrained in a container. In full sun at the garden it is prone to scorching from May to September. In shade it keeps its crisp good looks but may still become leggy and want cutting back almost to the ground more than once during the season. The green-and-white streaked leaves—the reason for growing this plant—are a striking contrast to a dark-leaved rhododendron, holly, or hemlock.

Another possible light-gathering grassy groundcover for moist shady sites is the seldom glimpsed, indescribably slow-growing *Hakonechloa macra* 'Aureola', whose foot-high, windswept, yellow-and-white streaked leaves give the plant the appearance of a cross between bamboo and liriope. It thrives (after a fashion) in moist, humusy shade.

At the garden's spring plant sale horticultural director Al Privette talked me into buying my first sedge, *Carex* (probably *morrowii*) 'Old Gold', a mophead-sized swirl of spaghetti-thin leaves edged in olive green with a central pale yellow stripe. I suspect the stripe might live up to the clone's moniker in stronger light, but I love the way this delightfully shaggy little plant glows in the shade as if lit by a spotlight. The long, wispy leaves give structural contrast with those of other shade-brighteners like variegated hosta and ivy.

There are numerous other variegated carexes. The variegated black carex (*C. nigra* 'Variegata') grows to twelve inches and might be snappy with the silvery white *C. albicola* from New Zealand. Two other New Zealand imports, *C. testacea* (to eighteen inches) and bronze hair sedge (*C. flagellifera*), develop a rich auburn color when grown in sun and may hold the color over winter.

The larger (to two feet), somewhat more upright *C. stricta* 'Bowles' Golden' is probably the most popular carex presently available (this grass is also listed as *C. elata* 'Aurea').

Variegated carex makes a potent visual cocktail when mixed with strong dark colors like those of ajuga, *Heuchera micrantha* var. *diversifolia* 'Palace Purple' (don't let the heuchera swallow it whole!), the garrish Japanese blood grass (*Imperata cylindrica* 'Red Baron'), and black mondo grass (*Ophiopogon planiscapus* 'Nigrescens').

Most sedges do well in humus-rich soil in either sun or shade as long as they have ample water.

Nothing Attempted, Nothing Done

The Halloween pumpkin goes out on the compost heap now, and the kids take cruel pleasure in watching its agonizing decline.

Frosted beds must be tidied, weeded (more violets! more lamium!), and mulched. The foliage of established daffodils is coming up, a reminder to get the rest of our bulbs into the ground. You can still hold off awhile on tulips. Just don't let the bulbs dry out. And, of course, there the pansies still sit in their nursery flats....

November is an excellent time to set out trees and shrubs. Remember that more young transplants perish from thirst than from cold, so mulch them well and water them whenever they go without rain for more than five days.

If you simply must have camellias, cover budded bushes on frosty nights and protect the swollen buds from early morning sun as well. Or, better yet, go down to the coast, where they're starting to bloom now, and enjoy to you heart's content.

Many shrubs (including roses) and some trees can be propagated from six-inch cuttings of year-old wood taken in late fall and early winter. Clip the cutting just above and below a leaf node, dip the bottom (be sure it's the bottom) into rooting hormone, and insert the cutting almost up to the top bud either directly into the soil or into a hole or trench filled with well-drained medium—garden soil, sand, peat moss, vermiculite, or any combination thereof works fine. Keep the cutting moist and lightly shaded until it's actively growing and can be potted up or relocated to a permanent site.

LATE BLOOMERS

The sporadic winter flowers of certain of the twining honeysuckles are even more welcome than the spate of spring and summer bloom. When grown in sun, the semievergreen native trumpet, or coral, honeysuckle (*Lonicera sempervirens*) produces a few dangling whorls of two-inch-long trumpets in shades of yellow and red during mild spells all winter long. It is slow to establish in dry shade but takes off like gangbusters in rich, moist soil in full sunshine, streaking to twenty feet or so. Long popular as a mailbox or lamppost vine, coral honeysuckle is equally valuable to shade an arbor or gussy up a boring chain-link fence.

Lonicera heckrottii, with yellow-flushed purplish flowers, is similar in looks and is a suspected hybrid between *L. sempervirens* and *L. americana*. The native yellowish orange-flowered *L. flava* is not merely a yellow-flowered version of *L. sempervirens* but a separate, less vigorous species.

If we look carefully, we'll find more secretive cold weather bloomers. Almost hidden by the fading orange leaves, the spidery yellow flowers of the native witch hazel (*Hamamelis virginiana*), a denizen of damp woodlands, streamsides, and low ground throughout the eastern United States, perfume the chilly air.

And, close to the ground, its hairy little stem barely stretching above the mat of freshly fallen leaves, is a scalloped, blue-white disk. Can it be? A hepatica in bloom!

December

Winter descends by subtle degrees. Migrating birds drift on, the downward rush of leaves subsides, their clatter soothed by chilling rain into a dark, sodden carpet of silence. The woods grow gray and still but for the flicker of a chickadee here, the spattered bright red of a possum haw there. Yet if we brush aside the leaf litter, we see the shooting stars are already coming up, and we might again catch the sunny wink of a hepatica or false rue anemone, heralding winter's end even before its beginning.

When I step outside to feed the birds, the early morning garden may be a study in white-on-white as the lacelike frost lies veiled in fog, and the frost-killed stems of *Salvia coccinea* exude a cotton candy web of spun ice at each leaf node.

Sometimes in December one fears that some passing celestial object has set the world to wobbling in its course, for the weather is eerily unsettled. Balmy days in the seventies coax tiny white flowers from the autumn-scorched stems of *Spiraea thunbergii*, and even the forsythia breaks into golden bloom. Pansies frolic with alyssum, and over at the busy intersection of McClung Avenue and California Street Jean Spencer's little corner patch of rosy *Phlox subulata* bursts into exuberant bloom.

Then drenching rainstorms tear through, ripping down holiday decorations and bringing temperatures and wind chills more befitting Montana than Zone 7. The sequence may repeat over and over so that, while Christmas Day may find children in shorts and shirtsleeves trying out their new bikes and Rollerblades, the subzero freeze that often ushers in the New Year is preceded by tornadic storms, which toss poor, used-up Christmas trees down the street like tumbleweeds.

Favorite Plants for Decorating

I believe I mentioned earlier that one should grow a few plants of cotton (*Gossypium* species) just to have the dried stems bearing their great, linty bolls on hand for holiday decorating. Of course, if you have crop failure (as I sometimes do), you can fake it by fluffing up store-bought cotton balls and attaching them to the split-open capsules of other mallow family members, like hibiscus or hollyhock.

My favorite-in-all-the-world plant for use in Christmas decorating is the nandina. (I jumped the gun and wrote about it in the February chapter.) I've a make-do planter on the front porch constructed of an (I hope) artfully arranged stack of bricks in the center of which is concealed a three-liter soft drink bottle with the top sawed off. Around Thanksgiving I fill the bottle with water and insert a few branches of nandina, clip away any excess leafage, and—voilà!—a lush arrangement that, weather permitting, will stay green-leaved and red-berried until March if I remember to keep it from going dry. Panicles of nandina berries can be cut into bright, airy sprays for insertion among other holiday greenery, too.

By far the easiest plant to use in decorating is Jackson vine (*Smilax lanceolata* or *S. smallii*). Many a southern porch is draped with a swag of this beautiful, slightly prickly cousin of the hellishly thorny assorted catbriers. Jackson vine climbs by tendrils to cloak railings, fences, and trellises with a graceful curtain of dark green, glossy, lancelike leaves. The flowers and fruit are not particularly showy. Once established, it thrives unattended in most soils, sun or shade.

It is our great good luck that December is considered the perfect time to prune this sleek evergreen climber, for, like ivy, the limber stems can be braided into a wreath, arranged in elegant strands around a centerpiece, or simply laid across a mantel.

DECIDUOUS HOLLY

The deciduous native hollies make a seasonal splash of color in the garden, and a berried stem or two inserted into a container with a few dried stems of cotton make an easy and festive holiday arrangement.

Ilex decidua, the common possum haw, is a suckering shrub or small multitrunked tree, which resembles privet in leaf and in fall is generously sprinkled with scarlet or bright orange fruits (drupes). If the wildlife allows, these may last until spring. Possum haw is tolerant of most reasonably moist soils in sun or even heavy shade, though the berrylike fruits are far less numerous in shade. 'Council Fire' and 'Warren Red' are good female clones bearing liberal quantities of long-lasting orange or red fruit, respectively, when in the company of a willing male like 'Red Escort'.

The swamp-dwelling winterberry (*I. verticillata*) is a superb choice for perpetually wet acid soil and is especially effective by water, which reflects the colorful berry clusters. 'Winter Red' is one of the best female clones, with persistent vivid red fruits. 'Nana' (alias 'Red Sprite' or 'Compacta') maxes out at about four to five feet and offers larger-than-type, persisting red fruit. All of them require a male plant such as 'Jackson' or 'Quansoo' for pollination.

Texture, Form, and Color

Major emphasis at this season is placed on evergreens—hollies, conifers, and *Magnolia grandiflora* in particular—but as ornamental and useful as they are, an overabundance of evergreens is claustrophobic and monotonous. Deciduous plants let welcome light into the winter garden and add much interest to the landscape with their diverse forms, textures, and colors.

The ornamental grasses have wonderful winter character, at least until flattened by ice. Miraculously, this doesn't happen some years and even the mighty plumes of pampas grass keep their fluff.

The hydrangeas have excellent winter appeal, with rough, reddish, exfoliating stems and great, papery brown fluffs of flower heads.

The featherlike skeletons of deciduous conifers lend an exclamatory vertical accent to the garden. Dawn redwood (*Metasequoia glyptostroboides*) sheds its Christmas-tree-scented needles to reveal the cinnamon-colored, peeling bark of its sprawling, thirsty roots and flared trunk, which narrows to a single, arrow-straight leader perforated with upward-angling, pinlike branches. A rapid grower, dawn redwood must have moist, well-drained, acid soil.

Similar in form though paler and softer in leaf are bald cypress (*Taxodium distichum*) and its cousin the pond cypress (*T. ascendens*). *Taxodium distichum* 'Shawnee Brave' and *T. ascendens* 'Prairie Sentinel' are strikingly columnar and are especially impressive when massed in "groves" of three of more. Though adaptable to many soils, this genus is an unsurpassed choice for a low, poorly drained area.

Probably no tree cuts a more arresting figure against the winter sky than the weeping willow (*Salix babylonica* and related species and hybrids). With sinuous, arching branches, which sweep the ground and stir continuously, sensitive to the faintest breeze, this most graceful of trees ripples with a liquid vitality. It is best situated beside a pond, stream, or other moist area, not only because such a setting maximizes its lithe beauty, but because otherwise the rapaciously thirsty roots wreak havoc with the nearest sewer or water line.

The weak branches of this fast-growing tree are vulnerable to damage by wind and ice. Winter is short for these willows, for they hold their slender leaves well into the season and leaf out anew before the last freeze.

Willow seeds may germinate within a day of dropping onto moist ground; cuttings root readily in damp earth or even a jar of water. Indeed, "willow water" is said to hasten the rooting of cuttings of other plants.

Dragon's claw willow (*S. matsudana* 'Tortuosa') is a fascinating small tree with curvaceous, contorted branches that add novelty and intrigue to the winter scene. Its rapid growth makes this willow superior to Harry Lauder's walking stick (*Corylus avellana* 'Contorta') as a source of curly stems for floral arrangements.

Salix caprea 'Pendula Weeping Sally' is perfect for the spot where you need a touch of spectacle. This small (to eight feet), exceedingly weepy tree is most commonly trained or grafted to a standard to prevent its floundering about like a mop without a handle. In late winter, it twinkles with jewellike catkins, like a chandelier in soft focus.

The coral embers willow (*Salix alba* 'Britzensis') makes a colorful contribution to the winter garden if it's cut back hard in late winter, since only the twiggy new growth bears the explosive scarlet coloration so valued in the winter landscape.

Hardy orange (*Poncirus trifoliata*) is a shrub or small tree with both unique form and strong winter color. The crazily twisting stems are vivid green and spiked with matching, pencil-thick thorns. Pruned or not, it makes an impregnable hedge and is menacingly handsome espaliered against a wall. When grown beneath a window, this unfriendly plant is more effective than a set of burglar bars. The small, sour, yellow fruits ripen in fall and can be used to flavor tea. Hardy throughout the South, this accommodating shrub accepts most well-drained, acid situations, even poor, dry ones. 'Flying Dragon' is the only cultivar I know of.

At our Ewing Street home the backyard (and, indeed, the neighborhood) was dominated by a leviathan American sycamore (*Platanus occidentalis*), a moisture-loving survivor of the time before a community drainage project rescued the property from the city's flood zone maps. Surely there could have been no more stirring winter sight than to have gazed up the mottled trunk of this giant and marveled at the soaring, stark white branches thrust against a sharp blue sky.

Still, I would recommend this tree only for a streambank or other reliably moist area well away from one's dwelling. Sycamores are messy trees, forever tossing down sticks, seedballs, and dead limbs. In July they shuck their bark in curled strips that can be gathered and broken into an attractive mulch, if one doesn't mind the work. The foot-wide maplelike leaves cast a dense, dry shade.

On a more manageable scale both the stewartias and the ubiquitous crapemyrtles reveal attractively mottled, exfoliating bark. Of the stewartias, the Japanese stewartia (*Stewartia pseudocamellia*) is perhaps the best of the lot. It is less amenable to the heat of Zone 8, however, than either the tall stewartia

(*S. monadelpha*), also from Japan, or our rare southeastern native silky camellia (*S. malacodendron*).

The sinuous multiple trunks of the Japanese stewartia are a patchwork of orange, green, and gray laid over silver-cream. Wayside Gardens offers *S. pseudocamellia* var. *koreana* 'Ballet', with larger-than-the-type (to three-and-a-half inches) white, golden-anthered, camellialike blossoms and a warm-hued fall performance.

Stewartias thrive in partial shade in moist, acid soil. Mulch well as you would with camellias.

In Zone 7 and below, where it's less likely to be killed to the ground in winter, crapemyrtle (*Lagerstroemia indica*) can be grown either as a leggy shrub or small specimen tree with or without multiple stems. Crapemyrtle is a year-round show-off. In winter the sinewy stems stand out, the sleek, pale, pearl gray or tan underbark splashed with warm cinnamon and rich coffee brown.

If the plant is sited in full sun (mandatory for maximum bloom and overall symmetry, for it strives toward the light), summer brings a nonstop display of vivid, clustered flowers from June until frost, by which time the leaves will be enflamed with autumnal hues of yellow, orange, or maroon.

The cultivar 'Natchez', with its huge trusses of gleaming white flowers, grows to be a tree and looks especially sharp in front of red brick, with the white-flowering groundcover *Liriope muscari* 'Monroe White' offsetting its piebald bark. 'Natchez' has exceptionally beautiful exfoliating bark and flowers for approximately a hundred days in our area.

'Seminole' is a bright pink selection with a compact habit and good mildew resistance. Michael Dirr recommends cutting off the first flush of blooms as soon as they fade to promote further profuse flowering.

'Apalachee' is a fine lavender, and 'Catawba' an excellent dark purple. 'Centennial Spirit' has smoldering dark red inflorescences borne on especially strong stems that don't bend to the ground when weighted by rain. 'Victor' is a compact three-foot dwarf with dark red flowers that lends itself to mass plantings.

According to David Byers of Byers Nursery Company, one of the country's largest wholesale producers of crapemyrtles, crapemyrtles are hardiest when neglected. Pruning, fertilizing, and watering all encourage tender growth which is easily winter-killed. Byers fertilizes his crapemyrtles only in fall and waters only when wilting or a decline in flowering indicates stress. He advises planting selections that naturally exhibit the desired growth habit rather than resorting to "crapemurdering," his term for drastic pruning, though he allows that crapemyrtles can be cut to the ground and started over. February is the best time to prune. While cutting off spent blossoms may prolong summer bloom, removing the attractive spherical seed capsules in winter does not increase flower production the following summer.

Most of the birches (*Betula*) would rather be watered with Drano than have to live in the steamy South. River birch (*B. nigra*) is the primary exception.

With a natural range extending from Massachusetts to Florida and west to Kansas, this streambank and bottomland dweller has much to offer the southern gardener.

The tan and russet peeling bark is its greatest attribute. The trunk appears to have been dipped in glue and rolled in multihued wood shavings. The most meritorious cultivar currently available is 'Heritage', which ultimately develops into a mid-sized tree with a fluttering grace and, in most years, cheerful yellow fall color. Moist, even wet, acid soil produces the healthiest specimens. This species offers good resistance to borers and is extremely cold hardy. Dirr cautions that birches bleed excessively if pruned in spring when the sap is flowing.

I am quite taken with the Asian white birch (*B. platyphylla*), particularly the variety *szechuanica*, which, when young, at least, has smooth bark that looks as though it has been spray-painted silver. This species is prone to borer infestation, though I don't know how prevalent the pest is in the South, since birches are not used extensively here. The specimens on the Alabama A&M campus look fine (knock on wood…).

Bark of similar character can be had with the paperbark maple (*Acer griseum*), a slow-growing tree that thrives in most soils from the lower South northward. The cinnamon colored outer bark of this elegant small tree curls back to reveal the ruddy new bark within. The leaves, each divided into three distinct leaflets, typically take on rusty red hues late in autumn.

Coralbark maple (*Acer palmatum* 'Sango Kaku') is a delicate small tree renowned for the vivid coloration of its young stems. Regular pruning is necessary, however, to promote this flamboyant new growth, for older stems fade to gray. This and other Japanese maples are at their best in lightly shaded, protected sites with moist, acidic, well-drained soil rich in organic matter.

The red-stemmed dogwood (*Cornus alba*) gives a similar effect if the oldest stems are removed each year to preserve the brilliant red winter color. This moisture-loving shrub is striking when reflected in water or in the company of evergreens, but is not at all suited to the lower South, and I've seen mixed results here in Zone 7. A little shade would probably be beneficial during our hot summers.

Another beautifully barked plant strictly for the upper South and points north is the Amur chokecherry (*Prunus maackii*). Many cherries wear their skin so tight one wonders they don't burst. In the Amur chokecherry's case they sometimes do, and the shiny, horizontally banded bark splits away in great shaggy shreds.

Green-stemmed, deciduous plants bring a welcome touch of mystery to the winter garden. Japanese kerria (*Kerria japonica*) gracefully arches its crooked, slender, apple-green stems—a study in delicacy. A shade-tolerant shrub content with any well-drained garden soil, kerria thrives throughout the South. The yellow flowers, in both single and double forms, appear in spring, arranged in an alternating pattern all along the stems. There are several variegated forms, the nicest, being 'Picta', whose saw-edged leaves are traced in white, lightly setting off the flowers, with their five soft-yellow petals. I find the egg-yolk yellow of the double form 'Pleniflora' harsh by comparison.

Variegated cultivars may revert to type if the occasional solid green-leaved stems aren't soon removed. Fall color is a late, excellent yellow.

One must *discover* the American euonymus (*Euonymus americanus*); it won't leap out at you. With its sparse, thin, green stems, this plant melts into the background during most of the year. But in fall strawberrylike seed capsules split open to reveal bright scarlet seeds within. The unique fruit gives the plant its common names, strawberry bush and hearts-a-bursting.

The fruit is preceded by tiny, pale greenish flowers, which hover above the paired leaves on filamentous stalks, giving an unsettling, slightly-out-of-alignment, 3-D effect.

American euonymus lurks unobtrusively about the woods throughout much of eastern North America and needs no special care. In deep winter each wiry, olive green branch is tipped with a rosy, fine-pointed bud like the flame on a candle.

With its floppy, umbrellalike leaves a foot across and stringy panicles of pale green flowers and fruit, Chinese parasol tree (*Firmiana simplex*) looks entirely too tropical to live around here. Yet it seems to thrive with little care, at least in protected locations. The slender multiple trunks with their smooth olive green skin have few branches, so that the winter aspect is austere. I suspect that a bit north of here Chinese parasol tree would function, if at all, more like an herbaceous perennial.

E V E R G R E E N   G R O U N D C O V E R S

Evergreen groundcovers and vines, just like the taller evergreen trees and shrubs, can tie together elements of the winter garden and give it a look of fullness and liveliness. Trees and shrubs with ornamental bare stems are especially striking against an evergreen groundcover.

I use a lot of English ivy (*Hedera helix*), not because I'm particularly fond of it, but because it was already on the premises when we arrived and because every square foot of ground covered by ivy is a square foot we won't have to mow.

Ivy, of course, is lovely on brick, imparting something of an Old World gentility to a setting. I can never decide whether I want my ivy on or off the house, though. Truly I wouldn't mind if it covered every brick, but when it glues its aerial rootlets to the wood trim and crawls in and out of the shutter slats, trouble starts, for I can't remove the ivy without removing the paint, and I can't paint without removing the ivy. And prying ivy off either wood or brick is a tedious strand-by-strand operation, requiring the patience of a saint and knuckles of steel. Would that the English ivy peeled easily away in great sheets like the deciduous Virginia creeper (*Parthenocissus quinquefolia*). Or would that we had vinyl trim.

If a tree is already swaddled in clinging vine, I wouldn't try to peel it off, for the bark would come away with the vine, making matters worse. Clipping off the ivy at the tree's base is an unsatisfactory response, too, for if, indeed, the vine does die, it will turn brown and hideous and cling accusingly for years. But I would think twice before I let it enshroud a tree I truly loved, for a weighty, moisture-hugging veil of ivy would likely increase the risk of wind and ice damage and favor fungal diseases.

Allowed to climb, mature ivy eventually develops a different, rather ovate leaf shape and blooms with clusters of tiny, scented, greenish cream flowers followed by dark, poisonous, berrylike fruit.

English ivy does best in shade to part-shade in rich, moist, well-drained soil but is not fussy about soil pH and, once established, becomes a permanent fixture. It can be trained over a topiary form or clipped to create a beautiful edging for a walkway. Strands of ivy can easily be braided into a holiday wreath or swag. It is hardy throughout most of the contiguous United States, but even in the South may occasionally be damaged by severe cold—a real disappointment, for an ivy-covered chimney may take several seasons to regain its former lush glory after a sudden subzero plunge.

'Thorndale', a cultivar with larger-than-average leaves, 'Bulgaria', and 'Hebron' are noted for hardiness. For a small bed or patio wall one might choose a miniature ivy like 'Gnome', with leaves no larger than a quarter. Or you could try a refined vine of a different color like 'Marginata' with gray-green leaves edged with white, or 'Buttercup' with pale veins and yellow new growth.

Colchis ivy (*Hedera colchica*) is more tender, being rated hardy only from Zone 7 southward. It is a lovely plant, with deep green heart-shaped leaves, and features some handsome cultivars: 'Dentata-variegata' with a gray and yellow variegation and 'Sulphur Heart' with a yellow blotch are two.

I'm not fond of wintercreeper (*Euonymus fortunei*) as a groundcover, for the species type, though tough and persistent in sun or shade, becomes too shrubby, and its stubbornly rooted offspring crop up all about the yard, and the dwarf and variegated sorts, for the most part, are puny and sad in winter. I much prefer the vincas, which, though similar in appearance, provide solid, healthy-looking, year-round coverage without stapling themselves to every tree and post.

Vinca minor, the common periwinkle, is a neat, low-growing filler with glossy, dark oval leaves. It works best carpeting pools of shade beneath deciduous trees and shrubs. Inge Paul uses a great deal of *V. minor* to fill in between shrubs and around spring wildflowers which go dormant shortly after bloom. In February her vinca is dotted with small lavender blooms, which complement the sunny yellow of the daffodils with which it is interspersed. As a child I played in a vinca patch that was enlivened in late summer by the scarlet flames of the red spider lily (*Lycoris radiata*).

Vinca major is a larger, looser version of *V. minor*. I'm especially taken with *V. major* 'Variegata', which, with its light green leaves edged with cream, brightens the shadowy haunts surrounding dark-leaved evergreens. It has a graceful, trailing habit that makes it a pleasing choice for an outdoor planter or an addition to an indoor arrangement.

I very seldom encounter a truly satisfactory bed of pachysandra. The Japanese pachysandra (*Pachysandra terminalis*) is not well suited to much of the South, resenting our heat and harsh sunlight and readily falling prey to fungal diseases. But in the middle and upper South it can make a fair showing even in extremely dense shade. *Pachysandra procumbens*, Allegheny spurge, is a native southerner suited to moist, rich soil in complete or partial shade. It is less sickly than its Japanese cousin, but the beautifully mottled leaves are not reliably evergreen. This species has an attractive little pinkish white flower spike in spring.

We've a toothwort along the nature trail at the botanical garden which, while dormant in summer, is lush and vigorous over winter and would, I believe, make us a better winter groundcover than pachysandra. The dusky green leaves are deeply cut into three broad, toothy leaflets and are prominently veined, their backside a sleek purple. The plant spreads by rhizomes into a low, solid mat, topped briefly in early spring by sprays of bell-like, pinkish-white flowers. Mike Gibson identifies it as an especially good form of *Cardamine* (formerly *Dentaria*) *diphylla*.

Both the lilyturfs (*Liriope muscari* and *L. spicata*) and their cousins the mondo grasses (*Ophiopogon*) do what they are supposed to do very well, filling in thickly around shrubs and trees in shade where grass is a struggle and softening, yet accentuating, the edges of walks and other paved areas. I know one visionary who planted his small, shaded front yard entirely in mondo grass and sold his lawn mower—not a bad idea at all unless you go in for croquet.

These slowly spreading, grasslike members of the lily family with their narrow, arching leaves do reasonably well in sun or shade, though liriope prefers shade. Ophiopogon is slower-growing and benefits from a richer, more humusy soil. Liriope hosts scale, but it's seldom serious. Both are touted as evergreen but often die down in winter just the same. Mondo grass may not survive winter above Zone 7. Well-organized people shear these plants back before spring, a notion I applaud, for it prevents the lush new growth from wearing a fringe of dead brown leaves all summer like mine does. Liriope bears its late summer flower spikes well above the foliage, while those of ophiopogon are nestled among the leaves.

Liriope muscari 'Monroe White' bears strapping dark green leaves and frothy spikes of sparkling white flowers which are replaced by glistening black berrylike fruits in fall. *Ophiopogon jaburan vittata* 'Aureus', with its yellow-striped leaves, is stunning in combination with ageratum or other blue flowers. *Ophiopogon japonicus* bears lavender flowers and beautiful pea-sized blue fruits. Dwarf mondo grass is superb in combination with dwarf conifers or even with cultivars of liriope or other mondo grasses. 'Gyokuruu' is barely there at two inches high; 'Shiroshima Ryu', with great white striped leaves, towers over it at four inches. The strangest, perhaps, is *O. planiscapus* 'Nigrescens', the "black" mondo grass, a planting of which looks at first glance like a small oil spill. At six inches it is a dandy companion for dwarf fescue (*Festuca glauca* 'Elijah's Blue', for example) or for anything small and yellow: *Coreopsis auriculata*, *Chrysogonum virginianum*, *Hypoxis hirsuta*.

Though it needs protection above Zone 8, cast-iron plant (*Aspidistra elatior*), another member of the lily family, can be employed in winter much the way hosta is used in summer, as a big-leaved, somewhat upright groundcover or small accent plant. It looks a bit peculiar, particularly when jutting with tropical fecundity above the occasional blanket of snow, but there it is.

Cast-iron plant creeps about rhizomatously and is valued for its tolerance of heavy, dry shade and poor soil, though it doesn't object at all to richer fare. Variegated cultivars are apt to go plain green if pampered, however.

Still another seldom-seen evergreen lily relative is lily of China, or Nippon lily (*Rohdea japonica*), which I've seen used to great winter effect beside a small waterfall at the Birmingham Botanical Garden. It looks a bit like a young corn plant, with long, tough, pointed leaves with parallel veins. In rich, moist soil it produces a short aroidlike spike of pale yellow flowers followed by striking red berries.

Arum italicum 'Pictum' is actually a "wintergreen" rather than an "evergreen." It is hard to fathom how this cousin of the caladium, with its white-veined, arrow-shaped leaves, so much like those of the tropical syngonium we grow indoors, can ignore the cold. And yet it is strictly a winter creature, coming up in autumn, blooming, and setting scarlet berries in much the same way as a jack-in-the-pulpit, then disappearing in spring.

It would be easy to explain this behavior as mere "confusion" if the plant hailed from the southern hemisphere, where winters and summers are reversed, but in fact it ranges from England to the Mediterranean region.

When we first began the wildflower area at the botanical garden, we had a housewarming of sorts and members of the state wildflower society, in town for their convention, brought gift plants and set them into a shady berm. Someone gave us a pair of Lenten roses (*Helleborus orientalis* or, more correctly, *H. ×hybridus*), natives not of Alabama, of course, but exotics from the ancient lands between the Mediterranean and Black Seas.

From time to time we look at these intruders, shake our heads, and remark, "We really ought to get them out of here; they don't belong here at all." But in midwinter, when their sleek, toothy, palmately divided leaves are overhung with nodding cups of speckled mauve and cream, we lift their downcast faces with their ring of startling stamens and we know, of course, that they are safe with us. Still, they are for most of us an acquired taste, having, as writer Helen Dillon has noted, a "slightly sinister, brooding charm."

In sunshine or partial shade perennial candytuft (*Iberis sempervirens*) starts blooming sporadically in midwinter and by April is going great guns, frothing along at the feet of the azaleas. With its wiry, almost woody, sprawling stems and dark green, narrow evergreen leaves, it reminds me of rosemary but for its racemes of crisp, white flowers, which advance up the stem as it grows.

Though we tend to combine candytuft to marvelous effect with our azaleas and dogwoods, it can be even showier with leaner soil and more sun—an effect of its Mediterranean origins. It is not particular about pH and never complains if no one waters it.

It's a good idea to cut back candytuft after bloom, particularly if you want to preserve the integrity of a cultivated variety, for it seeds itself with abandon. Cutting back also forces the plant to branch, creating a thicker, fuller plant. The stem I'm holding in my hand as I write was pruned back last year, and just below the stub five new stems have erupted and each, no doubt will bloom this spring. I'm going to slip this cutting into moist sand and set it outside in the terrarium. In a few weeks I'll have a new plant for the garden.

The cultivar 'Christmas Snow' is said to bloom a second time in autumn, while 'Purity' is extra low-growing with larger-than usual flowers.

Heirloom Houseplants

A hundred years ago (seems like) my Aunt Thelma Parris gave me a cutting of what she said was Christmas cactus (*Schlumbergera bridgesii*). Actually, I suppose it could be Thanksgiving cactus (*S. truncata*) or possibly Easter cactus (*Rhipsalidopsis gaertneri*) or, even more likely, given its smallish stem sections, dwarf Easter cactus (*R. rosea*)—all of which are epiphytic cacti from Brazil with bright, seasonal blossoms. I wouldn't know for sure because my plant is obviously an agnostic. It has never bloomed for any holiday, not even Groundhog Day, and I've played all the light/dark, hot/cold, wet/dry tricks to snap it into bloom that I've read about over the years. Finally I gave up and started hanging little balls on it at Christmastime.

When Elsabe Webster and I visited Bellingrath Gardens recently, I noticed a schlumbergera in the greenhouse that was lavishly budded for bloom. Greenhouse worker Flossie Miller, a delightful lady, informed me that it was a Thanksgiving cactus. She uses no special tricks to prod it into bloom, she said; just waters it every day in summer and Monday, Wednesday, and Friday in winter.

There is no earthly reason for one of these succulents to ever die unless it is chronically overwatered (so that it rots), underwatered, or allowed to freeze. If you notice rot setting in, break off a still-healthy stem section or two and root it in any clean, barely moist medium.

Speaking of heirloom plants, one that is easily started from seed, makes an adorable gift (I needed an excuse to include it in this chapter), rarely drops spent leaves, can safely be neglected (unwatered) for weeks, and always elicits compliments and a measure of wonder from visitors is the ponytail palm (*Beaucarnea recurvata*).

This peculiar member of the agave family grows to thirty feet in the warm, arid wilds of Texas and Mexico and with encouragement would no doubt do the same indoors. Mine is three feet high and requires a similarly tall pedestal to display the grasslike, six-foot-long leaves, which emerge fountain-style from the top of the banded gray trunk. The base of the trunk is swollen and crazed like a cantaloupe.

I feed and water this plant as little as possible, for moving it in and out of doors at the change of seasons is chore enough already. I think in summer it is actually happier on the sheltered, shaded front porch than on the more exposed, desertlike back porch.

A Gardener's Work Is Never Done

If you can still find healthy bulbs of tulip, hyacinth, lily, and the like, a stockingful will make a welcome gift for a gardening friend (and it isn't fattening, and it will never need dusting).

Most perennials, whether they're dormant or not, can be set out or moved in December, and hardwood cuttings still can be taken. Poppy, larkspur, bachelor's button, and other hardy annuals may be sown.

December is an excellent time to prune evergreens (spring-blooming rhododendrons being an obvious exception), using the trimmings in decorating or as protective cover for plants of borderline hardiness.

A garden is never really at rest. Even at the turn of the year when the old frying-pan-turned-birdbath in the backyard is frozen solid, the garden is enlivened with the motion of birds and shadows. Already the scent of winter honeysuckle and the magenta glimmer of *Verbena canadensis* hint at the explosive growth so soon to come. We must sit down with that stack of new catalogs and daydream while we can.

Index